■ ALL THE
Aires
FRANCE

Many thanks to the following Aire Heads, who provided information and pictures about Aires they have visited.

Barrie Wilson; John and Daryl; Paul Lammoil; Vicky and Nick Church; Phil Peyton; John Barry; Carol and Duncan Weaver; Ken Croft; Samantha Gardner; Mr and Mrs A Whitehead; Pete Schider; Peter Gordon and Steve Pyke of motorhomeandaway.co.uk

Special thanks to: Janice Sadler; Carol Weaver; Ken Croft and Chris Gladman.

First published in Great Britain by Vicarious Books LLP, 2007.

ISBN 978-0-9552808-1-8

The reader should confirm the legality or safety of any undertaking. All information is followed at the individual's own risk and no responsibility is accepted by the authors or publishers for any loss, damage, injury or inconvenience whatsoever, howsoever caused to anyone using this book.

Vicarious Books LLP, PO Box 72, Minehead, TA24 9AL. Tel: 0131 208 3333
www.vicariousbooks.co.uk

Cover pictures:
Main Picture Copyright © Ken Croft.

Small pictures:
Copyright © Carol and Duncan Weaver and Vicarious Books LLP.

Back cover:
Main Picture: Copyright © Ken Croft.

Small pictures Copyright © Carol and Duncan Weaver and Vicarious Books LLP.

Design and artwork by: Chris Gladman Design, 07745 856652.

Printed by: The Alden Group Limited www.alden.co.uk

© R Moss

Welcome to the first edition of All the Aires France. We have been busy in 2007 travelling the whole of France and have compiled a guide with 600 inspected Aires. We have also been given permission to publish information on another 500.

What is an Aire?

A direct translation is area. Most people have seen French motorway signs indicating Aires from lay-bys to service areas. We are not providing details of these but are providing the Aires de services that are found in the towns, villages, coastal and rural areas. In the main the local community, sometimes due to motorhome numbers, sometimes to attract motorhome tourism, provide them. It is down to local goodwill to keep them open and maintained. In reality they are carparks with service facilities.

1100 Aires makes this guide as comprehensive as any but our aim is to make this the best Aires guide possible. Firstly it's in English - we can't write in any other language. For each visited Aire we have provided simple directions with onsite GPS co-ordinates, colour photos, detailed information about both the service points and the parking areas. To help you make a choice we have commented on the ambience and local amenities; how far the town is, whether there are play parks for children, green space for exercising dogs, fishing, walking and cycling.

This is just the beginning, and we need your help. Aires are constantly changing therefore new ones appear and old ones deteriorate and some are improved or moved. We need you to tell us about the Aires you visit, especially new and un-inspected ones. It is equally important to tell us when changes need to be made, when things stay the same and better photos are really appreciated.

We hope you enjoy using this guide and have many enjoyable motorhoming experiences.

How to use this guide

This guide is divided into fourteen regional sections and entries are listed alphabetically by place name within each region. All sites can be located on a coloured map at the beginning of each region.

Explanation of an entry

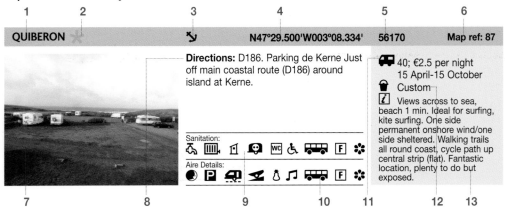

| 1 | 2 | 3 | 4 | 5 | 6 |

| **QUIBERON** ✳ | ↘ | N47°29.500'W003°08.334' | 56170 | Map ref: 87 |

Directions: D186. Parking de Kerne Just off main coastal route (D186) around island at Kerne.

🚐 40; €2.5 per night
15 April-15 October
⚓ Custom
ℹ️ Views across to sea, beach 1 min. Ideal for surfing, kite surfing. One side permanent onshore wind/one side sheltered. Walking trails all round coast, cycle path up central strip (flat). Fantastic location, plenty to do but exposed.

Sanitation:
🐾 🏛️ 🚽 ☠️ 🚻 ♿ 🚌 F ❇️

Aire Details:
● P 🚐 ⬎ 🌡️ 🎵 🚌 F ❇️

| 7 | 8 | 9 | 10 | 11 | 12 | 13 |

1 Town name.
2 Asterisked if special.
3 Ambience (type of area), see symbol key below.
4 GPS co-ordinates.
5 Postcode.
6 Map reference.
7 Colour photo of Aire.

8 Directions to Aire starting with road name or number.
9 At a glance Sanitation symbols, see key below.
10 At a glance Aire symbols, see key below.
11 Number of places; time limitations; cost per night.
12 Type of service point; cost; payment type.
13 Additional information including; green space; play parks; distance to town; availability of LPG.

Additional entries listed at the end of regions

Directions and other details regarding number of places, cost and facilities where supplied

| | 1 | Overnight stop | Service point | 5 | 6 |

| **VIELLE-SAINT-GIRONS** | ● ⚓ | 40560 | Map: 87 |

Directions: Lac (Lake) de Leon- Plage (beach) de Vielle; Near Lake Leon. • 25 • €7 • March - Oct

KEY TO SYMBOLS

Ambience (type of area)

↘	Coastal	🌲	Rural	🐄	Farm
🏛️	Residential	🏘️	Village	🏃	Park
🏢	Urban	⛵	Riverside or lakeside		

Sanitation and Aire

🐾	Water	F	Free of charge	🚐	Hard surface
🏛️	Grey water disposal	❇️	Open all year (Water may be off during winter)	⬎	Sloping
🚽	Toilet disposal			🌡️	Illuminated
☠️	Electric hook up	●	Overnight parking possible	🎵	Noisy
🚻	Toilets	P	Designated motorhome parking	🚌	Large motorhomes*
♿	Disabled toilet				

Note: Symbols in Grey = unavailable

Abbreviations

'text'	text in speech marks refers to extracts from signs
5 mins	all times are estimated walking times
Adv	advance
Back on	necessary to reverse onto service point
CL style	like a field
Diff	difficult
Dir	direction
Green area	Suitable for exercising children and dogs
Mairie	Town Hall
Opp	opposite
Playpark	young children's playground
Poss	possible
Pp	per person
Pt	part
Rd	road
Sign(ed)	Aire is signed by a motorhome symbol
Sp	sign posted
Sq	square
Suggested	not official but possible option
Visited	indicates an Aire that was submitted to us

*Large motorhomes

Very few French people own motorhomes over 7 metres, 6 meters appears to be the average. Most Aires are designed to accommodate 6-meter motorhomes. A symbol is provided to say it should be possible for larger motorhomes (those over 7 meters) to use the Aire. During busy periods access may not be possible, then there is the moral question, should large motorhomes take more than a space?

A second symbol tells you that it should be possible to get near the service point with a large motorhome. Most service points are designed specifically for emptying cassette style toilets and onboard grey water tanks. Few are designed for emptying onboard toilet tanks. In reality many are very poorly designed and maintained. It is your responsibility to organise your disposal to suit these widely varying systems.

Directions

These have been written to provide the simplest, most main route but have not been tested with a large vehicle. Therefore it is your responsibility to confirm in advance that access is suitable. Please let us know how you get on, we will be happy to update and include your information. Every effort is made to ensure directions are correct however route national and route departmental road numbers are currently being changed in France.

Using Aires

Aires symbolise the freedom of motorhoming. You are welcomed into local communities, where you can stay overnight at unique locations unavailable to other travellers. These are a luxury not a right, so park sympathetically to your neighbours, use the service point and facilities responsibly and try to support the local community.

Updates

It has been impossible for us to visit all the Aires in France, and we may have some inaccurate information in this first guide. So we need your help. At the back of the book there is a form to fill in, please update us with any information. Telling us that things have stayed the same is just as important as telling us things have changed. If you don't have a form, emails, scraps of paper and pigeons are accepted. We particularly need good photographs, try to take as true an overview as possible. Often taking a picture from the road or having a feature in the background like the church will help people to find it.

We make every effort to ensure the information is accurate, however we do have both gremlins and humans in the office so errors can occur. Vicarious Books LLP cannot be held accountable for the quality, safety or operation of the Aire concerned, or for the fact that conditions, facilities, management or prices may have changed.

If something is wrong, the directions or information incorrect or changed, please tell us. We can then update it. It's your guide, make a difference, make it the best.

© CDT Gard

50m
à Gauche

© CDT Gard

Contents

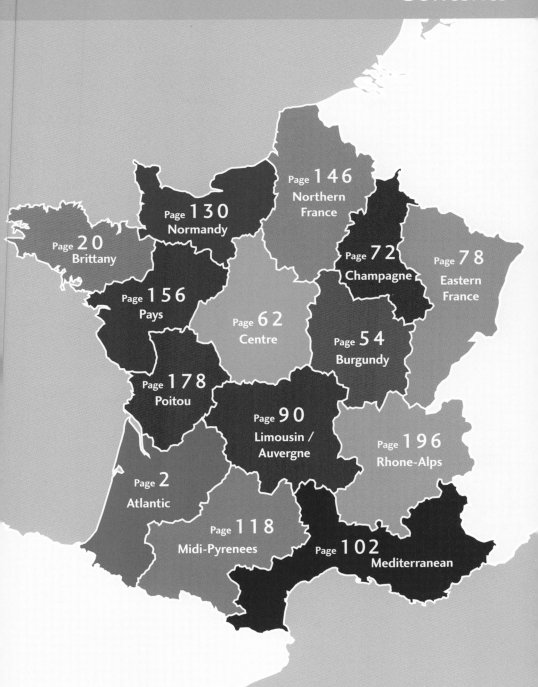

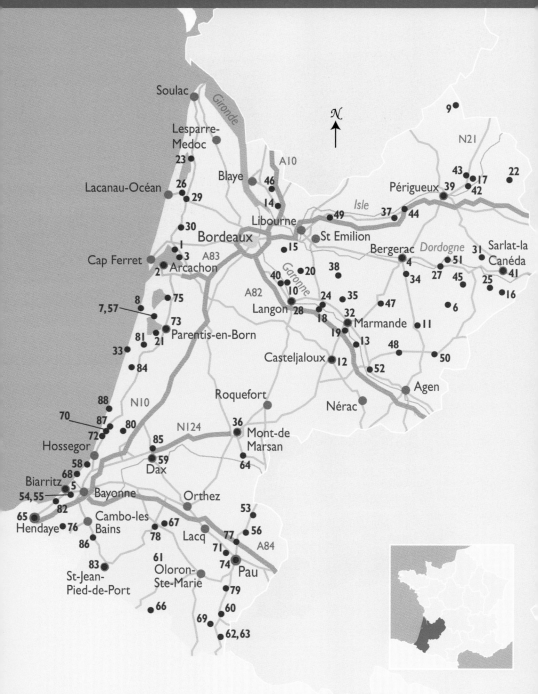

Soulac

Lesparre-
Medoc

23

Lacanau-Océan   26
                29

Blaye   46

14

Libourne

30

1   Bordeaux
3
Cap Ferret   2   A83
Arcachon

15   St Emilion

Bergerac   31   Sarlat-la
                      Canéda
        4   51
        27   45   41
        34   25   16
38   47
40   20
A82   10   24   35   6
Langon   28   32
18   Marmande   11
19   13   48
Casteljaloux   12   52   50

75
8
7,57
73
81   Parentis-en-Born
21
33
84

Roquefort

Nérac   Agen

88   N10
70   87   80
72
Hossegor
58
68   N124   36
Biarritz   5   85   Mont-de
54,55   59   Marsan
65   82   Dax   64
Hendaye   76   Bayonne   Orthez
        Cambo-les   67   53
        Bains   78   Lacq   77   56
86   71   A84
61   74   Pau
83   Oloron-
St-Jean-   Ste-Marie   79
Pied-de-Port   66   60
                69
                62,63

Gironde

A10

Isle   Périgueux   39   9   N21
                            43   17   22
                            42

37   44
49

Dordogne

Garonne

N

© John Barry

A mild climate and the most diverse geography in France, makes the Atlantic region an ideal year round motorhome destination.

100 miles of sandy coast is home to the Great Dune of Pyla (or Pilat) the highest dune in Europe. This coast also hosts the world circuit surf competitions but beginners can learn at the surf schools of Biarritz, Anglet, Bidart, Guéthary and Hendaye.

Bordeaux grapes are grown in the north of the region along the banks of the rivers Gironde, Garonne and Dordogne.

Just inland from the coast grows Europe's largest man-made pine forest, with miles of flat cycle paths and large lakes ideal for water sports.

European aristocracy transformed the seaside resort of Biarritz in the 19th century, leaving a legacy of beautiful architecture, and mainland Europe's second oldest golf course.

France meets Spain at the Pyrenees, providing skiing in the winter and hiking in the summer.

© Carol and Duncan Weaver

© Carol and Duncan Weaver

© Carol and Duncan Weaver

Atlantic

ANDERNOS-LES-BAINS N44°44.652'W001°06.516' 33510 Map ref: 1

Directions: Port Osteicole. From D3 (main road through) follow sp to 'port', then sp 'Aire de Camping Car' to Port Osteicole.

Sanitation:

Aire Details:

🚐 10

€8; max 24hrs. Raclet; Tokens

ℹ️ Views of port with pleasure/fishing boats. Oysters available for sale. Sea front 5 mins. Self cleaning toilet - the cleanest with loo paper!

ARCACHON N44°39.096'W001°08.893' 33120 Map ref: 2

Directions: D650. On entering town. Opp Citroen/Total garage next to Lidl outside stadium.

Sanitation:

Aire Details:

🚐 5

Raclet

ℹ️ Not ideal, on busy main area. Noisy, no views.

AUDENGE N44°41.066'W001°00.293' 33980 Map ref: 3

Directions: In municipal campsite carpark. From D3 turn onto D5 sp 'municipal camping' and 'camping cars'. Drive to roundabout and turn first right. Campsite adj to roundabout.

Sanitation:

Aire Details:

🚐 6

€8 - €11; 24hrs Euro Relais; Tokens

ℹ️ 5 mins from town.

BERGERAC N44°50.760'E000°29.275' 24100 Map ref: 4

Directions: Quai Garrigat. From north or south enter town on N21. On the north side of the river, at roundabout by river bridge turn off towards town sp Aire. The Aire is directly on left, signed.

Sanitation:

Aire Details:

🚐 7; 24hours

Custom

ℹ️ 5 min walk to town along river. River views and riverside picnic tables. Large green area adj to Aire along river. Restaurant adj.

BIARRITZ | N43°27.912' W001°34.302' | 64200 | Map ref: 5

Directions: Parking de la Milady.

© John Barry

🚐 40; €6 - 10
Custom
ℹ️ Roadside parking. 15 May - 15 Sept; Free 16 Sept - 14 May. May need long cable for elec. Visited 2007.

Sanitation:

Aire Details:

BIRON | N44°37.843' E000°52.247' | 24540 | Map ref: 6

Directions: Adj to road as exit village by information panel.

© Carol and Duncan Weaver

🚐 10
Flot blue; €2
ℹ️ Rural views and views of château, pleasant. Château worth a visit, 5mins. Visited 2005.

Sanitation:

Aire Details:

BISCAROSSE LAC | | - | 40600 | Map ref: 7

Directions: Port de Navarrosse; Adj to Marina, under trees.

© Carol and Duncan Weaver

🚐 100; €7
Euro Relais
ℹ️ Near marina; in wooded, shaded area; views of boats. Visited 2005.

Sanitation:

Aire Details:

BISCAROSSE PLAGE | | - | 40600 | Map ref: 8

Directions: Rue des Becasses; at Parking du Vivier.

© Carol and Duncan Weaver

🚐 200; €7
Euro Relais
ℹ️ Shaded area under trees. Visited 2005

Sanitation:

Aire Details:

Atlantic

BUSSEROLLES
 N45°40.616'E000°38.562'   24360   **Map ref: 9**

Directions: D90. Just off D90 in centre of village. Signed. Tight Access.

Sanitation:

Aire Details:

🚐 5

♿ Euro Relais; Tokens

ℹ️ In village centre near bar, Nice woody, hilly region.

CADILLAC
 N44°38.319'W000°19.011'   33410   **Map ref: 10**

Directions: Allee du Park. Follow signs from roundabout on D10. Aire located in the second carpark on one way street.

Sanitation:

Aire Details:

🚐 20

♿ Custom

ℹ️ Cadillac is a beautiful walled city surrounded by vines. Walking routes marked along river. Walled city 2 mins.

CANCON
 N44°32.192'E000°37.530'   47290   **Map ref: 11**

Directions: From the N21, follow sp 'Office de Tourism' and 'D124'.Turning next to Mairie (town hall) into carpark, facilities against barn wall, town sq adj.

Sanitation:

Aire Details:

🚐 10

♿ Custom

ℹ️ Very quiet night stop. 2 mins from shops. Possibility of cattle market. One 2 pin plug.

CASTELJALOUX
 N44°18.657'E000°04.760'   47700   **Map ref: 12**

Directions: D291. Turn off D933N onto D291 dir St Michel Castelnau, signed. Then turn left by the former railway line signed. To avoid town approach from South.

Sanitation:

Aire Details:

🚐 4

♿ Custom

ℹ️ 10 min walk to town centre. Large town, interesting church. Poss noise from fire station. LPG at Intermarche (D933 North).

CAUMONT-SUR-GARONNE N44°26.506'E000°10.781' 47430 Map ref: 13

Directions: D143. On D143 by canal as enter the village. Access made difficult by canal bridge.

Sanitation:

Aire Details:

2

Custom; €1

i Beautiful location worth the effort. Overlooking canal. Shaded by plane trees but should get afternoon sunshine. Boat moorings, towpath walks, village adj.

CAVIGNAC N45°05.964'W000°23.279' 33620 Map ref: 14

Directions: Rue des Lavandieres. Signed off D18 (main route through) in large carpark just off high street in centre of town.

Sanitation:

Aire Details:

10

Custom

i Town adj, Thursday market very large and fills whole town. Beware market arrives 5.30am Thurs.

CREON N44°46.592'W000°20.882' 33670 Map ref: 15

Directions: D671, Just off D671. Clearly signed. In carpark.

Sanitation:

Aire Details:

5

Flot Bleu; Tokens

i Cycle path adj; Boulangerie adj, town 2 mins. Next village, Le Sauve, has ruined abbey.

DOMME - 24250 Map ref: 16

Directions: Le Pradal; In village - follow the signs.

Sanitation:

Aire Details:

10

Euro Relais Junior

i Rural views; green space adj; Nice village; Visited 2004.

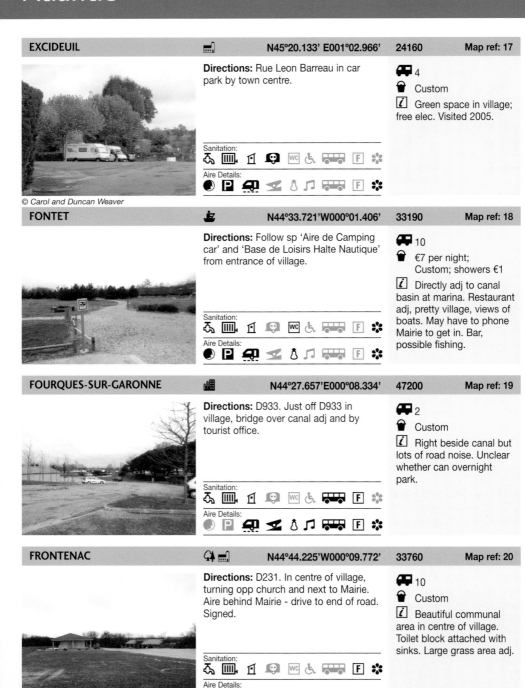

| EXCIDEUIL | | N45°20.133' E001°02.966' | 24160 | Map ref: 17 |

Directions: Rue Leon Barreau in car park by town centre.

🚐 4
🪣 Custom
ℹ️ Green space in village; free elec. Visited 2005.

Sanitation:
Aire Details:

© Carol and Duncan Weaver

| FONTET | | N44°33.721'W000°01.406' | 33190 | Map ref: 18 |

Directions: Follow sp 'Aire de Camping car' and 'Base de Loisirs Halte Nautique' from entrance of village.

🚐 10
🪣 €7 per night; Custom; showers €1
ℹ️ Directly adj to canal basin at marina. Restaurant adj, pretty village, views of boats. May have to phone Mairie to get in. Bar, possible fishing.

Sanitation:
Aire Details:

| FOURQUES-SUR-GARONNE | | N44°27.657'E000°08.334' | 47200 | Map ref: 19 |

Directions: D933. Just off D933 in village, bridge over canal adj and by tourist office.

🚐 2
🪣 Custom
ℹ️ Right beside canal but lots of road noise. Unclear whether can overnight park.

Sanitation:
Aire Details:

| FRONTENAC | | N44°44.225'W000°09.772' | 33760 | Map ref: 20 |

Directions: D231. In centre of village, turning opp church and next to Mairie. Aire behind Mairie - drive to end of road. Signed.

🚐 10
🪣 Custom
ℹ️ Beautiful communal area in centre of village. Toilet block attached with sinks. Large grass area adj.

Sanitation:
Aire Details:

GASTES 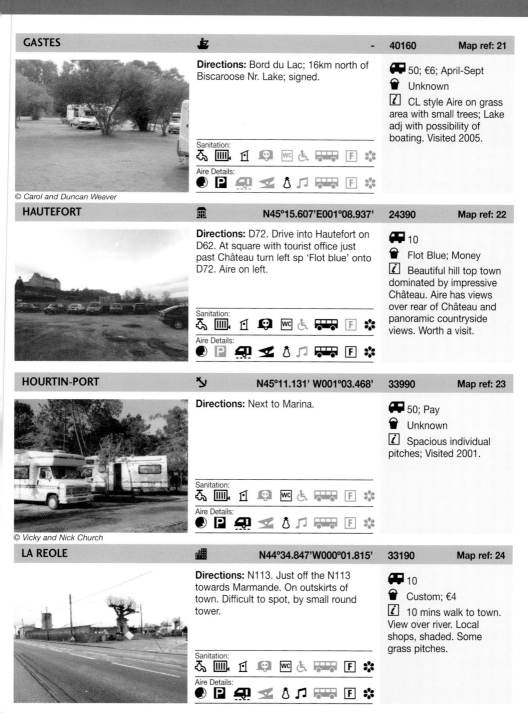 - 40160 Map ref: 21

Directions: Bord du Lac; 16km north of Biscaroose Nr. Lake; signed.

🚐 50; €6; April-Sept

💧 Unknown

ℹ️ CL style Aire on grass area with small trees; Lake adj with possibility of boating. Visited 2005.

Sanitation:

Aire Details:

© Carol and Duncan Weaver

HAUTEFORT N45°15.607'E001°08.937' 24390 Map ref: 22

Directions: D72. Drive into Hautefort on D62. At square with tourist office just past Château turn left sp 'Flot blue' onto D72. Aire on left.

🚐 10

💧 Flot Blue; Money

ℹ️ Beautiful hill top town dominated by impressive Château. Aire has views over rear of Château and panoramic countryside views. Worth a visit.

Sanitation:

Aire Details:

HOURTIN-PORT N45°11.131' W001°03.468' 33990 Map ref: 23

Directions: Next to Marina.

🚐 50; Pay

💧 Unknown

ℹ️ Spacious individual pitches; Visited 2001.

Sanitation:

Aire Details:

© Vicky and Nick Church

LA REOLE N44°34.847'W000°01.815' 33190 Map ref: 24

Directions: N113. Just off the N113 towards Marmande. On outskirts of town. Difficult to spot, by small round tower.

🚐 10

💧 Custom; €4

ℹ️ 10 mins walk to town. View over river. Local shops, shaded. Some grass pitches.

Sanitation:

Aire Details:

Atlantic

LA ROQUE GAGEAC
 - 24250 **Map ref: 25**

© John Barry

Directions: Parking Place Publique; just off main road as exit village.

Sanitation:

Aire Details:

🚐 30; pay; €5
Flot blue; €2
ℹ️ Green space adj; Parking 50 m from working river; Visited 2006.

LACANAU-OCEAN/LA HUGA
🔱 N45°00.430'W001°09.954' 33680 **Map ref: 26**

Directions: D6. Located just off D6, turn left as you enter La Huga. Large area with marked pitches.

Sanitation:

Aire Details:

🚐 50; €8 inc elec.
Custom
ℹ️ Large motorhome style campsite, pay at machine. Not glamorous, but convenient.

LALINDE
N44°50.365'E000°44.585' 24150 **Map ref: 27**

Directions: Avenue General Leclerc. From town centre follow sp 'SNCF'. Outside the train station. Suggested parking at the stadium, turn left after canal bridge and drive along tow path. N44*50.308'E000*44.153'

Sanitation:

Aire Details:

🚐 2
Custom
ℹ️ Pretty town nestled between river and canal. Canal walks/cycles. Plenty of restaurants. No parking restrictions anywhere in town.

LANGON
 - 33210 **Map ref: 28**

© Carol and Duncan Weaver

Directions: Parking adj to Canal du Berry; Just off main route.

Sanitation:

Aire Details:

🚐 5
Euro Relais; Tokens
ℹ️ Views over canal; parking directly alongside. Play area; picnic tables; visited 2006.

10

Atlantic

LE MOUTCHIC

N44°59.934'W000°08.431' 33680 Map ref: 29

Directions: C16. At end of village follow sp to 'Carreyre' and 'Camping La Teday'. Beside old dilapidated Chateau. Turn immediately right into gateway with memorial.

🚐 10

🛁 Custom; back on

ℹ️ Only open in Summer. Lake adj. Not suitable for children - dilapidated buildings on site. Village with restaurant 2 mins. Surrounded by wood with cycle paths.

Sanitation:
Aire Details:

LE PORGE

N44°52.362'W001°05.578' 33680 Map ref: 30

Directions: In central square, outside tourist office, church adj.

🚐 5

🛁 N/A

ℹ️ In village. No facilities available or visible at time of visit.

Sanitation:
Aire Details:

LES EYZIES-DE-TAYAC

N44°56.325' E001°00.552' 24620 Map ref: 31

Directions: Adj D47 in the valley of the Vezere. On communal car park; Signed.

🚐 25; €4

🛁 Raclet; 2

ℹ️ CL style feel; close to Museum of Prehistory; Visited 2004.

Sanitation:
Aire Details:

© Carol and Duncan Weaver

MARMANDE

N44°29.907'E000°09.576' 47200 Map ref: 32

Directions: Blvd Richard Coeur de Lion. From D933. Aire signed between river bridge/major traffic light junc. Turn opp SAAB/SUZUKI garage. Sp 'Parking Filhole'. Aire opp motorcross.

🚐 5

🛁 Custom

ℹ️ Town 2 mins, canal, fishing possible.

Sanitation:
Aire Details:

11

MIMIZAN PLAGE ⚓ - 40200 Map ref: 33

Directions: On town parking area; signed.

🚐 50; Pay

🛒 Euro Relais; Pay

ℹ️ In town; large sand dune adj; Beach 5 mins over sand dune; visited 2005.

Sanitation:

Aire Details:

© Carol and Duncan Weaver

MONBAZILLAC N44°47.321'E000°29.751' 24240 Map ref: 34

Directions: D13. Drive through village dir Ribenac, the Vinyard is on the right as you exit the village. Sp 'Domaine de la Lande'.

🚐 5

🛒 Custom

ℹ️ Views across vines. Wine tasting on site. Wine tasting at Château Monbazillac 5 mins. Free for France Passion members.

Sanitation:

Aire Details:

MONSEGUR 🏛 N44°39.056'E000°05.038' 33580 Map ref: 35

Directions: Place du 8 Mai 1945. Turn off the D668 on Duras side sp 'Centre Ville' at junc with monument behind sp. Aire on left opp park. Do not enter from any other way.

🚐 5; 48hrs

🛒 Custom

ℹ️ Park with view opp, town with interesting covered market 2 mins.

Sanitation:

Aire Details:

MONT DE MARSAN ⛴ N43°53.813' W000°31.216' 40000 Map ref: 36

Directions: Route de Sabres. Adj to the village pond.

🚐 3

🛒 Raclet

ℹ️ Views over pond; grass parking giving a CL style feel; trees. Visited 2005.

Sanitation:

Aire Details:

© Carol and Duncan Weaver

Atlantic

| MUSSIDAN | | N45°02.508'E000°21.137' | 24400 | Map ref: 37 |

Directions: At Super U. N89 South of town.

Sanitation:

Aire Details:

🚐 5
Euro Relais; Tokens
ℹ Supermarket, Pizzeria, LPG.

| PELLEGRUE | | N44°44.694'E000°04.483' | 33790 | Map ref: 38 |

Directions: D16E Clearly signed at the D15/D16 crossroads at the north of town. Signed from all directions.

Sanitation:

Aire Details:
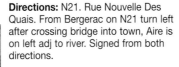

🚐 4
Euro Relais
ℹ Rd adj, town 5 mins. Walking trail from village. N21 Total Garage sells LPG. D672 to Ste Foy la Grande nice drive through grapevines.

© Carol and Duncan Weaver

| PERIGUEUX | | N45°10.982'E000°43.440' | 24000 | Map ref: 39 |

Directions: N21. Rue Nouvelle Des Quais. From Bergerac on N21 turn left after crossing bridge into town, Aire is on left adj to river. Signed from both directions.

Sanitation:

Aire Details:

🚐 20
Custom
ℹ Adj to river, with views, town 2 mins. LPG at Total garage.

| PREIGNAC | | N44°35.125'W000°17.731' | 33210 | Map ref: 40 |

Directions: On N113. Signed off N113 - main route through. Drive through Square with Mairie (town hall) past trees, Aire before sports ground. Parking area away from road noise.

Sanitation:

Aire Details:

🚐 8
Custom
ℹ Nice views of rooftops/church from Aire. Town adj.

13

SARLAT-LA-CANEDA — N44°53.747'E001°12.747' — 24200 — Map ref: 41

Directions: Parking Flandres Dunkerque. On D704 at the north of town. Shortly after D6 and D704 meet at the roundabout go straight across on the D704 sp Aire. The Aire is on left 100m away.

24h €5; 48h €12!

Euro Relais Junior; €2

15 mins walk from town. Credit card barrier system; unable to establish whether British credit cards accepted as barrier broken. Far from an ideal location.

Sanitation:

Aire Details:

SARLIAC-SUR-L'ISLE — N45°14.155'E000°52.448' — 24420 — Map ref: 42

Directions: N21. Just off 1st Roundabout as enter town on N21 from north - sp 'Aire de Repos'. Overlooking football pitches.

10

Custom

Large area of football pitches adj. Town 2 mins.

Sanitation:

Aire Details:

SORGES — N45°18.332'E000°52.371' — 24420 — Map ref: 43

Directions: N21. Located just off N21, just as you exit Sorges to the south on right.

5

Euro Relais; In adj layby

Tennis adj to parking, village 2 mins. Also coach parking.

Sanitation:

Aire Details:

SOURZAC — N45°03.097'E000°23.715' — 24400 — Map ref: 44

Directions: N89. Adj to Church and bridge across river just off N89.

10

Custom

Views of either church or across river and surrounding countryside. Aire only let down by the proximity of main road. Very close to A89 motorway - ideal stopover.

Sanitation:

Aire Details:

ST CYPRIEN

N44°52.102'E001°02.663' | 24220 | Map ref: 45

Directions: Place Machenheim C201. Sp from all directions 'P du centreville'.

8; €5 per night, max 24h

Custom

No motorhomes are allowed to stay outside of the Aire between 7pm - 9am. Town 1 min. LPG at total garage on D703 towards Sarlat-la-Caneda.

Sanitation:

Aire Details:

ST MARIENS

N45°06.915'W000°23.947' | 33620 | Map ref: 46

Directions: D18/D22. Aire signed off D18 on outskirts of St Mariens. Sp Aire des Lagunes.

2; 48hrs

Custom

In residential area, ideal for night stop.

Sanitation:

Aire Details:

ST PARDOUX ISAAC

N44°36.816'E000°21.585' | 47800 | Map ref: 47

Directions: At Intermarche. From town follow sp Bergerac then sp Intermarche sp off D933.

10

Custom

15 mins to town. Supermarket. Fuel Station.

Sanitation:

Aire Details:

STE-LIVRADE-SUR-LOT

N44°23.760'E000°35.490' | 47110 | Map ref: 48

Directions: Place du Lieutenant Colonel Jean-Francois Calas. From D113 at roundabout with Casion supermarket, turn adj 'Tresor Public', signed, down road lined with plane trees. Aire at end of road past 'Terre du Sud'. Also sp 'Sapiers Pompiers' (fire station).

5

Custom

2 mins to town. Boules court adj. LPG at Intermarche Villeneuf sur Lot.

Sanitation:

Aire Details:

ST-MEDARD-DE-GUIZIERES
 N45°00.909'W000°03.489' 33230 **Map ref: 49**

Directions: N89. By D21/N89 junction. Near Church. Signed.

Sanitation:

Aire Details:

🚐 3
🏠 Custom
ℹ️ Just off main shopping area, Church adj.

ST-SYLVESTRE-SUR-LOT
 N44°23.765'E000°48.331' 47140 **Map ref: 50**

Directions: Avenue Jean Moulin. Access from D103 or D911. Aire behind Intermarche (Facilities by Petrol Station) adj to river.

Sanitation:

Aire Details:

🚐 10
🏠 Custom
ℹ️ Adj Intermarche, canal, boules court. View of canal possible. Town 2 mins. LPG at Intermarche Villeneuf sur Lot.

TREMOLAT
 N44°52.433'E000°49.853' 24510 **Map ref: 51**

Directions: D30. Enter village on D30 from Pezuls. Drive straight on, turning left opp Mairie at T junction. The Aire is on the left directly opposite La Poste. From D30 south, it is on right opp La Poste.

Sanitation:

Aire Details:

🚐 10
🏠 Custom
ℹ️ Beautiful little rural village with tourist facilities; art shop, bar, pizzaria, restaurant. River walk. Base Nautique has a campsite adj to river.

VILLETON
 N44°21.844'E000°16.376' 47400 **Map ref: 52**

Directions: D120. By bridge on D120 sp 'Musee de la Memoire Paysanne', 'Aire Camping Car' and 'Restaurant la Fluviale'. Located behind Mairie at marina.

Sanitation:

Aire Details:

🚐 4
🏠 Flot Bleu; €2
ℹ️ Directly beside canal, but no view. Pizzaria and museum adj. Very pleasant spot, poss fishing and canal walks/cycling. Boat moorings adj.

AIRE-SUR-L'ADOUR 🌐 🚰 40800 Map: 53

Directions: Parc Municipal.
• 20 • All year

ANGLET 🚰 64600 Map: 54

Directions: Aire de Camping Car Anglet Les Corsaires.
• July/Aug

ANGLET 🚰 64600 Map: 55

Directions: Espace Services Camping Car Anglet BAB2.
• All year

ARZACQ-ARRAZIGUET 🌐 🚰 64410 Map: 56

Directions: Place du Marcadieu.
• 20 • 72 hours • All year

HAVE YOU VISITED AN AIRE?

Don't forget to fill in the form at the back and return to Vicarious Books.

BISCARROSSE VILLE 🚰 40600 Map: 57

Directions: Centre Commercial Laouadie; Route de la Plage. • Free • No Parking

CAPBRETON 🌐 🚰 40130 Map: 58

Directions: Plage des Oceanides- Av. Des Alouettes.
• 120 • Max 48hrs

DAX 🌐 🚰 40100 Map: 59

Directions: Parking nouveau Pont - Berges Adour.
• 6 • 72hrs • Free • All year

EAUX-CHAUDES 🚰 64440 Map: 60

Directions: Route du Pourtalet.
• All year

ESPES-UNDUREIN 🌐 🚰 64130 Map: 61

Directions: ETCHE GOXOKI.
• 6 • March - Nov

GOURETTE 🌐 🚰 64440 Map: 62

Directions: Ley.
• 50 • All year

GOURETTE 2 🌐 🚰 64440 Map: 63

Directions: Cardet.
• 30 • All year

GRENADE-SUR-L'ADOUR 🌐 🚰 40270 Map: 64

Directions: Place du 19 Mars 1962.
• 1 night • All year

HENDAYE 🌐 🚰 64700 Map: 65

Directions: Rue Anseonia.
• 5 • 24 hrs • April - Sept

LA PIERRE SAINT-MARTIN 🌐 🚰 64570 Map: 66

Directions: At the ski station.
• 24 • July - Aug

LAAS 🌐 🚰 64390 Map: 67

Directions: Camping Le St Jacques.
• 20 • All year

LABENNE OCEAN 🌐 🚰 40530 Map: 68

Directions: Avenue de l'Ocean.
• 50 • June - Sept

LARUNS 🌐 🚰 64440 Map: 69

Directions: Avenue de la Gare.
• 30 • All year

LEON 🌐 🚰 40550 Map: 70

Directions: Les Berges du Lac.
• 50 • €8 • April - Sept

LESCAR 🌐 🚰 64230 Map: 71

Directions: 5 places for 24 hrs all year in the following places: Parking Jacques Monod; Place Royale; Place de la Hourquie; Place de l'Evêché and Place du Fronton.

MOLIETS-ET-MAA 🌐 🚰 40660 Map: 72

Directions: Avenue de l'Ocean.
• €4 • 40 • 24hrs • All year

PARENTIS-EN-BORN 🌐 🚰 40160 Map: 73

Directions: Route des Plages.
• 20 • All year

PAU 🌐 64000 Map: 74

Directions: Place de Verdun.
• 48 hrs • All year

SANGUINET 🌐 🚰 40460 Map: 75

Directions: Les Bardets and Parking du Pavillon both in Avenue de Losa. • 15 • Pay • June - Sept

SARE 🌐 🚰 64310 Map: 76

Directions: Bas de la Salle Polyvalente (community centre/village hall). • 15 • 48 hrs • All year

SAUVAGNON 🌐 🚰 64230 Map: 77

Directions: Place du Champ de Foire.
• 5 • All year

Atlantic

SAUVETERRE-DE-BEARN 🌐🛒 64390 Map: 78

Directions: Exact location unknown.
• 10 • All year

SEVIGNACQ-MEYRACQ 🌐🛒 64260 Map: 79

Directions: Aire de Camping Car du Gave d'Ossau;
Quartier Raguette. • 20 • All year

SOUSTONS PLAGE 🌐🛒 40140 Map: 80

Directions: Port d'Albret Sud - Avenue de la Petre. 50m
from Lake Marin. • 50 • €8

ST-EULALIE-EN-BORN 🌐🛒 40200 Map: 81

Directions: By the lake.
• €6 • 20 • April- Oct

ST-JEAN-DE-LUZ 🌐🛒 64500 Map: 82

Directions: Pont Charles de Gaulle.
• All year

ST-JEAN-PIED-DE-PORT 🌐🛒 64200 Map: 83

Directions: Avenue de Jai-Alai.
• 50 • 48 hrs • All year

ST-JULIEN-EN-BORN 🌐🛒 40170 Map: 84

Directions: Avenue du Phare a Contis.
• 48 • €8

ST-PAUL-LES-DAX 🌐🛒 40990 Map: 85

Directions: En bout de l'allee du Plumet.
• 8

ST-PEE-SUR-NIVELLE 🌐🛒 64310 Map: 86

Directions: At the Lake.
• 50 • 48 hrs • All year

VIELLE-SAINT-GIRONS 🌐🛒 40560 Map: 87

Directions: Lac (Lake) de Leon- Plage (beach) de Vielle;
Near Lake Leon. • 25 • €7 • March - Oct

VIEUX-BOUCAU 🌐🛒 40480 Map: 88

Directions: Boulevard du Marensin; near the plage
(beach) des Sableres. • 25 • €10

© Carol and Duncan Weaver

© Carol and Duncan Weaver

© Carol and Duncan Weaver

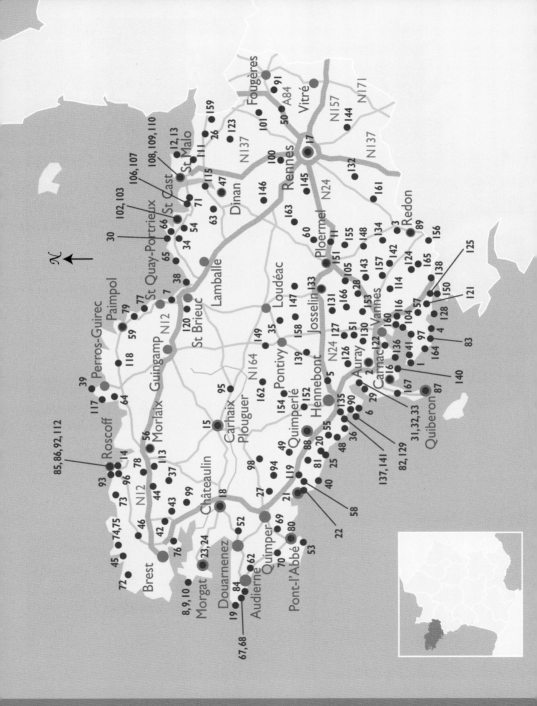

Brittany has a mild, dry climate, excellent Aires and scenery, making it an all year destination.

This is the best region in France for a motorhome beach holiday. With rocky coves to the north and large sandy beaches to the south, there are countless Aires with sea views.

Brittany's unusual light and wealth of prehistoric standing stones, give the region a mystic feel. The best examples can be seen at Carnac where row upon row stand like soldiers. Broceliande in the Foret de Paimpont is clamed to have been home to King Arthur. Merlins tomb can be reached from the D31.

The walled city of Dinan has something to offer every tourist and motorhome visitors can use the Aire at its beautiful river port.

The fascinating spit of Quiberon is a 'must see'. Though at its narrowest point little wider than the road there is a wild windy beach one side for the sporty and calmer warmer waters on the other. Walking, cycling and kite surfing are popular here and the rugged coastline is stunning at any time of year.

© Carol and Duncan Weaver

ARZON  N47°32.365'W002°52.841' 56640 Map ref: 1

Directions: Point du Crouesty. From the Super U roundabout on the D780 take C201 sp Kermor.

Sanitation:

Aire Details:

40; €6 per 24hrs; credit card; max 72 hrs.

Euro Relais; pin code req.

Footpath to beach 5 mins. Campsite style Aire, complete with gate and electric points. Tight entrance and bays only 7 meters. All operated by credit card. Daytime parking at Port du Crouesty.

AURAY N47°39.936'W002°59.411' 56400 Map ref: 2

Directions: Entering from south on the D768 follow sp to 'centre ville'. Turn right onto Rue Henry Dunant signed 'Picine' and 'centre cultural athina'. The Aire is up the next road on the left, signed.

Sanitation:

Aire Details:

3

Flot Blue

2 mins to town centre; difficult service point. LPG at Super U.

BAIN-SUR-OUST N47°42.316'W002°04.204' 35600 Map ref: 3

Directions: On C3 between church and football stadium, large gravel parking area just off of main Square. Service point hidden behind toilet block.

Sanitation:

Aire Details:

30

Custom

Close to village centre.

BANASTERE (SARZEAU) N47°30.877' W002°40.043 56370 Map ref: 4

Directions: Rue du Palud Bihan; Signed.

Sanitation:

Aire Details:

6

Aire Service; Pay

Sandy beach adj; Visited 2006.

© Carol and Duncan Weaver

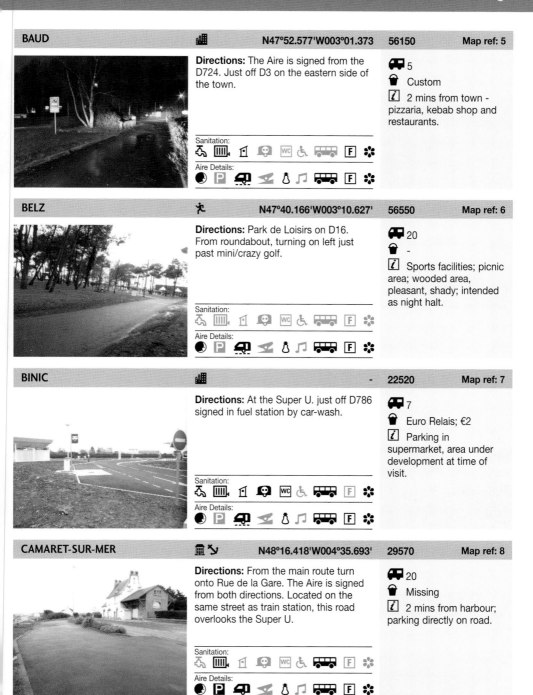

| BAUD | | N47°52.577'W003°01.373 | 56150 | Map ref: 5 |

Directions: The Aire is signed from the D724. Just off D3 on the eastern side of the town.

🚐 5
🗑 Custom
ℹ️ 2 mins from town - pizzaria, kebab shop and restaurants.

Sanitation:

Aire Details:

| BELZ | | N47°40.166'W003°10.627' | 56550 | Map ref: 6 |

Directions: Park de Loisirs on D16. From roundabout, turning on left just past mini/crazy golf.

🚐 20
🗑 -
ℹ️ Sports facilities; picnic area; wooded area, pleasant, shady; intended as night halt.

Sanitation:

Aire Details:

| BINIC | | - | 22520 | Map ref: 7 |

Directions: At the Super U. just off D786 signed in fuel station by car-wash.

🚐 7
🗑 Euro Relais; €2
ℹ️ Parking in supermarket, area under development at time of visit.

Sanitation:

Aire Details:

| CAMARET-SUR-MER | | N48°16.418'W004°35.693' | 29570 | Map ref: 8 |

Directions: From the main route turn onto Rue de la Gare. The Aire is signed from both directions. Located on the same street as train station, this road overlooks the Super U.

🚐 20
🗑 Missing
ℹ️ 2 mins from harbour; parking directly on road.

Sanitation:

Aire Details:

CAMARET-SUR-MER 2

N48°16.442'W004°36.525'   29570   Map ref: 9

© Carol and Duncan Weaver

Directions: Rue du Georges Ancey. Signed through town. Aire is at top of cliffs by stone circle, near Pointe de Penhir, well signed.

Sanitation:

Aire Details:

75; €4 per 24 hrs april/oct

Aire Service; €2; tokens

On hilltop surrounded by open spaces with stone circle adj, town 10-20 mins away, coastal path; Sandy beach 10 mins walk, rugged, interesting coastline, ruins, ideal for active people, football pitches.

CAMARET-SUR-MER 3

N48°16.644'W004°36.306'   29570   Map ref: 10

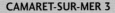

If you have a suitable picture for this Aire, please email to: gomotorhoming@hotmail.co.uk

Directions: Outside camping municipal/minigolf, 1 block towards the harbour from Camaret-sur-Mer 2 Aire, signed.

Sanitation:

Aire Details:

None

Euro Relais; €2

Service point only

CAMPENEAC

N47°57.461'W002°17.319'   56800   Map ref: 11

Directions: Rue de la Fontaine. service point: Signed off D134 and D724 adj to church and Mairie. Parking: 5 'car' spaces in coach/car park. Better parking on Rue de Ecoles; follow signs 'Salle Polyvente' or 'Ecole Notre Dame' or 'Plan d'eau', sp from N24. Parking overlooking lake. N47°57.408'W002°17.623'

Sanitation:

Aire Details:

5 , town car park

Custom; raised service point

Pleasant village with amenities and cycle path from lake. unofficial parking gravel opposite lake/river outside school - pleasant.

CANCALE

N48°40.735' W001°51.911'   35260   Map ref: 12

Directions: D355 at Super U. In car park at Super U, signed.

Sanitation:

Aire Details:

18

€2.5; token

Supermarket car park; Bays 7m; Laundrette self service open 7am-9pm, 7 days a week; LPG at supermarket.

CANCALE - LA VILLE-BALLET 🏴 N48°40.198'w001°51.930' 35260 Map ref: 13

Directions: Rue Des Francus Lubres. Signed off the D76 as you approach Cancale after picnic spot, take next left and the Aire is 200m on left.

Sanitation: 🛁 🚽 1️⃣ ☠️ WC ♿ 🚌 F ✳️

Aire Details: ⚫ P 🚐 ⬋ 🏕️ 🎵 🚌 F ✳️

🚐 144; €3 per day, max 3 days

🛢️ Aire Service; €2

ℹ️ 15 mins from town; hilltop location; road noise. Campsite for motorhomes, well organised but lacks charm. No spaces for motorhomes over 7 meters.

© Carol and Duncan Weaver

CARANTEC 🏢 N48°39.578'W003°54.845' 29660 Map ref: 14

Directions: Rue de Kerrot. Sp 'tennis club', 'sports complex'. Drive towards water tower. Parking and service point at base of water tower, signed. Clearly signed at all turnings from D73.

Sanitation: 🛁 🚽 1️⃣ ☠️ WC ♿ 🚌 F ✳️

Aire Details: ⚫ P 🚐 ⬋ 🏕️ 🎵 🚌 F ✳️

🚐 20

🛢️ Euro Relais; Tokens - Boulangeries

ℹ️ 5-10 minutes from town, 10-20 mins from beach (down hill); no views; area under renovation at time of visit.

CARHAIX PLOUGUER 🏢 N48°16.700'W003°34.326 29270 Map ref: 15

Directions: Les Augustins. Enter town on the D54, at the roundabout in the town turn left (you should see a large church that you would reach if you went straight on), the Aire is in a small car park immediately on the right.

Sanitation: 🛁 🚽 1️⃣ ☠️ WC ♿ 🚌 F ✳️

Aire Details: ⚫ P 🚐 ⬋ 🏕️ 🎵 🚌 F ✳️

🚐 5

🛢️ Custom

ℹ️ On busy road but good access to town and supermarket; difficult to find. The next turning on right leads to Casino Supermarket and is the quickest route on foot to town.

CARNAC 🏢 N47°35.103'W003°04.939' 56340 Map ref: 16

Directions: On D781 as you enter-town. Just past Lidl, opp office Notarial, behind/beside Gendamerie National.

Sanitation: 🛁 🚽 1️⃣ ☠️ WC ♿ 🚌 F ✳️

Aire Details: ⚫ P 🚐 ⬋ 🏕️ 🎵 🚌 F ✳️

🚐 10

🛢️ Raclet; €2

ℹ️ Town adj; 5-10 mins walk to large collection of standing stones. From Aire follow sp to 'Auray'. Parking available at stones.

CESSON-SEVIGNE
 N48°06.773'W001°35.380' 35510 Map ref: 17

Directions: Carrefour Supermarket - in Petrol Station. Exit 2 from the E50/N136 sp 'Cesson', turn left onto D32 and at the large roundabout turn left into Carrefour Supermarket and the centre commercial.

Sanitation:

Aire Details:

 10

Euro Relais; €1; token - petrol station

ℹ️ Out of town retail park. Other shops available. LPG available.

CHATEAULIN
N48°11.787'W004°05.146' 29150 Map ref: 18

Directions: Rue de ty Carree. At Intermarche Supermarket. Chateaulin operates on a one-way system so when you cross the bridge on the D887 enter the town (some tight turns) and follow the road up the hill to the Intermarche supermarket.

Sanitation:

Aire Details:

 6

Station Sanitaire; €2

ℹ️ Near busy road; supermarket; clothes shops; petrol station; noisy but only 2 mins walk down hill to town, not worth the difficulty in finding!

CLEDEN-CAP-SUZIN
N48°02.915'W004°39.030' 29770 Map ref: 19

Directions: On D43. Drive through village, opp cemetery; signed.

Sanitation:

Aire Details:

 20; night cost on service point

 Aire Service; €2

ℹ️ Remote village; 2 mins from village; boulongery in town; likely to be quiet in summer.

CLOHARS-CARNOET
N47°47.887'W003°35.113' 29360 Map ref: 20

Directions: Follow sp 'Quimperle' on D16 - northern edge town signed/next to 'Salle Omni sports'.

Sanitation:

Aire Details:

4

Aire Service; €2

ℹ️ 2 mins from town; market on Saturday; Area is a bit scrappy; No views.

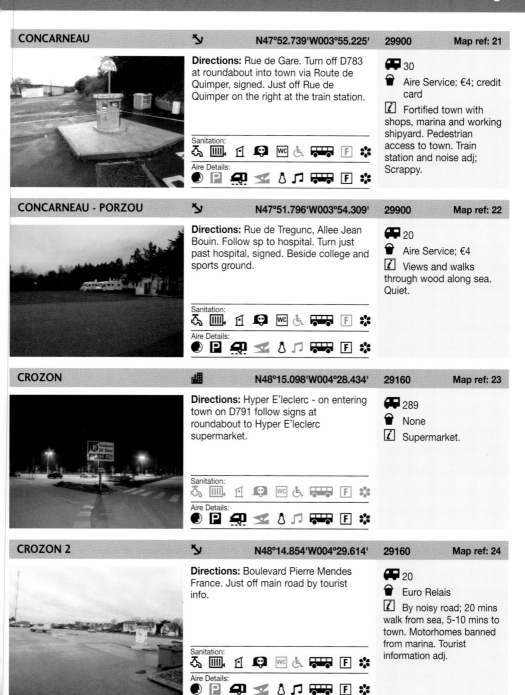

CONCARNEAU
N47°52.739'W003°55.225' 29900 Map ref: 21

Directions: Rue de Gare. Turn off D783 at roundabout into town via Route de Quimper, signed. Just off Rue de Quimper on the right at the train station.

Sanitation:

Aire Details:

🚐 30
Aire Service; €4; credit card
ℹ️ Fortified town with shops, marina and working shipyard. Pedestrian access to town. Train station and noise adj; Scrappy.

CONCARNEAU - PORZOU
N47°51.796'W003°54.309' 29900 Map ref: 22

Directions: Rue de Tregunc, Allee Jean Bouin. Follow sp to hospital. Turn just past hospital, signed. Beside college and sports ground.

Sanitation:

Aire Details:

🚐 20
Aire Service; €4
ℹ️ Views and walks through wood along sea. Quiet.

CROZON
N48°15.098'W004°28.434' 29160 Map ref: 23

Directions: Hyper E'leclerc - on entering town on D791 follow signs at roundabout to Hyper E'leclerc supermarket.

Sanitation:

Aire Details:

🚐 289
None
ℹ️ Supermarket.

CROZON 2
N48°14.854'W004°29.614' 29160 Map ref: 24

Directions: Boulevard Pierre Mendes France. Just off main road by tourist info.

Sanitation:

Aire Details:

🚐 20
Euro Relais
ℹ️ By noisy road; 20 mins walk from sea, 5-10 mins to town. Motorhomes banned from marina. Tourist information adj.

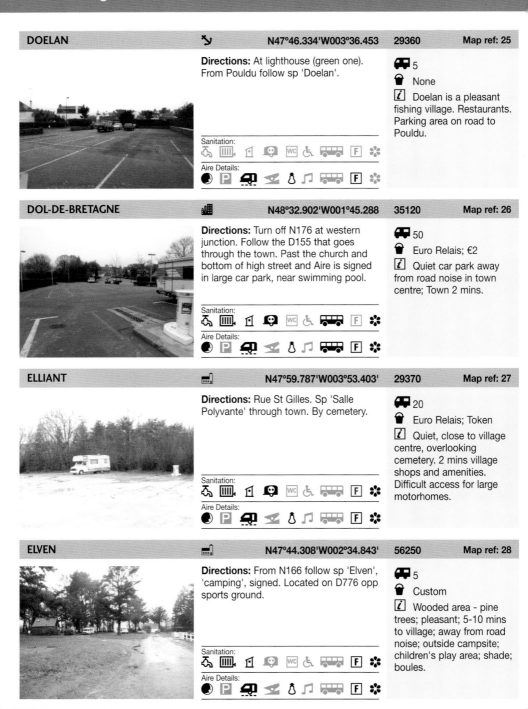

DOELAN — N47°46.334'W003°36.453 — 29360 — Map ref: 25

Directions: At lighthouse (green one). From Pouldu follow sp 'Doelan'.

Sanitation:

Aire Details:

5

None

Doelan is a pleasant fishing village. Restaurants. Parking area on road to Pouldu.

DOL-DE-BRETAGNE — N48°32.902'W001°45.288 — 35120 — Map ref: 26

Directions: Turn off N176 at western junction. Follow the D155 that goes through the town. Past the church and bottom of high street and Aire is signed in large car park, near swimming pool.

Sanitation:

Aire Details:

50

Euro Relais; €2

Quiet car park away from road noise in town centre; Town 2 mins.

ELLIANT — N47°59.787'W003°53.403' — 29370 — Map ref: 27

Directions: Rue St Gilles. Sp 'Salle Polyvante' through town. By cemetery.

Sanitation:

Aire Details:

20

Euro Relais; Token

Quiet, close to village centre, overlooking cemetery. 2 mins village shops and amenities. Difficult access for large motorhomes.

ELVEN — N47°44.308'W002°34.843' — 56250 — Map ref: 28

Directions: From N166 follow sp 'Elven', 'camping', signed. Located on D776 opp sports ground.

Sanitation:

Aire Details:

5

Custom

Wooded area - pine trees; pleasant; 5-10 mins to village; away from road noise; outside campsite; children's play area; shade; boules.

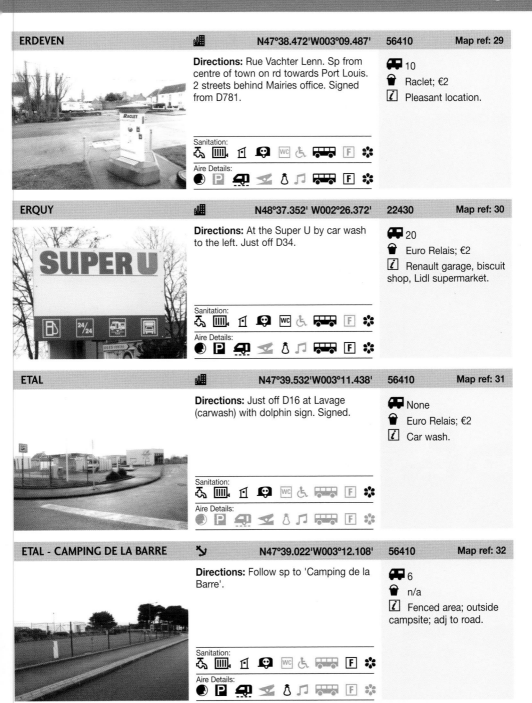

ERDEVEN		N47°38.472'W003°09.487'	56410	Map ref: 29

Directions: Rue Vachter Lenn. Sp from centre of town on rd towards Port Louis. 2 streets behind Mairies office. Signed from D781.

🚐 10
🔧 Raclet; €2
ℹ️ Pleasant location.

Sanitation:

Aire Details:

ERQUY		N48°37.352' W002°26.372'	22430	Map ref: 30

Directions: At the Super U by car wash to the left. Just off D34.

🚐 20
🔧 Euro Relais; €2
ℹ️ Renault garage, biscuit shop, Lidl supermarket.

Sanitation:

Aire Details:

ETAL		N47°39.532'W003°11.438'	56410	Map ref: 31

Directions: Just off D16 at Lavage (carwash) with dolphin sign. Signed.

🚐 None
🔧 Euro Relais; €2
ℹ️ Car wash.

Sanitation:

Aire Details:

ETAL - CAMPING DE LA BARRE		N47°39.022'W003°12.108'	56410	Map ref: 32

Directions: Follow sp to 'Camping de la Barre'.

🚐 6
🔧 n/a
ℹ️ Fenced area; outside campsite; adj to road.

Sanitation:

Aire Details:

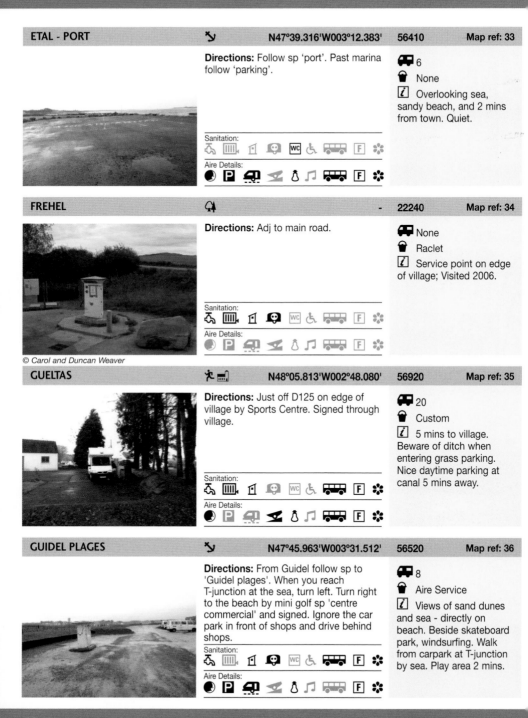

ETAL - PORT ⚓ N47°39.316'W003°12.383' 56410 Map ref: 33

Directions: Follow sp 'port'. Past marina follow 'parking'.

🚐 6
🚰 None
ℹ️ Overlooking sea, sandy beach, and 2 mins from town. Quiet.

Sanitation:

Aire Details:

FREHEL 💧 - 22240 Map ref: 34

Directions: Adj to main road.

🚐 None
🚰 Raclet
ℹ️ Service point on edge of village; Visited 2006.

Sanitation:

Aire Details:

© Carol and Duncan Weaver

GUELTAS N48°05.813'W002°48.080' 56920 Map ref: 35

Directions: Just off D125 on edge of village by Sports Centre. Signed through village.

🚐 20
🚰 Custom
ℹ️ 5 mins to village. Beware of ditch when entering grass parking. Nice daytime parking at canal 5 mins away.

Sanitation:

Aire Details:

GUIDEL PLAGES ⚓ N47°45.963'W003°31.512' 56520 Map ref: 36

Directions: From Guidel follow sp to 'Guidel plages'. When you reach T-junction at the sea, turn left. Turn right to the beach by mini golf sp 'centre commercial' and signed. Ignore the car park in front of shops and drive behind shops.

🚐 8
🚰 Aire Service
ℹ️ Views of sand dunes and sea - directly on beach. Beside skateboard park, windsurfing. Walk from carpark at T-junction by sea. Play area 2 mins.

Sanitation:

Aire Details:

Brittany

| GUIMILAIU | 🏃 | N48°29.199'W003°59.811' | 29400 | Map ref: 37 |

Directions: Follow sp to 'Salle Polyvalente' on edge of village just off D31.

Sanitation:

Aire Details:

🚐 20
🏺 Custom
ℹ️ Edge of village, quiet road, 2 mins walk to village.

| HILLION | 🏢 | N48°30.876'W002°40.027' | 22120 | Map ref: 38 |

Directions: Signed from main route D34, rear of town square, signed.

Sanitation:

Aire Details:
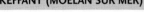

🚐 30
🏺 Custom
ℹ️ Rear of town square, away from road; pleasant.

| ILLE GRANDE | ⚓ | N48°47.942'W003°35.016' | 22560 | Map ref: 39 |

Directions: Outside camping municipal Ille Grand. signed.

Sanitation:

Aire Details:

🚐 10; €5 24hrs
🏺 Raclet; €2
ℹ️ Adj to beach, ideal for beach holiday; basically this is similar to campsite without amenities, may be more desirable/economical to stay in campsite if you really want to stay here.

| KEFFANY (MOELAN SUR MER) | ⚓ | N47°48.138'W003°41.541' | 29350 | Map ref: 40 |

Directions: Follow sp to 'Keffany', then to 'Keffany plages' (beaches) service point on left on D116 at the edge of the village.

Sanitation:

Aire Details:

🚐 5
🏺 Aire Service
ℹ️ On edge of village; main road adj.

KERNERS (ARZON)

 N47°33.181'W002°52.970' 56640 Map ref: 41

Directions: Sp 'Camping du Tindio', sp from main road. Service point outside campsite.

Parking in community

Custom

ℹ️ Dilapidated facilities. Small village, slightly inland.

Sanitation:

Aire Details:

LA MARTYRE

N48°26.949'W004°09.381' 29800 Map ref: 42

Directions: D35 towards Ploudury exactly as you exit the village, by Maison du Plaleau.

🚐 20

Euro Relais

ℹ️ Woody location; 2 minutes from village and restaurants; Next village 5/10 minutes cycle on flat cycle path.

Sanitation:

Aire Details:

LANDERNEAU

N48°26.818W004°15.423' 29800 Map ref: 43

Directions: Rue de Calvaire. Just off Route to Quimper, signed. As you exit the town centre towards Quimper, take the first turning on right as the D7 bears left away from the river. Close to the campsite.

🚐 6

Euro Relais; €2

ℹ️ Urban, on riverside but no view, 2 mins from town along river. By sports de combat dojo, on minor road away from road noise. children's playpark and grassy area. 3.5t restriction on entry road.

Sanitation:

Aire Details:

LANDIVISIAU

N48°30.607'W004°04.566' 29400 Map ref: 44

Directions: Enter town on D34/D712 roundabout, signed. At the next roundabout past the Super U turn left into Aire. Signed.

🚐 30

Custom

ℹ️ 2 mins to town via busy main road. Telephone.

Sanitation:

Aire Details:

LANNILIS

N48°33.420'W004°30.383' 29870 Map ref: 45

Directions: From the D13 follow sp 'Aire de Repos'. On site of former road junction but is not accessible from main road.

Sanitation:

Aire Details:

5

Euro Relais

ℹ️ Picnic site, on side of busy road - D13 - very noisy.

LE FOLGOET

N48°33'37"W004°20.06' 29260 Map ref: 46

Directions: Route de Gorrekear. Just behind church. From D788 drive towards church through green. Just past church the entrance is on right by Bishops statue. Signed, also sp 'omni sport'.

Sanitation:

Aire Details:

50

Euro Relais

ℹ️ View of church - green area edge of village. Access to toilets, museum, restaurants. Away from main road.

LE PORT DE DINAN

N48°27.252'W002°02.309 22100 Map ref: 47

Directions: Sous le viaduct D2. At the bottom of viaduct (the large bridge spanning river) on edge of river 2 min from beautiful river town.

Sanitation:

Aire Details:

50

Custom

ℹ️ Opportunity for walking. Steps up to hilltop Dinan. Nice peaceful sheltered location, riverside walk, restaurants and limited shops more facilities in Dinan; service point at toilettes 200m away by the marina; under development at time of visit.

LE POULDU PLAGE DE BELLAGENET

N47°46.043'W003°33.286' 29360 Map ref: 48

Directions: Plage de Bellagent; follow signs to 'Le Pouldu'/'Le Pouldu Plages' from Clohars-Carnet. Dedicated motorhome parking opposite beach.

Sanitation:

Aire Details:

20; 15/6-15/9; €4 22hrs-9hrs

None

ℹ️ Seaside town ideal for beach holiday. Likely to be busy in Summer - free day parking. Beach, restaurants, mini golf, play area and tourist info 2 mins.

LE TREVOUX
N47°53.796'W003°38.513' 29380 Map ref: 49

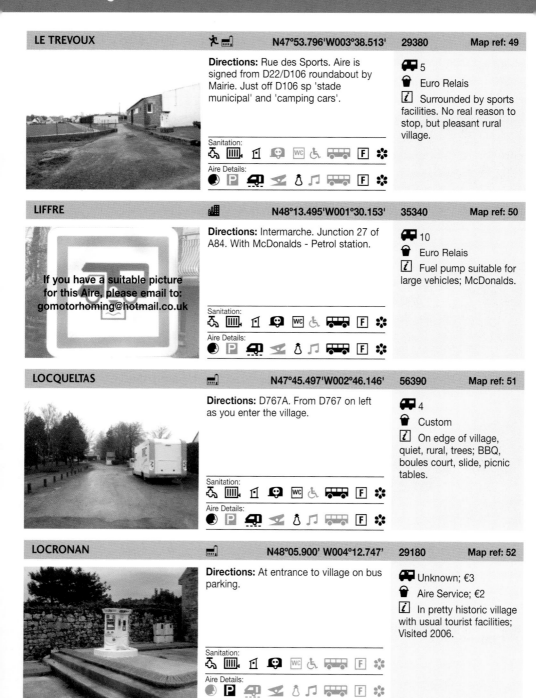

Directions: Rue des Sports. Aire is signed from D22/D106 roundabout by Mairie. Just off D106 sp 'stade municipal' and 'camping cars'.

🚐 5
Euro Relais
ℹ Surrounded by sports facilities. No real reason to stop, but pleasant rural village.

Sanitation:

Aire Details:

LIFFRE
N48°13.495'W001°30.153' 35340 Map ref: 50

If you have a suitable picture for this Aire, please email to: gomotorhoming@hotmail.co.uk

Directions: Intermarche. Junction 27 of A84. With McDonalds - Petrol station.

🚐 10
Euro Relais
ℹ Fuel pump suitable for large vehicles; McDonalds.

Sanitation:

Aire Details:

LOCQUELTAS
N47°45.497'W002°46.146' 56390 Map ref: 51

Directions: D767A. From D767 on left as you enter the village.

🚐 4
Custom
ℹ On edge of village, quiet, rural, trees; BBQ, boules court, slide, picnic tables.

Sanitation:

Aire Details:

LOCRONAN
N48°05.900' W004°12.747' 29180 Map ref: 52

Directions: At entrance to village on bus parking.

🚐 Unknown; €3
Aire Service; €2
ℹ In pretty historic village with usual tourist facilities; Visited 2006.

Sanitation:

Aire Details:

© Carol and Duncan Weaver

LOCTUDY - PLAGE DU COSQUER  N47°47.928'W004°11.842' | 29750 | Map ref: 53

Directions: Plage du Cosquer, 4 km south of Loctudy, signed from Loctudy to Lesconil road. Aire is clearly signed off this road at roundabout down Des Sables Blancs (white sands).

Sanitation:

Aire Details:

 8

Euro Relais; €2

ℹ Bottom of dunes, long sandy beach 2 min. Walks along top of dunes. Ideal for beach holiday. Service point completely destroyed at time of visit.

MATIGNON N48°35.977'W002°17.204' | 22550 | Map ref: 54

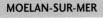

Directions: Exit Matignon on the D13 towards Saint Cast. The Aire is at the Super U.

Sanitation:

Aire Details:

🚐 2

€2

ℹ Service point in fuel station; selection of shops; 5 mins from town; Launderette next to service point; tight access for large motorhomes.

MOELAN-SUR-MER N47°49.286'W003°37.044' | 29350 | Map ref: 55

Directions: Intermarche. Follows signs to Intermarche on Route to Quimper. Overnight parking between 8pm and 8am.

Sanitation:

Aire Details:

🚐 5

€2

ℹ Service point difficult to access.

MORLAIX N48°34.447'W003°49.891' | 29600 | Map ref: 56

Directions: Rue de Brest. Signed, car park of Ecomarche.

Sanitation:

Aire Details:

🚐 20

Raclet

ℹ 2 mins from town centre, beside river; supermarket parking adj. Supermarket car park is pay (€1-1.5 hrs, free Monday) but adj car park appears free.

MUZILLAC   N47°33.538'W002°30.711'   56190   Map ref: 57

Directions: Super U. At D20/N165 roundabout.

🚐 20

Euro Relais

ℹ️ Not working at time of visit.

Sanitation:

Aire Details:

NEVEZ   N47°48.953'W003°47.362'   29920   Map ref: 58

Directions: Rue de Port Manec'h D77. Follow signs to Port Manec'h (might need to follow 'toutes directions' around one way system before Port Manec'h, beside sports ground. Signed. Also sp 'Salle Omnisport'.

🚐 20; 24hrs

Custom; €2

ℹ️ Clean, tidy ideal night halt. Edge of village, partial rural views, quiet.

Sanitation:

Aire Details:

PAIMPOL   N48°47.003'W003°02.821'   22500   Map ref: 59

Directions: parking Champ de Foire, signed. Located in wooded area just off D7, D789 roundabout. Entrance on Rue Pierre Loti. Further parking at end of road in carpark on left.

🚐 13

Aire Service; €3

ℹ️ Busy road, semi wooded, city park feel, 2 min from town, hedged pitches suitable for 7m motorhomes.

Sanitation:

Aire Details:

PAIMPONT   N48°01.377'W002°10.270'   35380   Map ref: 60

Directions: Rue Merlin L'Enchanteur D71. Signed from the D773, north side of lake by football pitch.

🚐 10

Aire Service; token - Mairie/campsite.

ℹ️ Edge of village, by sports facilities, part shaded; Lake and wood adj, town 5-10 minutes; reverse on service point.

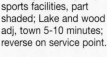

Sanitation:

Aire Details:

HAVE YOU VISITED AN AIRE?

FILL IN THE FORM AT THE BACK AND SEND TO VICARIOUS BOOKS.

ℹ️ We need your help to make this guide bigger and better. Don't forget to send us your Aires.

Sanitation:

Aire Details:

PHOUHINEC
 N48°00.963'W004°30.085' 29780 **Map ref: 62**

Directions: On D784 follow sp to Champion hypermarket.

🚐 5
🚿 Station Sanitaire; €2
ℹ️ Supermarket; near main road.

Sanitation:

Aire Details:

PLANCOET
N48°31.485'W002°14.357' 22130 **Map ref: 63**

Directions: On D768 from Plancoet towards Lamballe, at super U, signed from all points in town.

🚐 2
🚿 Euro Relais; €2
ℹ️ Plancoet is a pretty town around a river weir. Supermarket.

Sanitation:

Aire Details:

PLANETANUM DE BRETAGNE - PLEUMEUR BODOU
N48°46.989'W003°31.553' 22560 **Map ref: 64**

Directions: Planetanum de Bretagne, turn off D21, follow sp 'cosmopolis', drive towards large white ball and satellite dishes.

🚐 5
🚿 Raclet; €2
ℹ️ Creperie. Planetenum, Viking Museum, Museum of Telecommunication. Most level parking opp Viking museum.

Sanitation:

Aire Details:

PLENEUF-VAL-ANDRE ⭐   ⚓   N48°34.523'W002°34.000'   22370   Map ref: 65

Directions: At marina. follow road around marina, parking area on far side, turn off D786 to marina, sp 'yacht club Beureur de Port'. Signed.

Sanitation:

Aire Details:

🚐 50

Euro Relais; €3

ℹ️ On edge of marina, views across masts to town, town with shops, nice location close to water, pleasant views.

PLEVENON   N49°39.307' W002°19.939'   22240   Map ref: 66

Directions: D16. in village opp Mairie and tourist information signed on D16 at junction C3/D16.

Sanitation:

Aire Details:

🚐 5

Euro Relais; tokens - Mairie

ℹ️ Village centre, near church, no views, but pleasant and quiet. Telephone and village shops.

PLOGOFF 1   N48°02.243'W004°39.943'   29770   Map ref: 67

Directions: Head out of town on Route Cleden Cap Sizun, the Aire is by the church.

Sanitation:

Aire Details:

🚐 5

Aire Service; €2

ℹ️ Overlooking church in village; by road junction, pleasant.

PLOGOFF 2   N48°01.994'W004°39.731'   29770   Map ref: 68

Directions: From D784 turn left beside Boulangerie to stadium, signed. The Aire is on the left at the stadium.

Sanitation:

Aire Details:

🚐 50

▪ -

ℹ️ Choice of grass or gravel, terraced; partial sea views on edge of village, different rural France, ideal to escape the crowds, beach with parking just out of village, 5-10 min.

PLOMELIN N47°56.037'W004°09.093' 29700 Map ref: 69

Directions: From central square head south sp 'complexe sportif' then the first turning on left at the stadium, signed.

Sanitation:

Aire Details:

3
Euro Relais; €2
At sports complex, rural village, likelihood of kids hanging around. supermarket, few shops in town.

PLONEOUR-LANVERN N47°54.209'W004°16.763' 29720 Map ref: 70

Directions: Follow sp out of town to 'Pont-l'Abbe', after church square take first left opp Espace Raphalen and the Aire is 100m on your left.

Sanitation:

Aire Details:

50
Raclet; €2
2 mins from town but off main route. Bars, restaurants in small town square.

PLOUBALAY N48°34.829' W002°08.708' 22650 Map ref: 71

Directions: Place de la Gare Routiere. signed through village, edge of village, near cemetery.

Sanitation:

Aire Details:

5
Flot Blue; €2.50 in 50c pieces
Amenities in village.

PLOUDSLMEZEAU - PORSGUEN N48°33.961'W004°41.918' 29830 Map ref: 72

Directions: Follow D26 out of Ploudalmezeau towards Porguen. Signed entire route.

Sanitation:

Aire Details:

50
-
2 mins to sand dune and beach; similar to CL/campsite field.

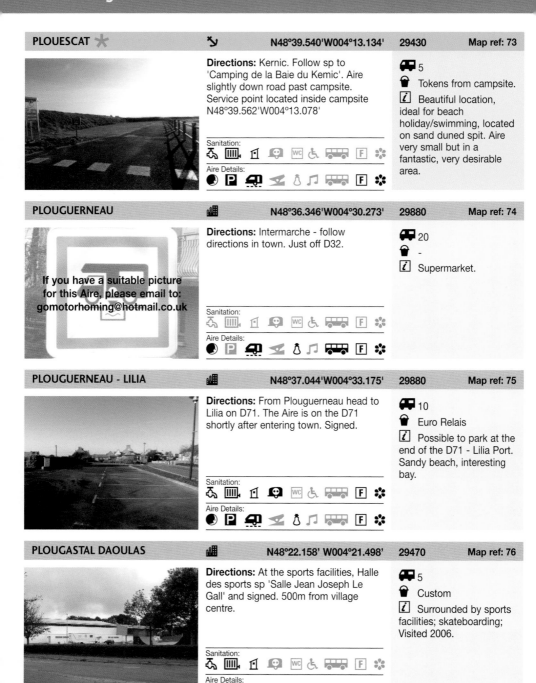

PLOUESCAT

N48°39.540'W004°13.134'   29430   Map ref: 73

Directions: Kernic. Follow sp to 'Camping de la Baie du Kemic'. Aire slightly down road past campsite. Service point located inside campsite N48°39.562'W004°13.078'

Sanitation:

Aire Details:

🚐 5
Tokens from campsite.
ℹ️ Beautiful location, ideal for beach holiday/swimming, located on sand duned spit. Aire very small but in a fantastic, very desirable area.

PLOUGUERNEAU

N48°36.346'W004°30.273'   29880   Map ref: 74

Directions: Intermarche - follow directions in town. Just off D32.

If you have a suitable picture for this Aire, please email to: gomotorhoming@hotmail.co.uk

Sanitation:

Aire Details:

🚐 20
🔑 -
ℹ️ Supermarket.

PLOUGUERNEAU - LILIA

N48°37.044'W004°33.175'   29880   Map ref: 75

Directions: From Plouguerneau head to Lilia on D71. The Aire is on the D71 shortly after entering town. Signed.

Sanitation:

Aire Details:

🚐 10
🔑 Euro Relais
ℹ️ Possible to park at the end of the D71 - Lilia Port. Sandy beach, interesting bay.

PLOUGASTAL DAOULAS

N48°22.158' W004°21.498'   29470   Map ref: 76

Directions: At the sports facilities, Halle des sports sp 'Salle Jean Joseph Le Gall' and signed. 500m from village centre.

Sanitation:

Aire Details:

🚐 5
🔑 Custom
ℹ️ Surrounded by sports facilities; skateboarding; Visited 2006.

© Carol and Duncan Weaver

PLOUHA  N48°40.554' W002°53.107' 22580 Map ref: 77

Directions: Drive down D32 to sea, the aire is on the right facing the sea, sp 'Plage du Paulas - la Palus'.

Sanitation:

Aire Details:

🚐 20

Euro Relais; €1

ℹ️ Overlooking stony beach, cliff top paths, restaurants, very pleasant rocky cove, suitable for swimming and rock pooling, motor homes banned from seafront. Volleyball court, playarea.

PLOUVORN N48°34.662'W004°01.815' 29420 Map ref: 78

Directions: Located on the edge of town just off the D19 towards Morlaix. Sp from D19 'plan d'eau'/ 'De Lanorgant' campsite on D19. The Aire is located in the parking area to the right before you reach the lake.

Sanitation:

Aire Details:

🚐 20

Euro Relais; €2

ℹ️ Ideal for sporty/outdoor types, walking or cycling. Skateboard park is hangout for children. Parkland with walks, facilities, lake.

PLOUEZEC N8°44.845'W002°59.104' 22470 Map ref: 79

Directions: D786, Place de 19 Mars 1962. Signed, outside top garage, village parking adjacent.

Sanitation:

Aire Details:

🚐 7

Euro Relais

ℹ️ Main road and garage noise, semi commercial area, 2 mins from town.

PONT L'ABBE N47°51.849'W004°14.152' 29120 Map ref: 80

Directions: Follow sp in town to E'leclerc supermarket.

Sanitation:

Aire Details:

🚐 5

Aire Service; €2

ℹ️ €2 7 hours electricity at rear 4 allotted bays; 5-10 mins walk to town; LPG at supermarket fuel; supermarket.

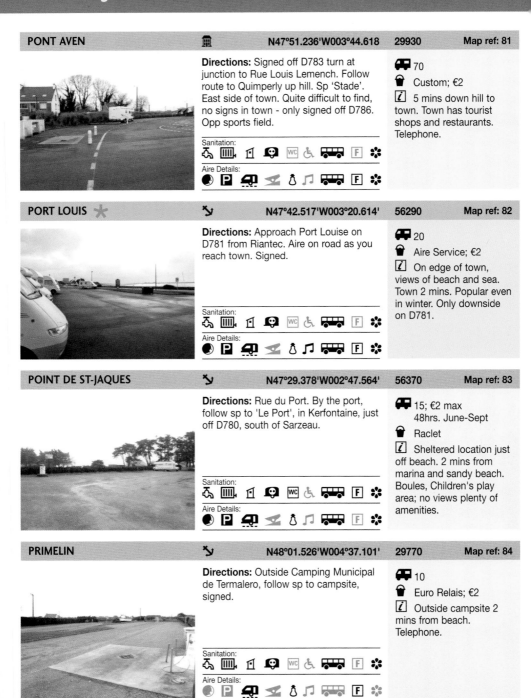

PONT AVEN

N47°51.236'W003°44.618   29930   Map ref: 81

Directions: Signed off D783 turn at junction to Rue Louis Lemench. Follow route to Quimperly up hill. Sp 'Stade'. East side of town. Quite difficult to find, no signs in town - only signed off D786. Opp sports field.

Sanitation:

Aire Details:

🚐 70

Custom; €2

ℹ 5 mins down hill to town. Town has tourist shops and restaurants. Telephone.

PORT LOUIS

N47°42.517'W003°20.614'   56290   Map ref: 82

Directions: Approach Port Louise on D781 from Riantec. Aire on road as you reach town. Signed.

Sanitation:

Aire Details:

🚐 20

Aire Service; €2

ℹ On edge of town, views of beach and sea. Town 2 mins. Popular even in winter. Only downside on D781.

POINT DE ST-JAQUES

N47°29.378'W002°47.564'   56370   Map ref: 83

Directions: Rue du Port. By the port, follow sp to 'Le Port', in Kerfontaine, just off D780, south of Sarzeau.

Sanitation:

Aire Details:

🚐 15; €2 max 48hrs. June-Sept

Raclet

ℹ Sheltered location just off beach. 2 mins from marina and sandy beach. Boules, Children's play area; no views plenty of amenities.

PRIMELIN

N48°01.526'W004°37.101'   29770   Map ref: 84

Directions: Outside Camping Municipal de Termalero, follow sp to campsite, signed.

Sanitation:

Aire Details:

🚐 10

Euro Relais; €2

ℹ Outside campsite 2 mins from beach. Telephone.

QUAI DE PEMPOUL (St Pol deLeon) ⚓   N48°47.046'W003°02.792'   29250   Map ref: 85

Directions: Rue Pierre Loti. At end of road, turn off roundabout with D7 and D789 signed. Turn off road just before cemetery, signed, and follow road.

Sanitation:
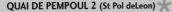

Aire Details:

🚐 15

🛖 See below

ℹ️ Partial view of harbour, away from road noise, 2 mins to harbour; 5 mins to town.

QUAI DE PEMPOUL 2 (St Pol deLeon) ⚓   N48°41.001'W003°58.269'   29250   Map ref: 86

Directions: Quai de Pempol. 2 mins further round from Pempoul, signed.

Sanitation:

Aire Details:

🚐 30; open 1-6 to 31-8

🛖 Euro Relais; €2

ℹ️ Restaurants, 5 mins walk to town, nice walk along waterfront. Pretty town. Phone; beautiful setting, sea views across to Rocher Ste Anne.

QUIBERON ✳   ⚓   N47°29.500'W003°08.334'   56170   Map ref: 87

Directions: D186. Parking de Kerne Just off main coastal route (D186) around island at Kerne.

Sanitation:

Aire Details:

🚐 40; €2.5 per night 15 April-15 October

🛖 Custom

ℹ️ Views across to sea, beach 1 min. Ideal for surfing, kite surfing. One side permanent onshore wind/one side sheltered. Walking trails all round coast, cycle path up central strip (flat). Fantastic location plenty to do but exposed.

QUIMPERLY 🏢   N47°51.967'W003°32.614   29300   Map ref: 88

Directions: Rue du Viaduct. Just off D16 sharp turn onto D49 sp 'Le Ploudu'. Where D16, Route de Moelan, meets/exits river. Signed from road, over narrow bridge.

Sanitation:

Aire Details:

🚐 5

🛖 Euro Relais

ℹ️ 2 mins from river and fairly large town centre. By stream but scrappy.

REDON

N47°38.704'W002°05.383'   35600   Map ref: 89

Directions: Rue de Vannes. On canal by lock and marina. At D775 and D775B roundabout, turn off onto D775 into town, sp 'Redon'. Follow this road into town and the Aire in on the right just in front of Marina.

🚐 10
Custom
ℹ️ On edge canal lock and marina. Walking distance to town. Possible to walk down canal path. Excellent town Aire.

Sanitation:

Aire Details:

RIANTEG-PLOUHINEC

N47°42.684'W003°17.931'   56670   Map ref: 90

Directions: D781. Off roundabout by Fishing boat named 'Rianteg'. Signed.

🚐 5
Aire Service; €2
ℹ️ Water feature, pond, picnic area, pleasant. Beach/town 5-10 mins walk.

Sanitation:

Aire Details:

ROMAGNE

N48°20.652'W001°16.453'   35133   Map ref: 91

Directions: N12 towards Forges. Picnic area on edge of town.

🚐 5
Custom
ℹ️ Town 2 mins walk. Service point by urinals.

Sanitation:

Aire Details:

ROSCOFF

N48°43.526'W003°58.224'   29680   Map ref: 92

Directions: Sp to 'Car Ferry', past car ferry follow road, at T junction turn right, follow road on right. From car ferry turn right and follow above.

🚐 50
Euro Relais
ℹ️ Service point is difficult to get to; need to back on, cars obstructing. Good location for walks, 2 mins to beach/fishing. Near church/viewpoint.

Sanitation:

Aire Details:

ROSCOFF - LABER   N48°42.744'W003°59.817'   29680   Map ref: 93

Directions: Route de Laber. Signed - follow directions to 'campsite de Perngray' and 'Laber'. On left when road runs alongside coast.

Sanitation:

Aire Details:

🚐 20
Euro Relais
ℹ️ By beach - swimming/bird life. Stoll down beach to town 5-10 minutes. On road, by garden and marked walks. Sea views, nice location. Picnic site and fields.

ROSPORDEN   N47°57.897'W003°51.176   29140   Map ref: 94

Directions: At Super U. Clearly sp through town - on D765 towards Quimper.

Sanitation:

Aire Details:

🚐 5
Aire Service; €2
ℹ️ Out of town retail area - on busy road.

ROSTRENEN   N48°13.995'W003°12.202'   22110   Map ref: 95

Directions: D790 sp through town with green info sp but follow D790 for accurate route. Sp 'Plouray' and canal 200m on right.

Sanitation:

Aire Details:

🚐 6
Euro Relais; Token - Bureau de Tabac/ Office de Tourism
ℹ️ Short walk to town; Main road noise, no view, very nice facilities.

SANTEC   -   29250   Map ref: 96

Directions: 5km Saint Pol de Leon. By Le Bistrot a Crepes.

Sanitation:

Aire Details:

🚐 10
€2; Tokens
ℹ️ 50 m from beach; Visited 2006.

© Carol and Duncan Weaver

Brittany

| SARZEAU | 🏢 | N47°31.795'W002°45.577' | 56370 | Map ref: 97 |

Directions: Rue des Venetes. Signed from main road D780. Clearly signed, sp 'Office Notarial'. Or from town turn by Office Notarial. Signed. Outside school Ecole Ste Anne.

🚐 20; €5 from 30 June
🚰 Raclet; €2
ℹ️ No parking during school terms.

Sanitation:

Aire Details:

| SCAER ✳ | ⛺ | N48°01.664'W003°41.695' | 29390 | Map ref: 98 |

Directions: Camping Municipal Kerisole. Follow sp to Camping municipal through town. Aire outside Camping municipal but in a separate designated area. Just off D782 - allee Croix Sinquin.

🚐 100
🚰 Custom
ℹ️ Wooded - cool in summer; 2 mins from town. walking trails, adj green land and fields.

Sanitation:

Aire Details:

| SIZUN | 🏃 | N48°24.018'W004°04.739' | 29450 | Map ref: 99 |

Directions: Sp 'Camping' and 'Picine'. By roundabout with D18/D30.

🚐 15
🚰 Euro Relais
ℹ️ 5-10 minutes walk uphill to town. Telephone; by noisy roundabout and football pitch.

Sanitation:

Aire Details:

| ST AUBIN D'AUBIGNE | 🏭 | N48°15.676'W001°36.387' | 35250 | Map ref: 100 |

Directions: Opp pharmacy on D175 before you enter the village from south. Signed at car park.

🚐 5
🚰 Custom
ℹ️ Town amenities; Water in toilets, WC disposal, point hidden in flower bed.

Sanitation:

Aire Details:

ST BRICE EN COGLES

 N48°24.684'W001°21.730' 35460 Map ref: 101

Directions: D102. Sp 'Gendarmerie' and signed. North of village.

 7

Custom

2 mins from town; backs on to cemetery; Water from 9am-10pm.

Sanitation:

Aire Details:

ST CAST LE GUILDO

 N48°37.738'W002°15.219' 22380 Map ref: 102

Directions: Rue de La Bataille. Turn off D19 at roundabout towards sea on to Rue Yves Dumanior, then take next left and the service point is on the left, by boules court.

 10

Euro Relais; €2

2 mins from sea. Boules court, very large golden sandy beach and seafront prom to town. Really just a service point but with scrappy parking available on side of road.

Sanitation:

Aire Details:

ST CAST LE GUILDO

N48°38.595'W002°14.767 22380 Map ref: 103

Directions: Rue De Semaphore. At the end of the peninsula, above harbour by coastguard building.

 20 marked bays

-

High above harbour, excellent views, exposed, walk across to cannon and down to marina. WC not for chemical disposal.

Sanitation:

Aire Details:

© Carol and Duncan Weaver

ST COLOMBIER

 N47°32.807'W002°43.295' 56370 Map ref: 104

Directions: Sp off D780 towards Sarzeau (second turning if miss first).

 5

€2

Play area, boules, cycle routes, village restaurant.

Sanitation:

Aire Details:

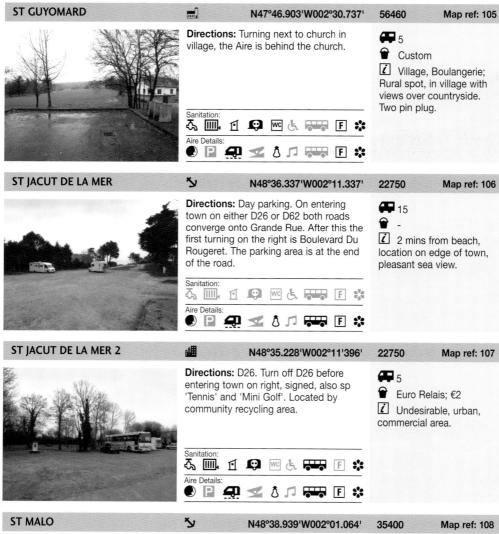

| ST GUYOMARD | | N47º46.903'W002º30.737' | 56460 | Map ref: 105 |

Directions: Turning next to church in village, the Aire is behind the church.

5
Custom
Village, Boulangerie; Rural spot, in village with views over countryside. Two pin plug.

Sanitation:

Aire Details:

| ST JACUT DE LA MER | | N48º36.337'W002º11.337' | 22750 | Map ref: 106 |

Directions: Day parking. On entering town on either D26 or D62 both roads converge onto Grande Rue. After this the first turning on the right is Boulevard Du Rougeret. The parking area is at the end of the road.

15
-
2 mins from beach, location on edge of town, pleasant sea view.

Sanitation:

Aire Details:

| ST JACUT DE LA MER 2 | | N48º35.228'W002º11'396' | 22750 | Map ref: 107 |

Directions: D26. Turn off D26 before entering town on right, signed, also sp 'Tennis' and 'Mini Golf'. Located by community recycling area.

5
Euro Relais; €2
Undesirable, urban, commercial area.

Sanitation:

Aire Details:

| ST MALO | | N48º38.939'W002º01.064' | 35400 | Map ref: 108 |

Directions: Avenue Louis Martin. Drive towards St Malo centre on the D1, which becomes Avenue Louis Martin. The parking runs parallel to the road, separated by a planted reservation and can be found before the marina.

10
-
2 mins from port, walled city; edge of busy road, backs onto park.

Sanitation:

Aire Details:

ST MALO 2
 N48°38.618'W001°59.618' 35400 Map ref: 109

Directions: Off the D12 signed from roundabout backs onto sports facilities and racecourse. Exit D301 onto D126 at first roundabout turn right, between the racecourse and train track.

30
Aire service
Parking under construction. €2 for 24 hours. Large motorhome campsite. 20 mins from town.

Sanitation:

Aire Details:

ST MALO 3
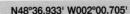 N48°36.933' W002°00.705' 35400 Map ref: 110

Directions: La Briantais. signed off D168 en route to Dinard, end wall chapel just past Dinard sign, sp 'La Briantais'. If heading into St Malo on D168 can go under underpass and then enter the D168 the right way.

50; 24 hrs
-
Reasonably remote and rural. Narrow entrance and exit.

Sanitation:

Aire Details:

ST MELOIR DES ONDES
 N48°38.081'W001°149' 35350 Map ref: 111

Directions: Signed from D76 in village, in front of the municipal campsite La Vallee Vert.

None
Euro Relais; €2
Outside campsite, 2 mins to village, no designed parking area but plenty of parking in the vicinity, semi industrial.

Sanitation:

Aire Details:

ST POL DE LEON
 N48°40.678'W003°59.905' 29250 Map ref: 112

Directions: E leclerc Supermarket. Behind supermarket on minor Rd. Follow E leclerc sp into town.

20 bays.
Aire Service; €2
Commercial, between garage and supermarket. Truck fuelling at E'leclerc (on slip road).

Sanitation:

Aire Details:

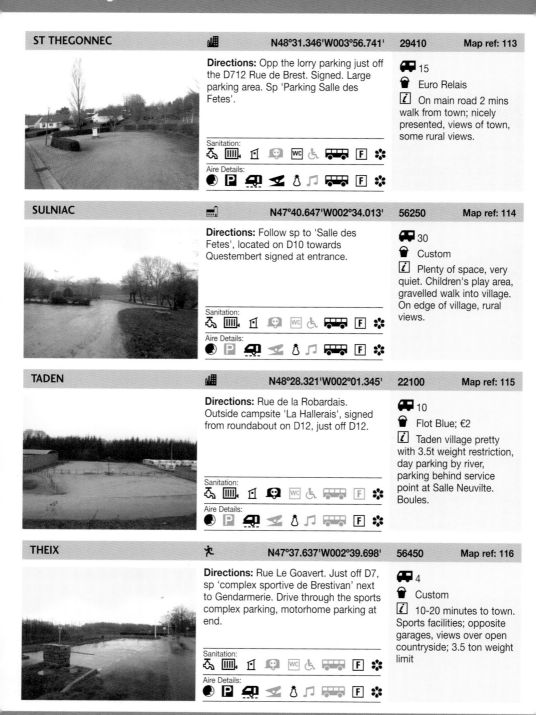

ST THEGONNEC

N48°31.346'W003°56.741' 29410 Map ref: 113

Directions: Opp the lorry parking just off the D712 Rue de Brest. Signed. Large parking area. Sp 'Parking Salle des Fetes'.

Sanitation:

Aire Details:

🚐 15

Euro Relais

ℹ️ On main road 2 mins walk from town; nicely presented, views of town, some rural views.

SULNIAC

N47°40.647'W002°34.013' 56250 Map ref: 114

Directions: Follow sp to 'Salle des Fetes', located on D10 towards Questembert signed at entrance.

Sanitation:

Aire Details:

🚐 30

Custom

ℹ️ Plenty of space, very quiet. Children's play area, gravelled walk into village. On edge of village, rural views.

TADEN

N48°28.321'W002°01.345' 22100 Map ref: 115

Directions: Rue de la Robardais. Outside campsite 'La Hallerais', signed from roundabout on D12, just off D12.

Sanitation:

Aire Details:

🚐 10

Flot Blue; €2

ℹ️ Taden village pretty with 3.5t weight restriction, day parking by river, parking behind service point at Salle Neuvilte. Boules.

THEIX

N47°37.637'W002°39.698' 56450 Map ref: 116

Directions: Rue Le Goavert. Just off D7, sp 'complex sportive de Brestivan' next to Gendarmerie. Drive through the sports complex parking, motorhome parking at end.

Sanitation:

Aire Details:

🚐 4

Custom

ℹ️ 10-20 minutes to town. Sports facilities; opposite garages, views over open countryside; 3.5 ton weight limit

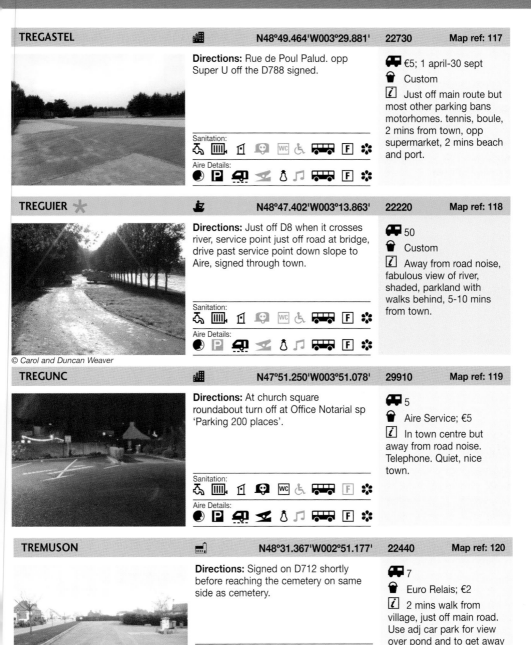

TREGASTEL   N48°49.464'W003°29.881'   22730   Map ref: 117

Directions: Rue de Poul Palud. opp Super U off the D788 signed.

€5; 1 april-30 sept

Custom

Just off main route but most other parking bans motorhomes. tennis, boule, 2 mins from town, opp supermarket, 2 mins beach and port.

Sanitation:

Aire Details:

TREGUIER ✳   N48°47.402'W003°13.863'   22220   Map ref: 118

Directions: Just off D8 when it crosses river, service point just off road at bridge, drive past service point down slope to Aire, signed through town.

50

Custom

Away from road noise, fabulous view of river, shaded, parkland with walks behind, 5-10 mins from town.

Sanitation:

Aire Details:

© Carol and Duncan Weaver

TREGUNC   N47°51.250'W003°51.078'   29910   Map ref: 119

Directions: At church square roundabout turn off at Office Notarial sp 'Parking 200 places'.

5

Aire Service; €5

In town centre but away from road noise. Telephone. Quiet, nice town.

Sanitation:

Aire Details:

TREMUSON   N48°31.367'W002°51.177'   22440   Map ref: 120

Directions: Signed on D712 shortly before reaching the cemetery on same side as cemetery.

7

Euro Relais; €2

2 mins walk from village, just off main road. Use adj car park for view over pond and to get away from road noise. Play area.

Sanitation:

Aire Details:

Brittany

AMBON 🌐 56190 Map: 121

Directions: Treherve.

ARRADON 🌐 56610 Map: 122

Directions: Pen Er Men.

BAZOUGES LA PEROUSE 🌐🪣 35560 Map: 123

Directions: Boulevard de Castel-Marie (near the centre).
• 7 • Free • All year

BEGANNE 🌐🪣 56350 Map: 124

Directions: Port de Folleux
• Custom

BILLIERS 🌐🪣 56190 Map: 125

Directions: Le Petit Teno.
• Custom

BREC'H 🌐🪣 56400 Map: 126

Directions: Rue du Pont Douar.
• Custom

COLPO 🪣 56390 Map: 127

Directions: Rue de Couba and Avenue du Bot Porhel.
• Custom

DAMGAN 🪣 56750 Map: 128

Directions: Boulevard de l'Atalante.
• Custom

GAVRES 🪣 56680 Map: 129

Directions: Aire de la presqu'ile de Gavres; Poche stade.
• Custom

GRAND-CHAMP 🌐 56390 Map: 130

Directions: Kermorio; Rue du General de Gaulle and 3, Rue de la Madeleine.

GUEHENNO 🪣 56420 Map: 131

Directions: Rue du Stade.

GUIPRY 🌐🪣 35480 Map: 132

Directions: Derriere la maison du port.
• 6 • Tokens • All year

JOSSELIN 🪣 56120 Map: 133

Directions: Place Saint-Martin.
• Aire Service

LA GACILLY 🪣 56200 Map: 134

Directions: Route de Sixt sur Aff.
• Euro Relais

LANESTER 🪣 56600 Map: 135

Directions: La Gerbe de Ble; Geant roundabout.
• Custom

LARMOR-BADEN 🌐 56870 Map: 136

Directions: Route d'Auray, Parking de l'atelier Municipal.

LARMOR-PLAGE 🌐🪣 56260 Map: 137

Directions: Outside Camping des Algues or Rue des Pins.
• Custom

LA-ROCHE-BERNARD 🪣 56130 Map: 138

Directions: Chemin du Patis.
• Custom

LES FORGES 🌐 56120 Map: 139

Directions: Place de l'eglise (church).

LOCMARIAQUER 🪣 56740 Map: 140

Directions: Les Pierres Plates.
• Euro Relais

LORIENT 🪣 56100 Map: 141

Directions: 12, rue Francois Tallec.
• Custom

MALANSAC 🪣 56220 Map: 142

Directions: Le Puits de Bas.
• Custom

MALESTROIT 🌐🪣 56140 Map: 143

Directions: Rue des Tanneurs; Service point, Ecluse; parking, Rue de la gare at Casino. • Flot Blue

MARTIGNE-FERCHAUD 🌐🪣 35640 Map: 144

Directions: Rue Lucien Vignelles in town centre.
• 6 • Free

MAURON 🪣 56430 Map: 145

Directions: Rue de la Liberation.
• Custom

MEDREAC 🌐🪣 35360 Map: 146

Directions: Le Bois Gesbert - Route de Becherel.
• 6 • €3 Token

MOHON 🪣 56490 Map: 147

Directions: Route de Josselin.
• Custom

MONTERREIN ⚫ 56800 Map: 148

Directions: Parking at the Mairie (town hall).

NEUILLIAC 🪣 56300 Map: 149

Directions: Impasse des Deux Croix; RD 767.
• Flot Blue

PENESTIN 🪣 56760 Map: 150

Directions: Parking at the tourist office.
• Borne Bayard

PLOERMEL ⚫🪣 56800 Map: 151

Directions: Parking at Lake Duc, circuit des Hortensias. • Service point; Rue Mystringue, near the post office (La Poste). • Custom

PLOUAY 🪣 56240 Map: 152

Directions: Rue Helene Le Chaton.

PLUMELEC 🪣 56420 Map: 153

Directions: Espace de la Madeleine; Route de Josselin.
• Euro Relais

PRIZIAC ⚫ 56320 Map: 154

Directions: Base de loisirs (leisure) du Bel Air.

REMINIAC ⚫ 56140 Map: 155

Directions: Rue de l'etang; near salle des fetes.

RIEUX 🪣 56350 Map: 156

Directions: Impasse du Chateau.
• Euro Relais

ROCHEFORT-EN-TERRE ⚫ 56220 Map: 157

Directions: Route de Malansac; parking des Grees.

ROHAN ⚫ 56580 Map: 158

Directions: Port de Plaisance; at the marina.

SAINS ⚫🪣 35610 Map: 159

Directions: Rue du Puits Rimoult, facing the school.
• Service €4

ST-ARMEL ⚫ 56450 Map: 160

Directions: Aire de Stationment.

ST JUST 🪣 35550 Map: 161

Directions: Les Landes de Cojoux by the sports facilities and campsite. • Free • All year

ST-AIGNAN 🪣 56480 Map: 162

Directions: Car park at the church.
• Flot Blue

ST-BRIEUC DE MAURON ⚫ 56430 Map: 163

Directions: Route de Gael - pond of Raffrais.

ST-GILDAS DE RHUYS ⚫🪣 56730 Map: 164

Directions: Parking; Route de la Baie d'Abraham, les Gohvelins. • Service point at Camping Municipal de Kerver • Euro Relais

ST-GORGON ⚫ 56350 Map: 165

Directions: Parking; La ville aux vents and La Croix des Landes.

ST-JEAN-BREVELAY 🪣 56660 Map: 166

Directions: Place de la Croix des Victimes.
• Custom

ST-PIERRE-QUIBERON ⚫ 56510 Map: 167

Directions: Rue des 2 Mers, Penthievre.

Burgundy

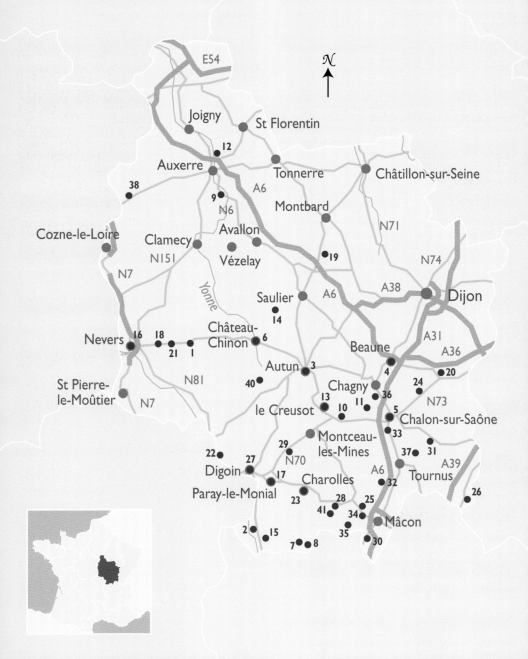

© Carol and Duncan Weaver

Burgundy, where pleasure can be found outside of the glass if you have the bottle. September and October are an ideal time to visit this historic and beautiful region. The vineyards are a hive of activity during the busy grape harvest and autumn colours of the vines are at their best.

Beaune is a popular quaffing destination where tasting and talk of wine goes as far back as the foundations of the towns jewel the Hotel-Dieu with its multi coloured roof.

© Carol and Duncan Weaver

© Carol and Duncan Weaver

When your pallet is suitably refreshed head south to Cluny and wonder at Europe's once largest, most powerful medieval abbey until Romans built St Peters.

© Carol and Duncan Weaver

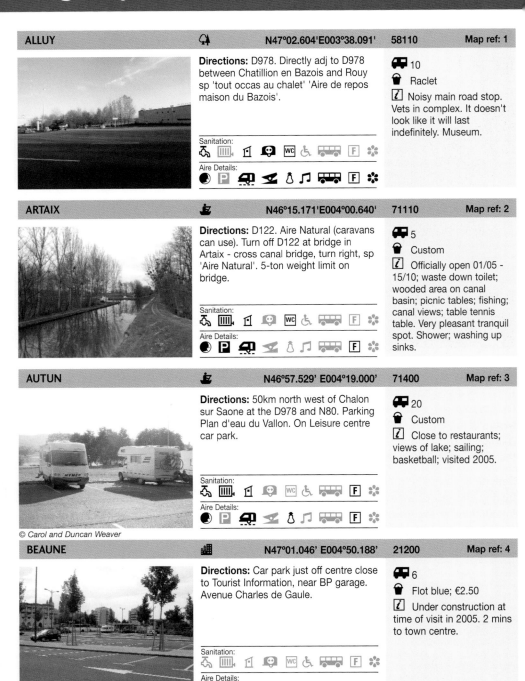

| ALLUY | ⛺ | N47°02.604'E003°38.091' | 58110 | Map ref: 1 |

Directions: D978. Directly adj to D978 between Chatillion en Bazois and Rouy sp 'tout occas au chalet' 'Aire de repos maison du Bazois'.

🚐 10
🛒 Raclet
ℹ️ Noisy main road stop. Vets in complex. It doesn't look like it will last indefinitely. Museum.

Sanitation:
🚿 ▥ 🔟 ☠ WC ♿ 🚌 F ❄️
Aire Details:
● P 🚐 ◀ 🍶 ♫ 🚌 F ❄️

| ARTAIX | ⛴ | N46°15.171'E004°00.640' | 71110 | Map ref: 2 |

Directions: D122. Aire Natural (caravans can use). Turn off D122 at bridge in Artaix - cross canal bridge, turn right, sp 'Aire Natural'. 5-ton weight limit on bridge.

🚐 5
🛒 Custom
ℹ️ Officially open 01/05 - 15/10; waste down toilet; wooded area on canal basin; picnic tables; fishing; canal views; table tennis table. Very pleasant tranquil spot. Shower; washing up sinks.

Sanitation:
🚿 ▥ 🔟 ☠ WC ♿ 🚌 F ❄️
Aire Details:
● P 🚐 ◀ 🍶 ♫ 🚌 F ❄️

| AUTUN | ⚓ | N46°57.529' E004°19.000' | 71400 | Map ref: 3 |

Directions: 50km north west of Chalon sur Saone at the D978 and N80. Parking Plan d'eau du Vallon. On Leisure centre car park.

🚐 20
🛒 Custom
ℹ️ Close to restaurants; views of lake; sailing; basketball; visited 2005.

Sanitation:
🚿 ▥ 🔟 ☠ WC ♿ 🚌 F ❄️
Aire Details:
● P 🚐 ◀ 🍶 ♫ 🚌 F ❄️

© Carol and Duncan Weaver

| BEAUNE | 🏢 | N47°01.046' E004°50.188' | 21200 | Map ref: 4 |

Directions: Car park just off centre close to Tourist Information, near BP garage. Avenue Charles de Gaule.

🚐 6
🛒 Flot blue; €2.50
ℹ️ Under construction at time of visit in 2005. 2 mins to town centre.

Sanitation:
🚿 ▥ 🔟 ☠ WC ♿ 🚌 F ❄️
Aire Details:
● P 🚐 ◀ 🍶 ♫ 🚌 F ❄️

© Carol and Duncan Weaver

CHALON-SUR-SAONE

 N46°47.052' E004°51.784'   71100   **Map ref: 5**

Directions: Prominade Sainte-Maire, Maison de Vins. Centre of village; sp 'P Ville Historique'.

 Unknown
 Raclet
Visited 2005.

Sanitation:

Aire Details:

© Carol and Duncan Weaver

CHATEAU-CHINON

N47°03.779'E003°56.167'   58120   **Map ref: 6**

Directions: Rue Jean Salonnyer. Enter town follow sp 'centre ville'. From D978 turn onto c1 signed then turn left sp 'parking' and the Aire is at the car park. Sp 'parking' 'equipement' through town.

20
Flot blue Fountaine
Fair on site at time of visit. Town 5 mins.

 Sanitation:

Aire Details:

CHATEAUNEUF

 N46°12.849'E004°15.304'   71740   **Map ref: 7**

Directions: D8. Enter village from Chauffailles follow the road and the Aire is on left just before the bridge across the river.

10
Custom
Adj to river; restaurant 2 mins; village centre 5 mins. Quiet peaceful spot; outdoor sink. Fishing in river.

 Sanitation:

Aire Details:

CHAUFFAILLES

 N46°12.096'E004°20.104'   71170   **Map ref: 8**

Directions: Chemin du Tour du Bois. Turn off D985 at traffic lights sp 'Aire de camping car' 'complex sportif'. Go across two bridges, past Park du Sports and Aire is on right, signed. Well signed.

15
custom
Park adj; football; basketball; town 5 mins; animals - deer and pony friendly to children; open air swimming pool adj; fishing pools - €5 per day; boules.

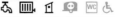 Sanitation:

 Aire Details:

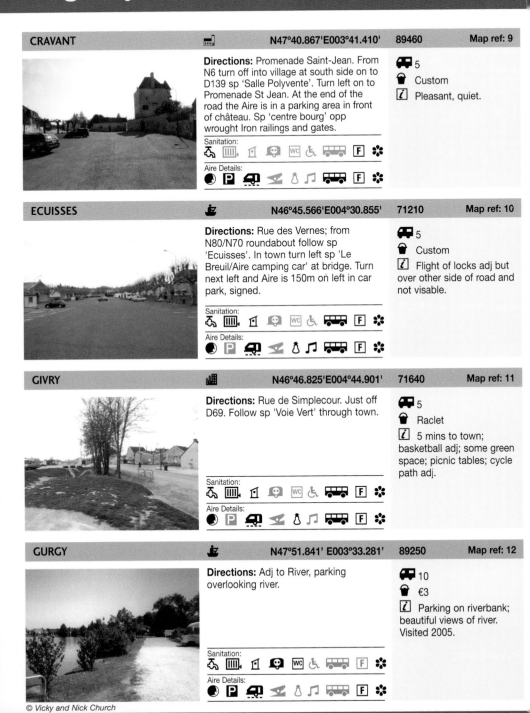

| CRAVANT | | N47°40.867'E003°41.410' | 89460 | Map ref: 9 |

Directions: Promenade Saint-Jean. From N6 turn off into village at south side on to D139 sp 'Salle Polyvente'. Turn left on to Promenade St Jean. At the end of the road the Aire is in a parking area in front of château. Sp 'centre bourg' opp wrought Iron railings and gates.

🚐 5
🪣 Custom
ℹ️ Pleasant, quiet.

Sanitation:
Aire Details:

| ECUISSES | | N46°45.566'E004°30.855' | 71210 | Map ref: 10 |

Directions: Rue des Vernes; from N80/N70 roundabout follow sp 'Ecuisses'. In town turn left sp 'Le Breuil/Aire camping car' at bridge. Turn next left and Aire is 150m on left in car park, signed.

🚐 5
🪣 Custom
ℹ️ Flight of locks adj but over other side of road and not visable.

Sanitation:
Aire Details:

| GIVRY | | N46°46.825'E004°44.901' | 71640 | Map ref: 11 |

Directions: Rue de Simplecour. Just off D69. Follow sp 'Voie Vert' through town.

🚐 5
🪣 Raclet
ℹ️ 5 mins to town; basketball adj; some green space; picnic tables; cycle path adj.

Sanitation:
Aire Details:

| GURGY | | N47°51.841' E003°33.281' | 89250 | Map ref: 12 |

Directions: Adj to River, parking overlooking river.

🚐 10
🪣 €3
ℹ️ Parking on riverbank; beautiful views of river. Visited 2005.

Sanitation:
Aire Details:

© Vicky and Nick Church

LE CREUSOT   🚶   N46°48.709'E004°24.842'   71200   **Map ref: 13**

Directions: Rue des Pyrenees. Follow 'Park Touristic des combes' blue sp through town. Well sp from all directions. Parking P2 for service point.

Sanitation:

Aire Details:

🚐 10 Parking P1

🔧 Custom

ℹ️ Theme park for children of all ages. 20 mins down hill or tourist train to large town. Walking - marked; play area and adventure playground in hills around.

LAC LES SETTONS   ⚓   N47°11.913' E004°03.794'   58230   **Map ref: 14**

Directions: Nr Montsauche Lac Les Settons - 26km south west of Saulieu on D193 in the regional Park du Morvan. By the lakeside.

Sanitation:

Aire Details:

© Carol and Duncan Weaver

🚐 12

🔧 Euro Relais; €3

ℹ️ Only 24hr in July and August. Visited 2005.

MELAY   ⚓   N46°13.298'E004°01.414'   71340   **Map ref: 15**

Directions: D122. Adj canal exit Melay on D122 towards Artaix on right before bridge over canal. Hault Nautique.

Sanitation:

Aire Details:

🚐 15

🔧 Custom

ℹ️ Some road noise; adj to canal - views canal boats/moorings; fishing; picnic tables; washing sinks; canal walks. Village 5 mins.

NEVERS   🏛   N47°00.594'E003°10.546'   58000   **Map ref: 16**

Directions: Ave Jean Jaures. Turn off A77 junc 34, follow sp 'Nevez' then follow sp E'Leclerc.

Sanitation:

Aire Details:

🚐 5

🔧 Flot blue; €2

ℹ️ Supermarket, in a residential suburb of Nevez.

Burgundy

PARAY-LE-MONIAL		N46°28.033'E004°06.794'	71600	Map ref: 17

Directions: N79. At the E'leclerc hypermarket.

🚐 50

🚰 Flot blue; €2

ℹ️ Hypermarket and other out of town shops. LPG at supermarket.

Sanitation:

Aire Details:

ROUY		N47°01.710'E003°32.057'	58110	Map ref: 18

Directions: D978. In Rouy adj D978 as exit village towards Chatillon-en-Bazois.

🚐 3

🚰 Custom

ℹ️ Adj to D978, so noisy. Views of fields. Village 2 mins walk.

Sanitation:

Aire Details:

SEMUR EN AUXOIS		N47°29.500' E004°19.883'	21140	Map ref: 19

Directions: Behind the Police Station with access from l'avenue Pasteur, on edge of village which is very pleasant.

🚐 8

🚰 Custom

ℹ️ Views across hills. Worth a walk around. Visited 2005.

Sanitation:

Aire Details:

© Carol and Duncan Weaver

SEURRE		N47°00.263'E005°08.609'	21250	Map ref: 20

Directions: Quai du Nord. Port Plesance. Follow A36 sp through town. Follow sp 'Salle Omnisports' 'Camping le Port'.

🚐 10

🚰 Unknown make

ℹ️ Adj to river and small marina some bays with partial views, quiet, rural views, lock nearby promenade along river to town. Play pk, green space adj.

Sanitation:

Aire Details:

ST BENIN-D-AZY

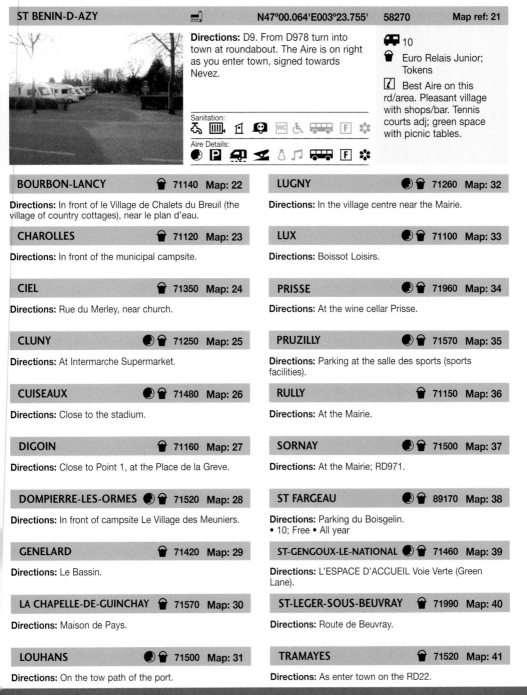

N47°00.064'E003°23.755'   58270   Map ref: 21

Directions: D9. From D978 turn into town at roundabout. The Aire is on right as you enter town, signed towards Nevez.

Sanitation:

Aire Details:

🚐 10

Euro Relais Junior; Tokens

i Best Aire on this rd/area. Pleasant village with shops/bar. Tennis courts adj; green space with picnic tables.

BOURBON-LANCY   71140   Map: 22

Directions: In front of le Village de Chalets du Breuil (the village of country cottages), near le plan d'eau.

CHAROLLES   71120   Map: 23

Directions: In front of the municipal campsite.

CIEL   71350   Map: 24

Directions: Rue du Merley, near church.

CLUNY   71250   Map: 25

Directions: At Intermarche Supermarket.

CUISEAUX   71480   Map: 26

Directions: Close to the stadium.

DIGOIN   71160   Map: 27

Directions: Close to Point 1, at the Place de la Greve.

DOMPIERRE-LES-ORMES   71520   Map: 28

Directions: In front of campsite Le Village des Meuniers.

GENELARD   71420   Map: 29

Directions: Le Bassin.

LA CHAPELLE-DE-GUINCHAY   71570   Map: 30

Directions: Maison de Pays.

LOUHANS   71500   Map: 31

Directions: On the tow path of the port.

LUGNY   71260   Map: 32

Directions: In the village centre near the Mairie.

LUX   71100   Map: 33

Directions: Boissot Loisirs.

PRISSE   71960   Map: 34

Directions: At the wine cellar Prisse.

PRUZILLY   71570   Map: 35

Directions: Parking at the salle des sports (sports facilities).

RULLY   71150   Map: 36

Directions: At the Mairie.

SORNAY   71500   Map: 37

Directions: At the Mairie; RD971.

ST FARGEAU   89170   Map: 38

Directions: Parking du Boisgelin.
• 10; Free • All year

ST-GENGOUX-LE-NATIONAL   71460   Map: 39

Directions: L'ESPACE D'ACCUEIL Voie Verte (Green Lane).

ST-LEGER-SOUS-BEUVRAY   71990   Map: 40

Directions: Route de Beuvray.

TRAMAYES   71520   Map: 41

Directions: As enter town on the RD22.

Centre

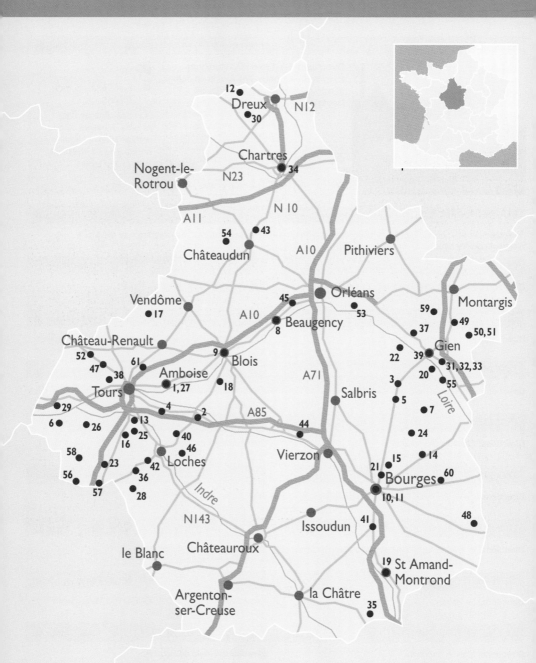

Dreux
12
30
N12

Chartres
34

Nogent-le-
Rotrou
N23

N 10

A11

54
43
Châteaudun

A10

Pithiviers

Vendôme
17
A10

45
Orléans
Beaugency
8

53

Montargis
59
49
37
50,51
Château-Renault
52
47
61
38
Amboise
22
39
Gien
31,32,33
Blois
9
18
A71
3
20
55
Tours
1,27
A85
Salbris
5
7
Loire
29
4
2
44
24
6
26
13
15
14
16
25
40
Vierzon
21
58
46
Bourges
60
23
42
Loches
10,11
56
36
57
28
Indre
48
41
N143
Issoudun
le Blanc
Châteauroux
19 St Amand-
Montrond
Argenton-
ser-Creuse
la Châtre
35

© Paul Lammoil

The Centre, just south of Paris is cut by the majestic Loire River used to irrigate the 'garden of France'. Set in stunning scenery, this region is a romantic reminder of the splendours of previous times.

© Carol and Duncan Weaver

Located south of Blois, Château de Chenonceau with its formal gardens, is regarded as one of the best in the region. The former watermill, now a beautiful renaissance building straddles elegantly over the river Cher.

© Carol and Duncan Weaver

The river proves popular for many aqua sports and the French passion for paddling is served by many canoe hire locations. Be it wine, goats cheese, the beautiful country houses or interesting towns the river is key to it all. Simply follow it and your holiday will be a journey of discovery.

© Carol and Duncan Weaver

© Carol and Duncan Weaver

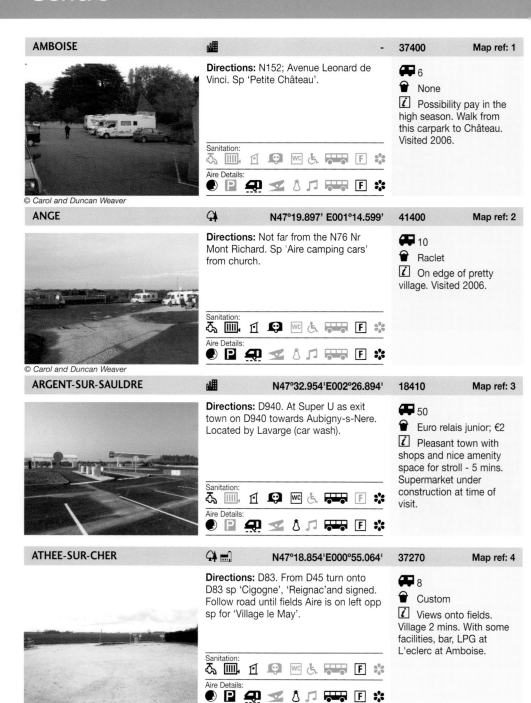

| AMBOISE | | - | 37400 | Map ref: 1 |

Directions: N152; Avenue Leonard de Vinci. Sp 'Petite Château'.

Sanitation:

Aire Details:

🚐 6
🍴 None
ℹ️ Possibility pay in the high season. Walk from this carpark to Château. Visited 2006.

© Carol and Duncan Weaver

| ANGE | | N47°19.897' E001°14.599' | 41400 | Map ref: 2 |

Directions: Not far from the N76 Nr Mont Richard. Sp 'Aire camping cars' from church.

Sanitation:

Aire Details:

🚐 10
🍴 Raclet
ℹ️ On edge of pretty village. Visited 2006.

© Carol and Duncan Weaver

| ARGENT-SUR-SAULDRE | | N47°32.954'E002°26.894' | 18410 | Map ref: 3 |

Directions: D940. At Super U as exit town on D940 towards Aubigny-s-Nere. Located by Lavarge (car wash).

Sanitation:

Aire Details:

🚐 50
🍴 Euro relais junior; €2
ℹ️ Pleasant town with shops and nice amenity space for stroll - 5 mins. Supermarket under construction at time of visit.

| ATHEE-SUR-CHER | | N47°18.854'E000°55.064' | 37270 | Map ref: 4 |

Directions: D83. From D45 turn onto D83 sp 'Cigogne', 'Reignac'and signed. Follow road until fields Aire is on left opp sp for 'Village le May'.

Sanitation:

Aire Details:

🚐 8
🍴 Custom
ℹ️ Views onto fields. Village 2 mins. With some facilities, bar, LPG at L'eclerc at Amboise.

AUBIGNY-SUR-NERE

 N47°29.482'E002°26.270' 18700 **Map ref: 5**

Directions: D940. Follow D940 through town towards La Chapelle d'Angillon. In car park adj to D940, signed.

Sanitation:

Aire Details:

🚐 50

🛖 Custom

ℹ️ Large town with shops 2 mins. Popular parking for locals on Saturday morning. Also used by trucks. 12 spaces; washbasin; elec points by turning.

AVOINE

 N47°12.767'E000°10.624' 37420 **Map ref: 6**

Directions: Route de la Republic. Sp picnique. Past church on D118 then turn right and follow road until end.

Sanitation:

Aire Details:

🚐 -

🛖 Custom

ℹ️ Unknown if this service point will reopen for 2007. Use as desperation only. No available parking. LPG at Bourguell Super U and Chinon L'eclerc.

BARLIEU

 N47°28.747'E002°37.891' 18260 **Map ref: 7**

Directions: D8. From Vailly-s-Sauldre exit on D8. The Aire is on left in 2 km. Very well signed.

Sanitation:

Aire Details:

🚐 20; €3 24hrs

🛖 Euro Relais

ℹ️ Very pleasant spot. Views across plan d'eau. Fishing in three ponds. Stroll around lake; play area; picnic tables. Cycle to Vailly-s-Saulere on road 5 mins. Elec €2.

BEAUGENCY

 - 45190 **Map ref: 8**

Directions: Quain Dunois - 300m from bridge that crosses river.

Sanitation:

Aire Details:

🚐 40

🛖 Unknown

ℹ️ Close to river, lots of trees; walk along river; can be crowded. Market on Sundays. Visited 2005

© Carol and Duncan Weaver

BLOIS

N47°35.372'E001°20.507'   41000   **Map ref: 9**

Directions: Promenade du Mail. Parking along rivers edge. From the central river bridge entering Blos from south turn right at roundabout, drive along tree lined parking area and turn right into parking area opp Hotel de Police at traffic lights. Big bays down ramp adj to river.

Sanitation:

Aire Details:

🚐 20
🪣 None
ℹ️ River views, Blois centre 2 mins, canoeing 5 mins. Blois is a beautiful riverside town with some lovely architecture.

BOURGES

N47°04.662'E002°23.855'   18000   **Map ref: 10**

Directions: Rue Jean Bouin. Follow D106 towards centre. At D106 roundabout adj to big round building follow sp 'centre historic gratuit'. Aire in lower part of free car park.

Sanitation:

Aire Details:

🚐 15; 48 hrs
🪣 Raclet
ℹ️ Nice tree lined green area in city opp stadium. Town 2 mins; castle; 5 mins to centre. Ideal city stop.

BOURGES 2

N47°04.330'E002°23.608'   18000   **Map ref: 11**

Directions: Boulevard de L'industrie. From N144 at traffic light junction turn right onto Boulevard de l'industrie. The Aire is on left just before campsite 'Camping Municipal de Bourges'.

Sanitation:

Aire Details:

🚐 3
🪣 Raclet
ℹ️ Not as nice as other Bourges Aire. Mainly a service point. Adj to cycle path.

BREZOLLES

N48°41.450' E001°04.183'   28270   **Map ref: 12**

Directions: On crossroads of Vermeuil sur Avre to Chartres.

Sanitation:

Aire Details:

🚐 5
🪣 Custom
ℹ️ Edge of village with shops; views of church. Visited 2005.

ESVRES

 N47°16.972'E000°47.096' 37320 Map ref: 13

Directions: D17. Turn off D17 at roundabout in village by church, the Aire is at the tennis club. Sp 'tennis', 'piscine', 'bibliotheque'.

 10

 Custom

 Tennis courts adj, river adj - no real views. Town adj.

Sanitation:

Aire Details:

HUMBLIGNY

 N47°15.267'E002°39.533' 18250 Map ref: 14

Directions: From D955 turn onto D44 sp 'Humbligny' follow D44 through village and Aire is on left as you exit.

 15

Euro relais junior; €2

Fantastic views of surrounding hills. Suffers wind, cold in winter. Picnic tables, green space adj. D923-955 nice drive, scenic route.

Sanitation:

Aire Details:

MENETOU-SALON

 N47°13.917'E002°29.409' 18510 Map ref: 15

Directions: Rue de la Mairie. In main town square, located just off D25.

 20

Flot blue fontaine

Adj boules court; play area.

Sanitation:

Aire Details:

MONTBAZON

 N47°17.504'E000°43.195' 37250 Map ref: 16

Directions: Allee de la Robinetterie. As you enter Montbazon on the N10 from Veigne turn left by Intermarche. Drive round behind Intermarche you'll find it. In residential area.

 3

Custom

Supermarket Intermarche adj, town sports facilities, 2 mins town 10 mins.

Sanitation:

Aire Details:

Centre

MONTOIRE-SUR-LE-LOIR N47°45.343'E000°51.834' 41800 Map ref: 17

Directions: D9. From D917 turn left onto D9 - signed through town. Located on D9 on left.

Sanitation:
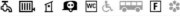

Aire Details:

 10

🚰 Custom - at toilet block

ℹ️ Very pretty town and adj village of Lauardin. Troglodyte evidence in hills. Town 2 mins. Coach parking adj. LPG L'eclerc supermarket in Vendome.

OUCHAMPS N47°28.762'E001°19.138' 41120 Map ref: 18

Directions: C1. Head out of the rear of Ouchamps village sp 'Plan d'eau'. Turn left past tennis courts sp 'Seur', 'Chopier'. The Aire is on left opp a lake.

Sanitation:

Aire Details:

🚐 5

🚰 Euro Relais

ℹ️ Sports facilities adj, views over lake, woods behind. Signed cycle trails 2 mins. Outside sports facilities - tennis, football. Fishing at lake.

ST AMAND MONTROND N46°43.097'E002°30.242' 18200 Map ref: 19

Directions: Quai Lutin. At roundabout on N144 over canal. Just as exit town to south side. Signed.

Sanitation:

Aire Details:
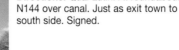

🚐 10

🚰 Custom

ℹ️ Lovely spot adj to canal. Town 5 mins. LPG available at supermarkets in town. Large town with cafes, shops, restaurants.

ST BRISSON-SUR-LOIRE N47°38.805'E002°40.815' 45500 Map ref: 20

Directions: D52. From D951 enter village on D52. Once entered village take the second turning on right sp 'salle polyvente' opp house no 33.

Sanitation:

Aire Details:

🚐 10

🚰 Raclet; €2

ℹ️ Basketball; village 2 mins; very interesting area. Briare has canal-aquaduct. Ideal for a walk and explore (2 mins drive). Shops in village.

ST GEORGES-S-MOULON

  N47°11.138'E002°25.079' 18110 **Map ref: 21**

Directions: Route de Charlay. Turn off D940 at traffic light, cross roads as exit village towards Bourges sp 'Espace Natural'. Aire is 500m on left.

🚐 3
🛈 Point Belle Eau
ℹ️ Football pitches; picnic tables. Plenty of large green spaces. Looks like old reservoir.

Sanitation:

Aire Details:

ST GONDON

  N47°41.888'E002°32.336' 45500 **Map ref: 22**

Directions: D951. Follow main route, D951, through village. Aire is adj to village pool by turning to 'Coullons'.

🚐 3
🛈 Custom
ℹ️ Village 2 mins, town of Gien 2 mins drive. Small river and pools adj. Shops in village.

Sanitation:

Aire Details:

STE MAURE DE TOURAINNE

  - 37800 **Map ref: 23**

Directions: Parking Ronsard. Access via Rue de Loches.

🚐 5
🛈 None
ℹ️ Visited 2005.

Sanitation:

Aire Details:

© Carol and Duncan Weaver

VAILLY-S-SAULDRE

  N47°27.449'E002°38.790' 18260 **Map ref: 24**

Directions: D923. Adj to D923 as enter town from Aubigny-s-Nere. On left sp. 'Aire Natural'.

🚐 10; €3
🛈 Custom
ℹ️ Elec €2.30; Showers €0.75; Caravans and motorhomes allowed. Views of fields. Picnic tables adj; town 2 mins; no twin axles. Showers; laundry/washing up sinks. River 1 min, no views.

Sanitation:

Aire Details:

| VEIGNE | ⚓ | N47°17.354'E000°44.090' | 37250 | Map ref: 25 |

Directions: Rue du Prieure, D50. At bridge crossing river at entrance/exit Veigne. Outside campsite.

None
Euro Relis; €2
No parking available. Canoe/kayaking possible in river.

Sanitation:

Aire Details:

| VILLAIRES-LES-ROCHERS | | N47°13.281'E000°29.723' | 37190 | Map ref: 26 |

Directions: Just off the D57 in the centre of town. Turn by La Poste, sp 'Mairie' and signed. Parking in the square outside Mairie (N47°13.284'E000°29.783'), service point to left of Mairie.

10
Custom
Troglodyte village, basket weaving, cycle route from square. Restaurant.

Sanitation:

Aire Details:

AMBOISE   37400 Map: 27
Directions: Parking autocars (bord de Loire).

BOSSAY-SUR-CLAISE   37290 Map: 28
Directions: Route de Martizay; at the exit of the village.

BOURGUEIL   37140 Map: 29
Directions: At the Hyper U supermarket.

BREZOLLES   28270 Map: 30
Directions: At the entrance of the village.

BRIARE   45250 Map: 31
Directions: Campsite.

BRIARE 2   45250 Map: 32
Directions: Port du Commerce Quai Mazoyer.
• All year

BRIARE 3   45250 Map: 33
Directions: Rue des Vignes.
• All year

CHARTRES   28000 Map: 34
Directions: At the campsite Les Bords de L'Eure.
• €2.50

CULAN   18270 Map: 35
Directions: Station service; Place du Champ de Foire.
• Free • All year

CUSSAY   37240 Map: 36
Directions: Domaine de la Pouge.

DAMPIERRE-EN-BURLY   45570 Map: 37
Directions: Exact location unknown.
• All year

FONDETTES   37230 Map: 38
Directions: Rue E.Branly; ZA la Haute Limougere.

GIEN   45500   Map: 39
Directions: Sortie de Gien - route de Briare.
• All year

LE LIEGE   37460   Map: 40
Directions: In the village.

LEVET   18340   Map: 41
Directions: Aire Caravaning; Chemin du crot a Thibault.
• Free • All year

LIGUEIL   37240   Map: 42
Directions: La Grange de Cercay.

MARBOUE   28200   Map: 43
Directions: In the village.
• €2

MERY-SUR-CHER   18100   Map: 44
Directions: Aire de Service camping cars.
• €3 • All year

MEUNG-SUR-LOIRE   45130   Map: 45
Directions: Exact location unknown.
• All year

MONTRESOR   37460   Map: 46
Directions: Facing the cemetery.

NEUILLE-PONT-PIERRE   37360   Map: 47
Directions: Parc Chauvin; near the gendarmerie.

NEUVY-LE—BARROIS   18600   Map: 48
Directions: Escale camping cars 'La Prairie'; Penisson.
• €6 • 01/04 - 30/10

NOGENT-SUR-VERNISSON   45290   Map: 49
Directions: Municipal.
• All year

OUZOUER SUR TREZEE   45250   Map: 50
Directions: Adj to canal.
• 1/04-31/10

OUZOUER SUR TREZEE 2   45250   Map: 51
Directions: Halte nautique. Parc de la Prairie St Roch.
• All year

SONZAY   37360   Map: 53
Directions: L'Arada Parc.

ST BENOIT-SUR-LOIRE   45730   Map: 54
Directions: At the port - facing the school Ste Marie and the gym. • All year

ST DENIS LES PONTS   28200   Map: 52
Directions: At the Mairie.

ST FIRMIN SUR LOIRE   45360   Map: 55
Directions: Place du Champ de Foire.
• All year

ST-EPAIN   37800   Map: 56
Directions: Aire des Deneux in town centre.

ST-MAURE-DE-TOURAINE   37800   Map: 57
Directions: Parking Ronsard.

TROGUES   37220   Map: 58
Directions: Chlorophylle Parc.

VARENNES-CHANGY   45290   Map: 59
Directions: Autoroute A77.
• All year

VILLEQUIERS   18800   Map: 60
Directions: Berrichonne; Le Petit Azillon.
• Free • All year

VOUVRAY   37210   Map: 61
Directions: Aire de Repos facing the campsite.

Champagne

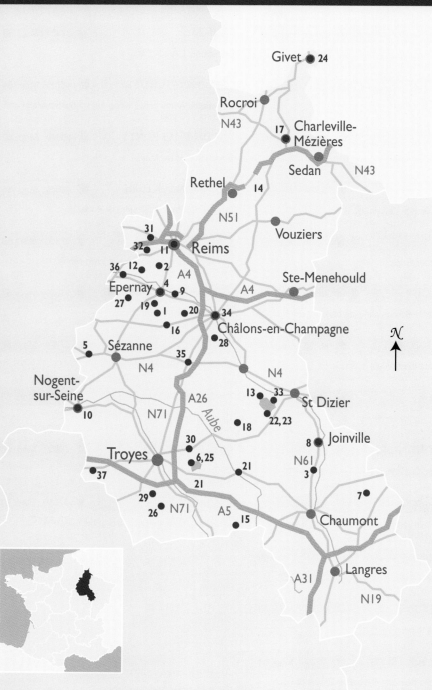

Givet ● 24

Rocroi ●

Charleville-
Mézières
17 ●

Sedan ●

N43

Rethel ● 14

N51

Vouziers ●

31 ●
32 ● 11 ●
Reims

36 ● 12 ● 2 ●
     A4
Epernay 4 ● 9 ●
27 ● 19 ● 1 ●
        20 ●
        16 ●
34 ●
A4

Ste-Menehould ●

Châlons-en-Champagne

28 ●

𝒩
↑

5 ● Sézanne ●
        N4
     35 ●

Nogent-
sur-Seine
10 ●

A26

N71

Aube

13 ● 33 ●
22, 23 ●

N4

St Dizier ●

18 ●

30 ●
6, 25 ●

8 ● Joinville

N61
3 ●

Troyes ●

37 ●

29 ●
26 ● N71

21 ●
21 ●
A5
15 ●

21 ●

7 ●

Chaumont ●

Langres ●
A31
N19

© R. Moss, CDT 8

Just 3 hours drive from Calais you can be relaxing, living life the French way, enjoying local cuisine, looking over vineyards as far as the eye can see.

© P Boillon, CDTaube

Champagne grapes march over the hills around the town of Epernay, home to several famous brands. Many of the Aires in this area are a short walk from wineries welcoming the public. Driving the tourist route gives you the opportunity for independent wine tasting at 26 producers.

© CDTaube

Architectural interest can be found in the towns of Chalons-en-Champagne and Troyes where half-timbered houses line the streets. Treasures can be bought in the antique shops and local specialities can be purchased to be enjoyed at home.

© Houplain, CDTaube

Foret d'Orient, just east of Troyes, offers a range of outdoor activities. You can partake in fishing, swimming, and sailing on the lakes or walking, cycling and horse-riding in the forest.

© R. Moss, CDT 8

| AVIZE | | N48°58.301'E004°00.593' | 51190 | Map ref: 1 |

Directions: Rue de Borg Joli. From D9 turn onto D19 sp 'Avize Centre'. Drive past 1914-1918 memorial on right then take next right. Follow one-way system around block and you will find Aire in first car park on right.

Sanitation:

Aire Details:

10

Custom

In Champagne producing town. Wine tasting possible. Car park with no outstanding features but ideal if Mareui-s-Ay is full.

| CHAMERY | | N49°10.453'E003°57.229' | 51500 | Map ref: 2 |

Directions: Salle Polyvente. Just off D26 at edge of village on left towards Ecueil. Signed.

Sanitation:

Aire Details:

5

Aire Services; €2

In champagne producing village - surrounded by vines. Tasting possible. Some views of vines but Aire nothing special.

| DONJEUX | | N48°21.994'E005°08.952' | 52300 | Map ref: 3 |

Directions: D13. Turn off N67 sp 'Donjeux' travel under railway bridge and Aire is in front of you adj to canal.

Sanitation:

Aire Details:

4

Custom

2 spaces with views over canal, free electric; cycling/walking adj canal. Pleasant; some rd noise. Picnic area 2 mins; village 2 mins; no shade. Fishing.

| EPERNAY | | N49°02.166'E003°57.072' | 51200 | Map ref: 4 |

Directions: Rue Dom Perignon. From D951 driving into town follow sp 'centre ville'. Turn right just before traffic lighted junction sp 'Palais des fetes' 'Piscine'. Aire on left behind church. Signed.

Sanitation:

Aire Details:

3

Euro Relais; tokens; tourist office

At rear of church. In champagne town with some of the most famous Brands. Town centre 10 mins.

Champagne

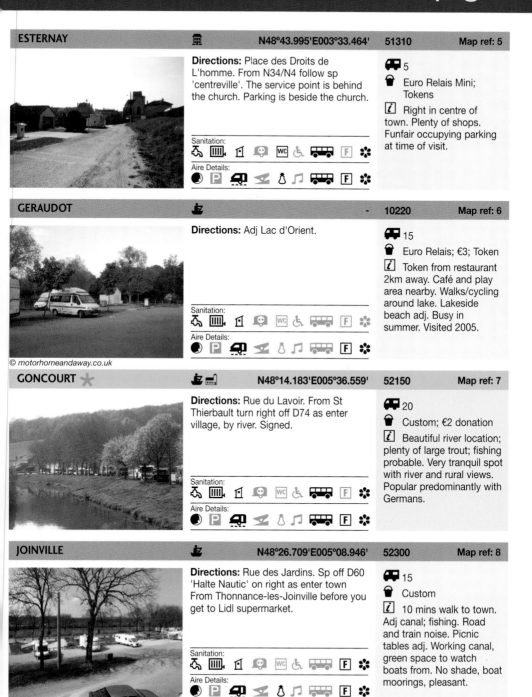

© motorhomeandaway.co.uk

ESTERNAY

N48°43.995'E003°33.464'   51310   Map ref: 5

Directions: Place des Droits de L'homme. From N34/N4 follow sp 'centreville'. The service point is behind the church. Parking is beside the church.

Sanitation:

Aire Details:

5

Euro Relais Mini; Tokens

Right in centre of town. Plenty of shops. Funfair occupying parking at time of visit.

GERAUDOT

-    10220   Map ref: 6

Directions: Adj Lac d'Orient.

Sanitation:

Aire Details:

15

Euro Relais; €3; Token

Token from restaurant 2km away. Café and play area nearby. Walks/cycling around lake. Lakeside beach adj. Busy in summer. Visited 2005.

GONCOURT

N48°14.183'E005°36.559'   52150   Map ref: 7

Directions: Rue du Lavoir. From St Thierbault turn right off D74 as enter village, by river. Signed.

Sanitation:

Aire Details:

20

Custom; €2 donation

Beautiful river location; plenty of large trout; fishing probable. Very tranquil spot with river and rural views. Popular predominantly with Germans.

JOINVILLE

N48°26.709'E005°08.946'   52300   Map ref: 8

Directions: Rue des Jardins. Sp off D60 'Halte Nautic' on right as enter town From Thonnance-les-Joinville before you get to Lidl supermarket.

Sanitation:

Aire Details:

15

Custom

10 mins walk to town. Adj canal; fishing. Road and train noise. Picnic tables adj. Working canal, green space to watch boats from. No shade, boat moorings, pleasant.

75

Champagne

MAREVIL-SUR-AY   N49°02.721'E004°02.062' 51160 Map ref: 9

Directions: Place Charles de Gaulle. From D1 main route through village turn into tree-lined village square, signed. Aire, adj canal on other side of square.

Sanitation:

Aire Details:

🚐 10

⚓ Custom; elec €5 3 hrs

ℹ️ Adj to working canal with views and shade in summer. Pleasant square adj. Canal walks possible. Several champagne producers (chateaux) in adj village.

NOGENT-SUR-SEINE N48°30.204'E003°30.504' 10400 Map ref: 10

Directions: Rue du Camping. Follow sp to 'piscine' and 'camping' - well signed through town. Tight access.

Sanitation:

Aire Details:

🚐 3 hrs only

⚓ Custom

ℹ️ Very industrial town, no river view; difficult access; town has restricted parking.

REIMS N49°14.936'E004°01.208' 51100 Map ref: 11

Directions: Esplanade Andre Malraux. From D980 or D31 head into Reims. After both roads merge into D31, turn right at traffic lighted junction opp Renault garage, signed. Then turn first left into barriered entrance. Signed. Go to reception, on left, to get barrier lifted. Also sp 'Reims Centre International de Sejour /CIS'.

Sanitation:

Aire Details:

🚐 7; 48hrs

⚓ Custom

ℹ️ Don't be put off by the barriered entrance. It is easy to get in and it is free. Located at youth hostel. Comedy club adj. Road noise but semi secure parking. Park adj; possible to walk to town centre. English spoken. WiFi.

VILLERS-SOUS-CHATILLON N49°05.787'E003°48.050' 51700 Map ref: 12

Directions: Rue du Park. Signed in village, turn off D501 by church.

Sanitation:

Aire Details:

🚐 5

⚓ Euro Relais; €3; tokens; bar

ℹ️ In champagne region - village surrounded by vines. Tennis courts adj. Champagne tasting adj. Bar 2 mins; on champagne route.

Champagne

ARRIGNY   🪣 51290   Map: 13

Directions: CAMPING CLUB LA FORET; Presqu'île de Larzicourt.

ATTIGNY   🌐🪣 08130   Map: 14

Directions: On D987.
• April-Sept

BALNOT SUR LAIGNES   🪣 10110   Map: 15

Directions: Aire de Balnot sur Laignes.

BEAUNAY   🌐🪣 51270   Map: 16

Directions: Rue principale Bel Air.

CHARLEVILLE-MEZIERES   🌐🪣 08000   Map: 17

Directions: Located 5 min walk from the town centre; outside of the campsite. • 14 • €2 • All year

CHAVANGES   🌐🪣 10330   Map: 18

Directions: Pierre Maitrot.

CHAVOT-COURCOURT   🌐🪣 51530   Map: 19

Directions: Rue des Vignes.
• All year

CHEVIGNY   🌐🪣 51130   Map: 20

Directions: Villeneuve Renneville. 12, Rue du plessis.

DOLANCOURT   🪣 10200   Map: 21

Directions: Parc d'attractions Nigloland; RN19 www.nigloland.fr

GIFFAUMONT-CHAMPAUBERT   🌐🪣 51290   Map: 22

Directions: By lake Der; Chemin de la Cachotte.

GIFFAUMONT-CHAMPAUBERT   🌐🪣 51290   Map: 23

Directions: By Lake Der; Chantecoq.

GIVET   🌐🪣 08600   Map: 24

Directions: Parking public au bord de Meuse.
• All year

GRAND LACS DE LA FORET D'ORIENT   🪣 10220   Map: 25

Directions: At the port and restaurant 'Marinka' adj to lake.

LANTAGES   🪣 10210   Map: 26

Directions: Aire de Lantages; 32, grande rue.

LEUVRIGNY   🪣 51700   Map: 27

Directions: 7, rue Douchy.

HAVE YOU VISITED AN AIRE?

Don't forget to fill in the form at the back and return to Vicarious Books.

NUISEMENT   🌐🪣 51240   Map: 28

Directions: On the banks of lake Der.
• €2

PAYS D'OTHE - CHAOURCOIS-VALD'ARMANCE   🪣 10210   Map: 29

Directions: Exact location unknown.

PINEY   🌐🪣 10220   Map: 30

Directions: Facing the station.

REIMS CHAMPAGNE NORD   🪣 51100   Map: 31

Directions: Autoroute A4; Direction Strasbourg / Paris.

REIMS CHAMPAGNE SUD   🪣 51100   Map: 32

Directions: Autoroute A4; Direction Strasbourg / Paris.

ST MARIE DU LAC   🌐🪣 51290   Map: 33

Directions: By lake Der; port de Nuisement.

ST MARTIN SUR LE PRE   🌐🪣 51520   Map: 34

Directions: STATION TOTAL; N44 Sortie Châlons-en-Champagne; Direction Reims.

SOMMESOUS   🪣 51320   Map: 35

Directions: Autoroute A26; Direction Troyes / Châlons-en-Champagne.

VANDIERES   🌐🪣 51700   Map: 36

Directions: 10, rue Bailly.

VILLEMAUR SUR VANNE   🪣 10190   Map: 37

Directions: 1, route de pâlis.
www.villemaur.com

Eastern France

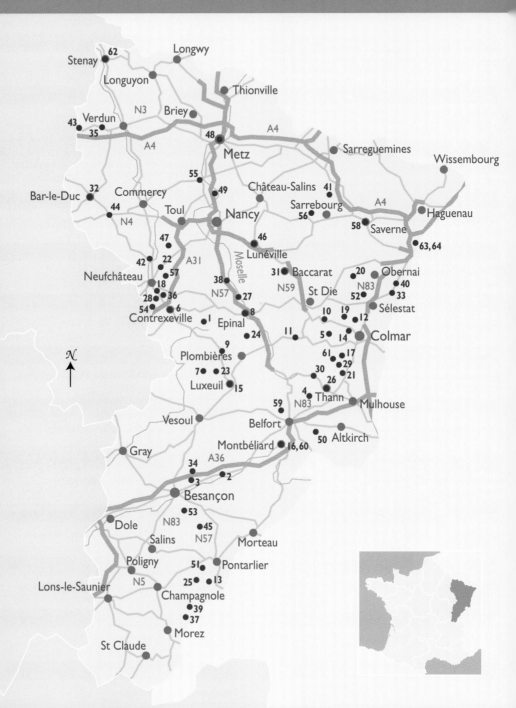

Stenay **62**
Longwy
Longuyon
Thionville
43 Verdun
35
N3
Briey
A4
Bar-le-Duc **32**
Commercy
44
Toul
N4
48
Metz
A4
Sarreguemines
Wissembourg
55
49
Château-Salins
41
Nancy
Sarrebourg
56
A4
Haguenau
58
Saverne
63, 64
47
46
Lunéville
42 **22**
A31
Neufchâteau
57
Moselle
31 Baccarat
20
Obernai
38
N59
St Die
N83
40
18
N57
52
33
28 **36**
27
Sélestat
54
6
8
10
19
12
Contrexeville
1
Epinal
11
5
14
Colmar
24
9
61
17
Plombières
30
29
7 **23**
26
21
Luxeuil
15
4
Thann
59
N83
Mulhouse
Vesoul
Belfort
Gray
Montbéliard
16, 60
50 Altkirch
34
A36
3
2
Besançon
53
Dole
N83
45
Salins
N57
Morteau
Poligny
51
Pontarlier
Lons-le-Saunier
N5
25
13
Champagnole
39
37
Morez
St Claude

N
↑

© motorhomeandaway.co.uk

Bordering Switzerland, Germany and Luxemburg there are many influences on this region. Sometimes the Germanic influence is so overwhelming it's hard to believe you are still in France, especially when all the motorhomes at the Aire are German.

The Royal Saltworks of Arc-et-Senans, near Besançon in the south, are a UNECSO world heritage site. Work begun in 1775 it was the first major achievement of industrial architecture, following the ideal of Enlightenment. The citadel of Besancon is also worth a visit.

© motorhomeandaway.co.uk

In the north of the region the Place Stanislas (Nancy), is listed as a Unesco World Heritage site, and considered to be the most beautiful royal square in Europe.

ATTIGNY

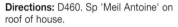 N48°03.555'E006°00.573' | 88260 | Map ref: 1

Directions: D460. Sp 'Meil Antoine' on roof of house.

Sanitation:

Aire Details:

 5

Custom

ℹ️ Honey farm, parking near main road under trees with picnic tables, free to France Passion. Non-member may need to buy honey. No English.

BAUME-LES-DAMES

N47°20.485'E006°21.572' | 25110 | Map ref: 2

Directions: D277. South side of town just off D50 by bridge over canal. Sp through town to 'Port' and signed.

Sanitation:

Aire Details:

25; €5 inc elec.

Custom; shower

ℹ️ Motorhome campsite-some pitches with canal views; showers €1. Full to overflowing over Easter mainly with Germans.

BESANCON MARCHAUX

N47°19.656'E006°07.721' | 25000 | Map ref: 3

Directions: A36. In motorway services each side of road dir Baume les Dames turn left sp 'coaches' for motorhome services. GPS in truck stop due to bad signage.

Sanitation:

Aire Details:

Overnight parking not recommended

Unknown

ℹ️ Badly signed. Usual motorway services.

BOURBACH LE HAUT

- | 68290 | Map ref: 4

Directions: Narrow winding roads to reach village from Thann. Next to picnic area, nursery school and village recycling bins. Small tarmac parking area-overlooking village.

5; March-Nov

Flot Blue

ℹ️ Good views across Vosges wooded hills to Alps in distance. Visited 2005.

COL DE LA SCHLUCHT — — Map ref: 5

Directions: Parking area located off RD 417.

Sanitation:

Aire Details:

© John Barry

🚐 20
🚰 None
ℹ️ Spectacular alpine views; altitude 1139m. Low overnight temperatures. Located at ski resort with ski lift within 100m. Hotel and restaurant adj. Visited 2007.

CONTREXEVILLE N48°11.267'E005°52.800' 88140 Map ref: 6

Directions: Rue des Magnolias. Off D429 towards Bulgneuville in 'Zone de Activities' situated behind L'Electric supermarket.

Sanitation:

Aire Details:

🚐 No designated parking
🚰 Custom - dilapidated
ℹ️ Pleasant Spa town with thermal bathing. Very dilapidated service point in industrial zone.

CORRE N47°54.935'E005°59.304' 70500 Map ref: 7

Directions: D44. Just off D44 on outskirts of village, turning by sports facilities. Follow sp 'Marina' 'camping car'.

Sanitation:

Aire Details:

🚐 14; €7 24hrs
🚰 Make unknown
ℹ️ Marina/boat yard adj; canal adj but no real views from all but a few pitches; café; walk along canal to village 5 mins; Motorhome campsite.

EPINAL N48°10.723'E006°28.133' 88000 Map ref: 8

Directions: Chemin du Petit Chaperon. Approach on D11, follow sp 'camping park du château' on left before town. Service point directly outside campsite.

Sanitation:

Aire Details:

🚐 Parking possible
🚰 Flot blue; Tokens
ℹ️ Football pitches adj; some parking with rural views; a way out of town.

FONTENOY LE CHATEAU

N47°58.625'E006°12.342'   88240   Map ref: 9

Directions: D434. Sp 'Bains les Bains' 'D434' from village centre.

Sanitation:

Aire Details:

🚐 10

Custom

ℹ️ Pretty village. Restaurant adj; village centre 2 mins; canal and river through village - no views from Aire. Some pretty walking in town.

FRAIZE

N48°10.928'E007°00.220'   88230   Map ref: 10

Directions: Adj N145 in village centre by tourist office and Ed supermarket. Sp 'office de tourisme' signed.

Sanitation:

Aire Details:

🚐 6

Euro Relais Mini

ℹ️ Ed supermarket adj; tourist office adj; builders yard adj.

GERARDMER

N48°04.350'E006°52.488'   88400   Map ref: 11

Directions: Boulevard D'Alsace. From D417 follow sp 'tourist office'. Directly adj ALDI supermarket carpark 100 m from tourist office. Service point opposite.

Sanitation:

Aire Details:

🚐 10

Flot Blue Euro

ℹ️ Town 2 mins; lake with pedaloes/motorboat hire/fishing/waterslides/ swimming 5 mins. Walking/cycling around lake.

KAYSERSBERG

N48°08.148'E007°15.740'   68240   Map ref: 12

Directions: Just off N415 follow sp 'P1' signed.

Sanitation:

Aire Details:

🚐 80; €6 24hrs; pay at ticket machine

Custom

ℹ️ On Alace wine route. Interesting architecture, plenty of wine caves. Aire complete suntrap. Town 2 mins; picnic tables; small amount green space; very popular.

LABERGEMENT STE MARIE — 25160 Map ref: 13

If you have a suitable picture for this Aire, please email to: gomotorhoming@hotmail.co.uk

motorhomeandaway.co.uk

Directions: Car park at Labergement Ste Marie.

🚐 8
🚰 €2
ℹ️ Likely to be crowded. Motorhomes banned from lakeside car park in Summer. Visited 2005.

Sanitation:

Aire Details:

LES TROIS EPIS — 68410 Map ref: 14

If you have a suitable picture for this Aire, please email to: gomotorhoming@hotmail.co.uk

motorhomeandaway.co.uk

Directions: Long winding climb up road from Turckheim. Aire adj to car park behind church and fire station. Not signed from main road.

🚐 8
🚰 €2
ℹ️ In town; Visited 2005.

Sanitation:

Aire Details:

LUXEUIL-LES-BAINS N47°49.036'E006°23.202' 70300 Map ref: 15

Directions: Rue Gambetta. From North keep on N57 at first town junction, turn at second junction and follow road straight on. At end of road turn left and follow road. At roundabout turn right and follow road. Aire on right adj to pond sp 'Aire de Vidage'.

🚐 30
🚰 Euro Relais; Tokens
ℹ️ Stroll around pond. Town 5 mins. No Fishing; play park 2 mins; pleasant spot. LPG at Auchan.

Sanitation:

Aire Details:

MONTBELIARD N47°30.426'E006°47.498' 25200 Map ref: 16

Directions: Rue du Champ de Foire. Follow sp 'P champ de foire' from junc 8 dir Montbeliard centre. Just off D438.

🚐 2; additional parking available
🚰 Raclet; Tokens
ℹ️ 500m town centre. Main road adj; canal adj; no views.

Sanitation:

Aire Details:

ORSCHWIHR
 N47°56.231'E007°13.872'   68500   **Map ref: 17**

Directions: Rue de la Source. Turn off N83 to 'Bergholtz' 'Orschwihr' go across bridge and at roundabout follow sp 'bergholzt' 'orschwihr' - 2nd exit. Follow road and at Orschwihr the service point is just off main road (D5) on left signed.

Sanitation:

Aire Details:

🚐 4

🚰 Flot blue; €4; credit card

ℹ️ Wine town - you could drink yourself silly here. Rural views of vines. Play area, tennis courts; picnic table's adj; wine tasting and village adj.

REBEUVILLE
 N48°20.120'E005°42.070'   88300   **Map ref: 18**

Directions: Rue du Cougnot. Enter village from D164. At T-junction turn left and follow road to end.

Sanitation:

Aire Details:

🚐 6

🚰 Custom

ℹ️ Adj with views over river, main road and railway provide some noise but very pleasant spot. Fishing; Horse riding adj. Gentle wide/shallow paddling river.

RIQUEWIHR
    -    68340   **Map ref: 19**

Directions: Parking on right hand side as enter town.

Sanitation:

Aire Details:

🚐 5; €6

🚰 Euro Relais; €2

ℹ️ Attractive but touristy half-timbered town. Also used by cars so manoeuvring of large motorhomes could be difficult. Visited 2005.

ROTHAU
    -    67570   **Map ref: 20**

If you have a suitable picture for this Aire, please email to: gomotorhoming@hotmail.co.uk

Directions: Aire outside municipal campsite.

Sanitation:

Aire Details:

🚐 8; €5 inc elec.

🚰 Flot Blue; €4

ℹ️ Near Le Struthof WW2 concentration camp (museum). May be cheaper to use campsite. Visited 2005.

ROUFFACH

 N47°57.325'E007°17.737' 68250 Map ref: 21

Directions: Place des Sports. From N83 sp 'Rouffach'. On entering town on D18 bis turn right sp 'Centre ville parking', 'camping municipal'. Then turn left, the Aire on right.

 10

Make unknown; tokens

ℹ Swimming pool/sports facility adj. Germanic style town with some interesting architecture, usual shops. Very short parking bays.

Sanitation:

Aire Details:

ST ELOPHE

 N48°24.559'E005°44.359' 88630 Map ref: 22

Directions: At the Mairie and sports field. Near church. Signed.

 5

Custom

ℹ Small village, rural views, green space and football pitches adj.

Sanitation:

Aire Details:
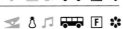

ST LOUP-S-SEMOUSE

 N47°53.178'E006°16.215' 70800 Map ref: 23

Directions: Rue des Jardins. Turn by church - follow main route through town and go behind church.

 2

Euro Relais; tokens

ℹ In undesirable residential area - view of flats. Town 2 mins.

Sanitation:

Aire Details:
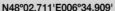

ST NABORD

N48°02.711'E006°34.909' 88200 Map ref: 24

Directions: Rue de la Croix St Jacques. Follow sp 'Gare' then cross railway track for service point. Parking area adj to the train station.

 50

Flot blue; Tokens; €3

ℹ Adj. to train station, scrappy, noisy area. Nothing compared to Thaon-les-Vosges.

Sanitation:

Aire Details:
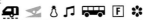

ST POINT LAC - 25160 Map ref: 25

© motorhomeandaway.co.uk

Directions: In small village on the west side of large lake. Large gravel parking area signposted from lakeside public car park in beach complex. Municipal campsite adj.

Sanitation:

Aire Details:

🚐 30; €5
🔧 Free
ℹ️ Adj beach complex with swimming, boating and windsurfing (crowded at weekend). Parking fee collected in evening by guardienne. Impressive Château de Joux nearby and Pontarlier claims to have 200 shops. Visited 2005.

THANN N47°48.650'E007°06.296' 68800 Map ref: 26

Directions: Rue Anatole Jacquot. From N66 - main route turn sp 'Centreville', signed, right at stop sign. Left at next junction signed, car park adj.

Sanitation:

Aire Details:

🚐 10
🔧 Custom
ℹ️ Pleasant spot adj to river; play park; walk into town along river 2 mins. Small town with usual facilities. Fishing possible.

THAON-LES-VOSGES N48°15.005'E006°25.521' 88150 Map ref: 27

Directions: Rue du Coignot. From Epinal on N57 take first exit sp 'Thaon-les-Vosges'. Drive through town straight over first roundabout; turn right at end of road. Turn left at roundabout and turn left immediately after crossing bridge. Follow road to end - Aire on left adj canal.

Sanitation:

Aire Details:

🚐 10
🔧 Custom
ℹ️ Adj to working canal with views. Boules; play park; table tennis adj; canal walks/cycles. Lock 500m. Town 5 mins - shops/restaurants/cafes. Very pleasant spot.

TILLEUX N48°17.972'E005°43.583' 88300 Map ref: 28

Directions: Grande Rue. Parking at the Church.

Sanitation:

Aire Details:

🚐 2
🔧 Water only
ℹ️ Small quiet village offering a night stop. Quiet pleasant rural views. Better stop and facilities at Rebeuville, 5 mins.

WESTHALTEN N47°57.376'E007°15.078' | 68250 | Map ref: 29

Directions: D18bis. On main road D18 as you drive past Westhalten.

🚐 4

🪣 Euro Relais; €2

ℹ️ Additional parking for large vehicles 200m; picnic tables; green space; beer factory adj; wine caves in the small pretty village.

Sanitation:

Aire Details:

WILLER-S-THUR N47°50.600'E007°04.370' | 68760 | Map ref: 30

Directions: Rue du Marechal Foch. Turn off N66 sp D13bis sp 'Goldback' 'Altenbach'. The Aire is on the left outside the church.

🚐 5

🪣 Flot blue

ℹ️ Village adj. Parking in church car park not ideal. Not as pleasant as Thann but not likely to be busy.

Sanitation:

Aire Details:

BACCARAT ● 🪣 54120 Map: 31
Directions: Place du Gal Leclerc.
• Free

BAR LE DUC ● 🪣 55000 Map: 32
Directions: Aire Communal
• Free • All year

BENFELD 🪣 67230 Map: 33
Directions: Concessionaire CLC Alsace; Adj RN83
• Free • Euro Relais Junior • All year

BESANCON-CHAMPOUX 🪣 25000 Map: 34
Directions: Motorway service station A36.

BLERCOURT ● 🪣 55120 Map: 35
Directions: Espace VDW; 16 Rue de la Gde Fontaine
• All year

CERTILLEUX ● 88300 Map: 36
Directions: Signed from D164.
• Free

CHAPELLE-DES-BOIS ● 25240 Map: 37
Directions: At the ski station.

CHARMES 🪣 88130 Map: 38
Directions: Port de Plaisance (Marina).

CHAUX-NEUVE ● 25240 Map: 39
Directions: Site des tremplins.

ERSTEIN 🪣 67150 Map: 40
Directions: At the municipal campsite; Free; Euro Relais Junior; April-Oct.

FENETRANGE ● 🪣 57930 Map: 41
Directions: Wally Services; Parc d'Activities; Route de Sarre-Union.

GREUX ● 88630 Map: 42
Directions: In village.
• Free

LES ISLETTES   55120   Map: 43

Directions: Centre Social D'Argonne Cat; Route Locheres.
• All year

LIGNY EN BARROIS   55500   Map: 44

Directions: Relais nautique.

LODS   25930   Map: 45

Directions: Aire Communal.

LUNEVILLE   54300   Map: 46

Directions: Allee des Chartreuses.
• Free • All year

MAXEY-SUR-MEUSE   88630   Map: 47

Directions: In village.
• Free

METZ   57000   Map: 48

Directions: Parking at the swimming pool.
• All year

MILLERY   54670   Map: 49

Directions: Avenue de la Moselle.

MONTREUX-CHATEAU   90130   Map: 50

Directions: Bassin de la Bourbeuse; 7;€5; 24hrs; Flot
blue; From April 2007; suitable for lge motorhomes.

MOUTHE   25240   Map: 51

Directions: Place du centre de secours.

NOTHALTEN   67680   Map: 52

Directions: Domaine Sohler; 80A, route des vins
• Custom • €2.

ORNANS   25290   Map: 53

Directions: Syratu Tourisme et Loisirs.

POMPIERRE   88300   Map: 54

Directions: In village.
• Free

PONT A MOUSSON   54700   Map: 55

Directions: Port de Plaisance (Marina).

RHODES   57810   Map: 56

Directions: Rue de l'Etang
• April-Sept

ROLLAINVILLE   88300   Map: 57

Directions: In village.
• Free

SAVERNE   67700   Map: 58

Directions: Rue de Pere Liebermann; Terrain municipal.
• Free • April-Sept

SERMAMAGNY   90300   Map: 59

Directions: Site du Malsaucy; close to Lake Malsaucy and
activity centre • 2 • €2 • All year • Adj mini golf; canoe; sailing

SOCHAUX   25600   Map: 60

Directions: At the Peugeot Museum.

SOULTZMATT   68570   Map: 61

Directions: As enter village on the RN83.
• Euro Relais • €2 • All year

STENAY   55700   Map: 62

Directions: Rue du Port.

STRASBOURG   67000   Map: 63

Directions: Parking de l'Auberge de Jeunesse des 2 Rives.
• Free • Euro Relais • All year

STRASBOURG 2   67000   Map: 64

Directions: Montagne Verte derriere l'Auberge de
Jeunesse Rene Cassin • Free • Euro Relais • All year

Vicarious Books LLP

One Stop Motorhome and Caravan Bookshop

Go Motorhoming Europe

Go Motorhoming Europe was the first in this series of groundbreaking motorhome books. It has earned the reputation as the motorhome bible, "a must read" no matter how experienced you are.

ACSI Camping Card

There are other low season discount schemes but none rival the quantity and freedom of this no commitment guide. Buy the book it's as simple as that and camp across Europe for a maximum of €14 a night. The card presses out of the cover.

Guida Camper

It's a little known fact that both motorhomes and caravans can use the mostly free overnight parking facilities throughout Italy. This is a guide to 1500 stopovers marked on a quality 1:300000 Italian road map.

Great Sea View Camping & Caravan Sites Britain

This exquisite guide features the best 150 sea view campsites around the British coast. The sites selected have amazing sea views but also have something special that makes them wonderful places to relax and make the most of your precious time.

France Passion

Like a glass of wine, then why not spend a night at the vineyard where you can see, smell and taste the process. Over 1000 farms to chose from where motorhomes of all sizes can stop the night for free. UK agent, see www.france-passion.co.uk

Campsite Guides Galore

We specialise in importing campsite guides from Europe, so no matter where your going we've got it covered. We also stock the superb Caravan Club Europe Guides, Alan Rogers and a range of other British Guides.

Stopover guides for all of Europe

We specialise in importing stopover guides from Europe, so no matter where your going we've got it covered. Reise Mobile Bord Atlas for Germany, Guida Camper for Italy and Camperstop Europe for a general guide across Europe.

0131 208 3333   www.vicarious-shop.co.uk

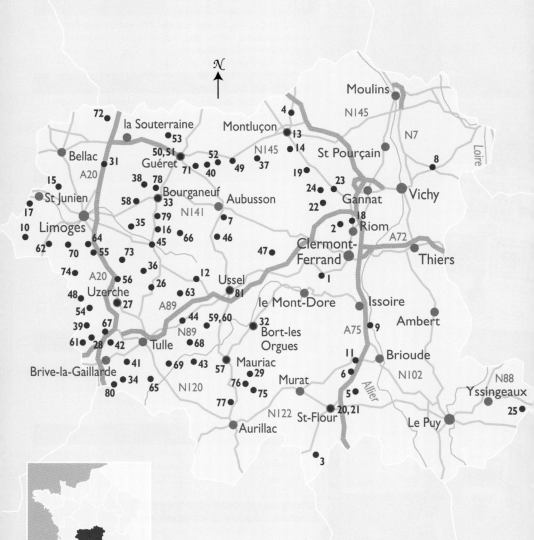

N

72

la Souterraine
53

Bellac
31

A20

50,51
Guéret
71
52
40
49

Montluçon
4
13
14

N145
37

Moulins
N145

N7

8

Loire

15
St Junien

38
78

Bourganeuf
33

58

35

79
16
45
66

Aubusson
N141
7
46

19
24
23
22

St Pourçain

Gannat
18
Riom
2

Vichy

A72

Thiers

17
10
Limoges
62
64
70
55
73

74
A20
56
36
26
63
12

48
Uzerche
54
27
A89

Ussel
81

47

Clermont-
Ferrand
1

le Mont-Dore

Issoire
9

Ambert

39
67
61
28
42
Tulle

44
N89
68

59,60
32
Bort-les-
Orgues

A75

11
6
5

Brioude
N102

N88
Yssingeaux

25

Brive-la-Gaillarde
80
34
65

41
N120

69
57
43
Mauriac
29
76
75

Murat

20,21
St-Flour
Le Puy

77

Aurillac

N122

3

© Pierre Soissons, CDT Correze

Hilly, wooded countryside adorns the centre of France. The short hot summers make for pleasant walking and fishing, once snow falls, cross-country skiing can be enjoyed. Massif du Cantal claims to be the largest volcano in Europe offering excellent mountain biking and horse riding.

© Tim Mannakee, CDT Correze

The beautiful town of Vichy is famed for its spa water and beauty products. Well-being is the key and a place to go for people wishing to pamper themselves. In the evening wander around the opulent architecture and enjoy a pleasant meal.

Oradour sur Glane 12 miles west of Limoges is a 'must see'. The village was destroyed by German soldiers in World War II and has been preserved as a memorial, in its decimated state ever since. No reason has ever been found for the massacre of the villagers.

© Ken Croft

© Tim Mannakee, CDT Correze

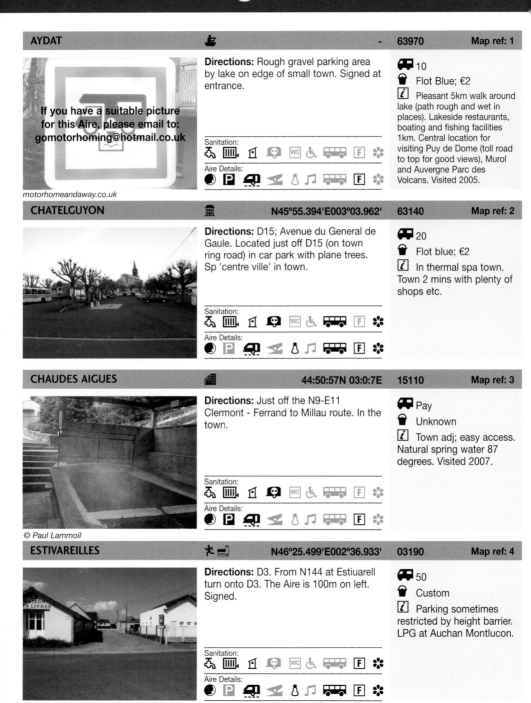

AYDAT	⚓	-	63970	Map ref: 1

Directions: Rough gravel parking area by lake on edge of small town. Signed at entrance.

Sanitation:

Aire Details:

🚐 10

🛉 Flot Blue; €2

ℹ️ Pleasant 5km walk around lake (path rough and wet in places). Lakeside restaurants, boating and fishing facilities 1km. Central location for visiting Puy de Dome (toll road to top for good views), Murol and Auvergne Parc des Volcans. Visited 2005.

If you have a suitable picture for this Aire, please email to: gomotorhoming@hotmail.co.uk

motorhomeandaway.co.uk

CHATELGUYON	🏛	N45°55.394'E003°03.962'	63140	Map ref: 2

Directions: D15; Avenue du General de Gaule. Located just off D15 (on town ring road) in car park with plane trees. Sp 'centre ville' in town.

Sanitation:

Aire Details:

🚐 20

🛉 Flot blue; €2

ℹ️ In thermal spa town. Town 2 mins with plenty of shops etc.

CHAUDES AIGUES	🏢	44:50:57N 03:0:7E	15110	Map ref: 3

Directions: Just off the N9-E11 Clermont - Ferrand to Millau route. In the town.

Sanitation:

Aire Details:

🚐 Pay

🛉 Unknown

ℹ️ Town adj; easy access. Natural spring water 87 degrees. Visited 2007.

© Paul Lammoil

ESTIVAREILLES	🏃🏘	N46°25.499'E002°36.933'	03190	Map ref: 4

Directions: D3. From N144 at Estiuarell turn onto D3. The Aire is 100m on left. Signed.

Sanitation:

Aire Details:

🚐 50

🛉 Custom

ℹ️ Parking sometimes restricted by height barrier. LPG at Auchan Montlucon.

LA CHAPELLE-LAURENT 🏃 N45°10.830'E003°14.635' 15500 Map ref: 5

Directions: D10. On D10 as exit town towards St Lauren Chabreuges. 20 mins from junc 25 A75.

Sanitation:

Aire Details:

🚐 10

☂ Custom; €1

ℹ️ Small village, rural location. Sports fields; green space adj; BBQ and football pitches. Plenty of small shops in town; café, bar and fromargerie. LPG at Champion St Flour.

LA FAYETTE (LORLANGES) A75 🏢 N45°20.127'E003°16.342' 43360 Map ref: 6

Directions: A75. Turn off A75 into Aire la Fayette. Follow sp to picnic area. Service point adj to picnic area.

Sanitation:

Aire Details:

🚐 20

☂ Euro Relais

ℹ️ Dog exercise point; play area; picnic tables; views; caravans allowed. By auto grill. LPG at Shell garage.

LAC D'ABUSSON ⛴ 45.75414N 3.61503E 23200 Map ref: 7

Directions: Very large parking area near reservoir, near base de loisirs.

Sanitation:

Aire Details:

🚐 20; €5

☂ Free

ℹ️ Near reservoir with bathing beach. Daytime parking charge Fri/Sat/Sun. Visited 2006.

© motorhomeandaway.co.uk

LAPALISSE 🏢 - 03120 Map ref: 8

Directions: Overnight parking allowed behind church, public wc and in town market square.

Sanitation:

Aire Details:

🚐 Unknown

☂ Custom

ℹ️ Virtually all shops closed on Mondays. Visited 2005.

© motorhomeandaway.co.uk

LE BREUIL-SUR-COUZE

N45°28.142'E003°15.663' · 63340 · Map ref: 9

Directions: Rue de la Gare. Just past train station. Well signed through town, turn off D726A signed and sp 'Mairie'. Follow road across railway track turn right drive past train station and Aire is on right.

Sanitation:

Aire Details:

🚐 5

Custom

ℹ️ Village with a few shops and what appears to be potable water from fountain. Play park; bar 2 mins; village 5 mins; LPG at Shell garage 'La Fayette' A75.

LES SALLES LAVAUGUYON

N45°44.422'E000°42.056' · 87440 · Map ref: 10

Directions: D33. On D33 one km before reaching village on left by two barns.

Sanitation:

Aire Details:

🚐 6, €4 per night; pay at honesty box

Euro Relis

ℹ️ Idyllic spot, countryside views, village with bar and boulangerie 5 mins.

MASSIAC

N45°15.178'E003°11.794' · 15500 · Map ref: 11

Directions: Rue de L'allagnon. At the train station. From A75 turn off sp 'Massiac' at junc 23. Follow sp 'centre ville' on N9. Then right at roundabout with Spa supermarket sp 'P', signed. The train station is on right and Aire is at far end of car park. Sp 'Gare SNCF'.

Sanitation:

Aire Details:

🚐 10

Custom; charge for electric

ℹ️ Town 2 mins with shops, cafes. Train station adj.

MEYMAC

Lat: 45,5402778 - Long: 2,1541667 · 19250 · Map ref: 12

Directions: Base Nautique de Sèchemailles; Out of village at lake de Sechemailles. Located at holiday village.

If you have a suitable picture for this Aire, please email to: gomotorhoming@hotmail.co.uk

Sanitation:

Aire Details:

🚐 20; 08/04 - 01/11

Flot Blue; €2; Tokens

ℹ️ Super views over lake with good walks. Likely to be busy July/Aug. Tokens from tourist office - at lake July and August; €2; Visited 2004-7.

Mr and Mrs Whitehead

Limousin & Auvergne

MONTLUCON
N46°21.304'E002°35.208' 03100 Map ref: 13

Directions: Place de la Fraternite. Enter town on D943. Just off D943, signed, in large square. Just before D916/D301 junctions.

Sanitation:

Aire Details:

🚐 50
Raclet
ℹ️ In tree lined square used for market Thursday. Large green space and play park adj. Boules court adj. Town centre 20 mins walk. LPG Auchan.

NERIS LES BAINS
N46°17.201'E002°39.144' 03310 Map ref: 14

Directions: D155. At camping du Lac - well sp through town. Located directly on D155.

Sanitation:

Aire Details:

🚐 7; €3
Raclet; Tokens; €2.50 Electric €2.50 per hour.
ℹ️ In thermal spa town. Shower. Beautiful centre 10 mins worth a visit. Thermal water, cafes and plenty of healthy activities.

ORADOUR-SUR-GLANE
N45°56.129'E001°01.531' 87520 Map ref: 15

Directions: Rue du Stade. At sports ground, well sp 'Aire de Repos'. Sp from D101 and D3.

Sanitation:

Aire Details:

🚐 14
Raclet; €2
ℹ️ 10 mins from town, every pitch has view over sports ground and countryside. BBQ, picnic tables, children's play area. Plenty of open space. Nice spot, sports ground adj.

PEYRAT-LE-CHATEAU
N45°48.881' E001°46.251' 87470 Map ref: 16

Directions: Place du Pre de l'age, just off the main road.

Sanitation:

Aire Details:

🚐 10
Custom
ℹ️ Rural views; visited 2005.

© Carol and Duncan Weaver

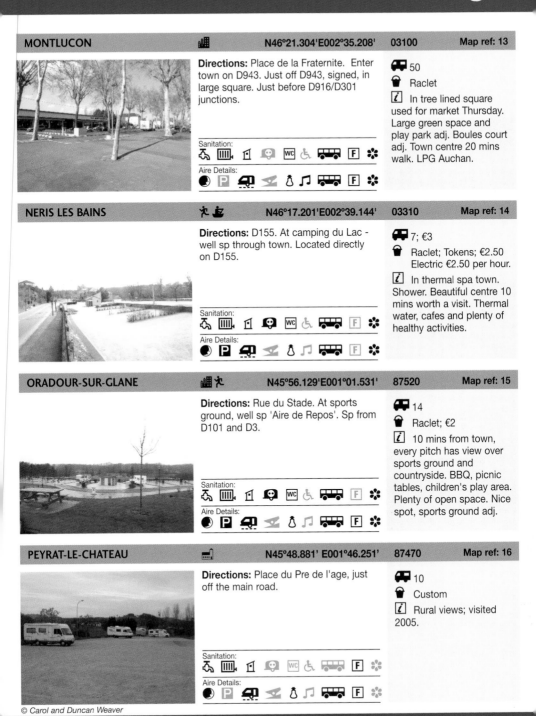

| SAILLAT-SUR-VIENNE | 🏭 | N45°52.330'E000°49.100' | 87720 | Map ref: 17 |

Directions: D235. Located just off the D235 by large factory.

🚐 90

👕 Custom

ℹ️ Called a camping municipal but probably set up as temporary accommodation for factory workers. Possibly not being operated as campsite any more. Factory very noisy. Emergencies only.

Sanitation:

Aire Details:

| ST BONNET-PRES-RIOM | 🏭 | N45°55.648'E003°06.809' | 63200 | Map ref: 18 |

Directions: N144. Behind the church just off N144 two entrances both easy to miss.

🚐 5; 24 hrs

👕 Custom

ℹ️ Town adj with shops and cafés. Views of countryside.

Sanitation:

Aire Details:

| ST ELOY LES MINES | ⚓ | N46°09.337'E002°50.152' | 63700 | Map ref: 19 |

Directions: Adj N144 as enter from south. Signed. Parking overlooking large lake.

🚐 50; 48 hrs

👕 Flot blue; €2

ℹ️ Views over lake possible. Town centre with shops/café 5 mins. Children's play area adj; green area adj; walks around lake possible. Swimming/fishing possible. Boules court, skateboarding.

Sanitation:

Aire Details:

| ST FLOUR 1 | 🏭 | N45°02.165'E003°05.904' | 15100 | Map ref: 20 |

Directions: Rue Marie-Aimee Maraville. Exit junc 28 A75 sp 'St Flour'. At roundabout follow sp 'St Flour'. Follow road until enter town (at bottom of hill). Turn right, signed. Follow road turning left crossing bridge and Aire is then on right.

🚐 10

👕 Euro Relais Maxi; €2

ℹ️ Views of hilltop town. St Flour has thermal water. Train track adj. Shops and bottom town centre 2 mins, walk along river. Walk to hilltop town 15 mins. LPG at Champion.

Sanitation:

Aire Details:

Limousin & Auvergne

ST FLOUR 2   N45°02.038'E003°05.250'   15100   Map ref: 21

Directions: Cours Chazerat (s). Take D926 up hill sp 'haute ville'. At top of hill go straight on. Aire in car park on right. Service point accessed by driving past parking area and at next roundabout take last left turn then first left and service point is on right. Located directly behind car park opposite bandstand.

Sanitation:
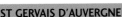

Aire Details:

🚐 50

Euro Relais Maxi; €2

At hill top town; bandstand; town 2 mins; LPG champion; small green area and shaded seating area.

ST GERVAIS D'AUVERGNE   N46°02.204'E002°49.096'   63390   Map ref: 22

Directions: D987. As exit town towards St Priest-des-champs. Places de Loires.

Sanitation:

Aire Details:

🚐 5

Euro relais junior; €2

At lake; walking; fishing; play area; campsite café bar; tennis; boules. Very pleasant. Might have to park at Shoppi supermarket in town in busy times.

ST PARDOUX   N46°03.624'E002°59.710'   63440   Map ref: 23

Directions: Enter village on N144 from St Eloy. Turn right sp 'aquil' and signed. Drive 1.5km turn left onto track sp 'etang des cayers'. Follow track to end.

Sanitation:

Aire Details:

🚐 4

Euro Relais; Tokens

Overlooks lake/pond. A remote, rural beautiful location for those that like it quiet. Fishing possible. Not suitable for RVs.

ST REMY DE BLOT   N46°04.624'E002°55.894'   63440   Map ref: 24

Directions: D99. From N144 turn up D109 sp 'St Remy de Blot' and signed. From D109 turn left onto D99 sp 'Remy de Blot' signed. Adj to D99 on left.

Sanitation:

Aire Details:

🚐 5

Flot blue

Isolated village up in hills. Interesting drive on D109 Gorges de la Sioule. Canoeing at D109 turning.

TENCE		45.11508N 4.29015E	43190	Map ref: 25

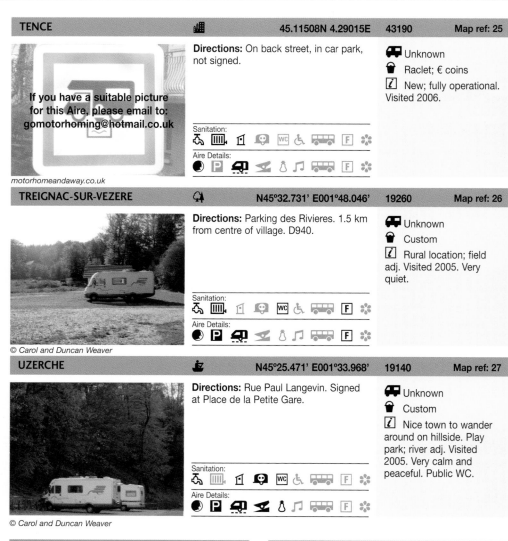

If you have a suitable picture for this Aire, please email to: gomotorhoming@hotmail.co.uk

motorhomeandaway.co.uk

Directions: On back street, in car park, not signed.

🚐 Unknown
🚰 Raclet; € coins
ℹ️ New; fully operational. Visited 2006.

Sanitation:

Aire Details:

TREIGNAC-SUR-VEZERE		N45°32.731' E001°48.046'	19260	Map ref: 26

Directions: Parking des Rivieres. 1.5 km from centre of village. D940.

🚐 Unknown
🚰 Custom
ℹ️ Rural location; field adj. Visited 2005. Very quiet.

Sanitation:

Aire Details:

© Carol and Duncan Weaver

UZERCHE		N45°25.471' E001°33.968'	19140	Map ref: 27

Directions: Rue Paul Langevin. Signed at Place de la Petite Gare.

🚐 Unknown
🚰 Custom
ℹ️ Nice town to wander around on hillside. Play park; river adj. Visited 2005. Very calm and peaceful. Public WC.

Sanitation:

Aire Details:

© Carol and Duncan Weaver

ALLASSAC	●🚰 19240 Map: 28

Directions: Avenue Victor Hugo; Service point facing the train station. • 4 • Free • Euro Relais Junior • All year

ANGLARDS DE SALERS	●🚰 15380 Map: 29

Directions: Near the Château Tremoliere.
• Opening 2007

AUBUSSON	●🚰 23200 Map: 30

Directions: Place du Champ de Foire (Fair Ground) - Rue des Fusillés (access via l'avenue d'Auvergne). • 2 at service point • Pay • Shaded • Additional parking at Champ de Foire (10)

BESSINES-SUR-GARTEMPE	●🚰 87250 Map: 31

Directions: Parking at Champ de Foire (fair ground) • 2

BORT LES ORGUES	🚰 19110 Map: 32

Directions: Parking at the Font Grande.
• Free • All year • www.bort-les-orgues.com

BOURGANEUF	●🚰 23400 Map: 33

Directions: Near the Champ de Foire (fair ground), access via RD912. • 10 • Free

BRIVEZAC 19120 Map: 34
Directions: Valeyran; Aire naturelle de camping situated in a meadow by the river Dordogne, 5 km from Beaulieu-sur-Dordogne. • Pay; 15/04-15/10

BUJALEUF 87460 Map: 35
Directions: Place du Champ de Foire (Fair Ground). • Custom.

CHAMBERET 19370 Map: 36
Directions: Route de la Font Blanche; 200m from town centre • 4 • Free • 01/06-30/10 www.chamberet.correze.net

CHAMBON-SUR-VOUEIZE 23170 Map: 37
Directions: At the campsite entrance. • 4 • Pay • Not Shaded

CHATELUS-LE-MARCHEIX 23430 Map: 38
Directions: Near the town centre • Free • Not Shaded

CONCEZE 19350 Map: 39
Directions: In town on Route du cimetière (road to cemetery) • 1 • Free • Custom • All year • www.conceze.com

CRESSAT 23140 Map: 40
Directions: At the Plan d'eau (village pond) • 5 • Not Shaded

DAMPNIAT 19360 Map: 41
Directions: At the Rugby Stadium; 1.5km from town centre. • 6 • Free • Euro Relais Junior • All year • www.brive-tourisme.com

DONZENAC 19270 Map: 42
Directions: Camping Municipal la Rivière; Parc des sports et loisirs; 1.5km from town centre at the sports and activities park. • 6 • Free • Electric €2.80 from campsite • All year • www.donzenac.correze.net

DRUGEAC 15140 Map: 43
Directions: Facing the train station. • 8 • €2 • All year

EGLETONS 19300 Map: 44
Directions: Parking de l'espace Ventadour; 500m from the centre of town; access via D1089 and A89 motorway exit 22. • 20 • Free • All year • www.mairie-egletons.fr

EYMOUTIERS 87120 Map: 45
Directions: Parking Casino - Route de Limoges.

FELLETIN 23500 Map: 46
Directions: Close to the town centre. • Free • Not Shaded

FLAYAT 23260 Map: 47
Directions: At Camping Etang de la Ramade - RD13. • 4 • Free • Shaded

GLANDON 87500 Map: 48
Directions: Place de la Bascule.

GOUZON 23230 Map: 49
Directions: Place du Champ de Foire (fair ground). • Free • Shaded

GUERET 23000 Map: 50
Directions: Outside the campsite. • Not Shaded

GUERET 23000 Map: 51
Directions: At l'Aire des Monts de Guéret (RN145). • Not Shaded

JARNAGES 23140 Map: 52
Directions: At the communal pond. • 6 • Free • Not Shaded

LA CELLE-DUNOISE 23800 Map: 53
Directions: At the entrance to the campsite; in the town; Parking tolerated. • Shaded

LUBERSAC 19210 Map: 54
Directions: Parking at supermarket Super U; Route de Pompadour; RD 901 500m from town. • All year

MAGNAC-BOURG 87380 Map: 55
Directions: Champ de Foire (fair ground). • Custom

MASSERET 19510 Map: 56
Directions: Aire Porte de Corrèze; Autoroute A20 • Tokens from petrol station • €2 • All year

MAURIAC 15200 Map: 57
Directions: Service Point Total petrol station; La Relais de Marsalou; Parking; near Val St Jean. • Free • €3

MONTBOUCHER 23400 Map: 58
Directions: At the tennis courts, behind the communal buildings. Access via the church. • 10 • Free • Not Shaded

NEUVIC 19160 Map: 59
Directions: Camping le Mialaret; Route d'Egletons. • Euro Relais • €3.50 • 01/06-30/09 • www.lemialaret.com

NEUVIC 2 19160 Map: 60

Directions: Camping Municipal du Lac. • 6 • €4; pay campsite or Mairie • 01/06-30/09 • www.haute-dordogne.com

OBJAT 19130 Map: 61

Directions: Espace loisirs (leisure space); barrier; entry by Mairie or Maison de Presse. • 15 • Euro Relais • Tokens • All year • www.objat.fr

PAGEAS 87230 Map: 62

Directions: Pageas - RN 21 • 6

HAVE YOU VISITED AN AIRE?

Don't forget to fill in the form at the back and return to Vicarious Books.

PEYRELEVADE 19290 Map: 63

Directions: Route de Chamboux; in town at municipal campsite. • € 2 • 01/03-15/11 • www.peyrelevade.correze.net

PIERRE-BUFFIERE 87260 Map: 64

Directions: Camping Municipal; camping de Chabanas. • 4

PLEAUX 15700 Map: 65

Directions: Place d'Empeyssine; Parc des Auzerals. • Free • All year

ROYERE-DE-VASSIVIERE 23460 Map: 66

Directions: Place Pierre Ferrand(adj RD3); Parking Tolerated. • Free

SADROC 19270 Map: 67

Directions: Place du Château; near A20 motorway. • 6 • Free • All year

ST-PANTALEON DE LAPLEAU 19160 Map: 68

Directions: Camping Municipal des Combes. • 5 • €5 per motorhome • €1.80 per person • All year

ST PRIVAT 19220 Map: 69

Directions: Lotissement des Chanaux; 200m from town; • 10 • €2 • All year • www.saint-privat-19.fr

ST-HILAIRE LES PLACES 87800 Map: 70

Directions: At Lac Plaisancel; At lake and campsite car park.

ST-LAURENT 23000 Map: 71

Directions: Town centre, close to the church. • 4 • Free • Not shaded • Due to open 2007

ST-SULPICE LES FEUILLES 87160 Map: 72

Directions: Aire de Boismande- A 20. • Custom

ST-VITTE SUR BRIANCE 87380 Map: 73

Directions: Place de la Mairie.

ST-YRIEIX LA PERCHE 87500 Map: 74

Directions: Parking Jean-Pierre Fabregue. • Custom

SALERS 15140 Map: 75

Directions: Route d'Aurillac. • Free • Opening 2007

ST BONNET DE SALERS 15140 Map: 76

Directions: Ferme de Chasternac. • Free • All year

ST CERNIN 15310 Map: 77

Directions: Details to be confirmed. • Opening 2007

ST-DIZIER-LEYRENNE 23400 Map: 78

Directions: Adj RD 912 at the entrance to the campsite. • 4 • Free • Not Shaded

ST-JUNIEN-LA-BREGERE 23400 Map: 79

Directions: Close to the town. Adj to RD13, near the RD 940. • 4 • Free

TURENNE 19500 Map: 80

Directions: In town near tourist office • Free • Euro Relais Junior • All year • www.brive-tourisme.com

USSEL 19200 Map: 81

Directions: Centre touristique de Ponty; opp camping municipal de Ponty • 15 • €2 • 01/03-31/10

© motorhomeandaway.co.uk

© Frédéric Magnoux, CDT Correze

© Carol and Duncan Weaver

Briançon

Guillestre

Barcelonnette

St-Etienne-
de-Tinée

16

Tende

Sospel

Menton

Monaco -
Monte-Carlo

NICE

Antibes

Cannes

St-Raphaël

Vence

Grasse

Fréjus

5

Castellane

N202

37

Digne

N85

96

Draguignan

60

97

70

le Luc

68

85

64

57

69

33

le Lavandou

8

St-Tropez

87

N98

Hyères

65

38

35

50

54

74

Brignoles

58,59

Toulon

89,90,91

86

Gap

Durance

A51

N94

Sisteron

39

Apt

Manosque

80

Aix-en-Provence

Aubagne

63

la Ciotat

A50

A8

Serres

Carpentras

51,52

76

62

66

Salon-de-
Provence

61

Martigues

MARSEILLE

Orange

55

78

A7

83

42

Avignon

St-Remy-de-P.

A54

Fos

30,88

7

9

31

10

Arles

Rhône

Pont-St-Esprit

94

34

Nîmes

Ste-Maries-
de-la-Mer

75

Alès

Gard

45

Aigues-
Mortes

2,3,4

72,73

27

Langogne

20

Florac

13

Mende

24

23

44

le Vigan

Hérault

Montpellier

Sète

36

Lodève

A75

A9

Agde

40

22

6

17

A75

19

Pézenas

43

29

26

14,15

Perpignan

Argelès

49

Cerbère

31

47

St-Pons

Béziers

18

Narbonne

A9

48

71

Céret

92

46

Castelnaudary

Carcassonne

32

41

A61

Aude

Quillan

12

N116

81

95

56

Mont-Louis

93

Font-
Romeu

79

84

61

77

53

Bourg-Madame

28

25

© tarisme gard

Enjoying the best weather in France this region is ideal for both summer and winter visitors. As a result there are many Aires adjacent to the beach but more increasingly a fee is levied.

© tarisme gard

The French Riviera stretches from Monaco to St Tropez, this is possibly the most famous and glamorous area of Mediterranean coast. Favoured by the rich and famous, ideal for anyone looking to add a little chic to his or her holiday.

To the north of the region the stunning Tarn gorges, interesting scenery, water sports and vultures make this an interesting place to visit.

© motorhomeandaway.co.uk

To the west lie the UNESCO sites of the midi canal with plenty of canal side Aires and the walled city of

© motorhomeandaway.co.uk

Carcassonne. Visitors can walk the ramparts, shop in the boutiques, and soak up the atmosphere over lunch or coffee.

© tarisme gard

ADGE — N43°17.954'E003°28.259' — 34300 — Map ref: 1

Directions: Route de Guiraudette. At Hyper U just off N112 towards le Cap d'Agde.

Sanitation:

Aire Details:

🚐 100

Raclet; €2.50; token; from cabin

ℹ️ Supermarket, garden centre, McDonalds. Adge has unrestricted canal parking - pretty.

AIGUES-MORTES — N43°33.985'E004°11.147' — 30220 — Map ref: 2

Directions: Rue du Port. Parking at port. Enter town from D62 and follow signs.

© Phil Peyton

Sanitation:

Aire Details:

🚐 40; €7

Flot Blue

ℹ️ Some river/boat views. Views of ramparts. Town 5 mins walk. Very busy over Easter weekend.

AIGUES-MORTES 2 — N43°33.969'E004°11.705' — 30220 — Map ref: 3

Directions: Located in car park P3. As enter town follow road alongside city wall to barrier car park P3. Signed.

Sanitation:

Aire Details:

🚐 50; €8.60

Flot Blue

ℹ️ Walled city adj with pristine walls all the way around. Central square with cafés and restaurants. Worth a visit. Likely to be a space here when Aires in other places full.

AIGUES-MORTES 3 — N43°34.650'E004°11.966' — 30220 — Map ref: 4

Directions: D979. Parking at Intermarche. On outskirts of town by D62/D979 and D58 roundabout. At rear of Intermarche signed. North of town.

Sanitation:

Aire Details:

🚐 10

None

ℹ️ Supermarket with LPG, out of town shopping area.

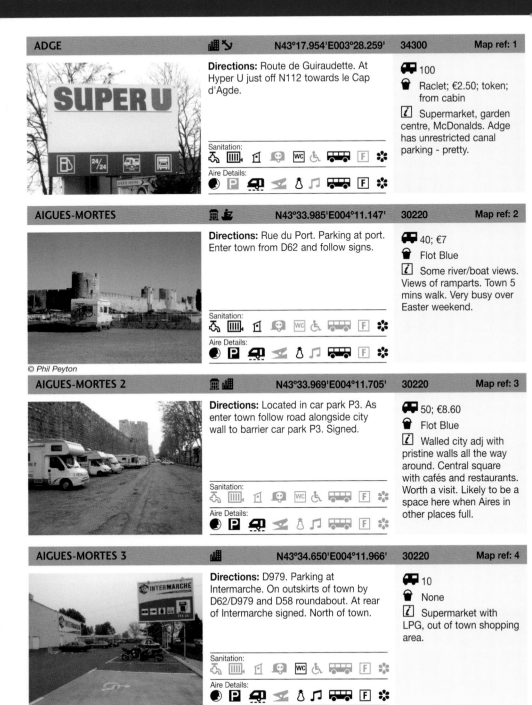

ANNOT
43.96505N 6.66545E   04240   **Map ref: 5**

Directions: Large parking area in woods signed from town centre across river bridge.

🚐 5
🚰 Unknown
ℹ️ New, in woods. Visited 2006.

Sanitation:

Aire Details:

© motorhomeandaway.co.uk

AUMONT AUBRAC
N44°44.418'E003°17.358'   48130   **Map ref: 6**

Directions: Turn off A75 at junc 35 follow sp 'centre commercial'. Supermarket ATAC adj A75. Service point in fuel station.

🚐 50
🚰 Custom
ℹ️ Not an ideal service point, supermarket.

Sanitation:

Aire Details:

BOLLENE
N44°19.344'E004°44.562'   84500   **Map ref: 7**

Directions: Intermarche Supermarket; D26. Turn off D26 into 'centre commercial' Intermarche. North of Bollene, road parallel to A7. By Lavarge (car wash). Signed.

🚐 20
🚰 Raclet
ℹ️ LPG; carwash; Hypermarket.

Sanitation:

Aire Details:

BORMES LES MINOSAS
-    83230   **Map ref: 8**

Directions: Small designated parking area in town behind church near underground parking.

🚐 20
🚰 None
ℹ️ Places likely to be filled with cars and vans. Visited 2005.

Sanitation:

Aire Details:

© motorhomeandaway.co.uk

CHUSCLAN  N44°08.733'E004°40.644' 30200 Map ref: 9

Directions: D138. From N580 at roundabout take turning sp 'Chusclan' 'D138'. Follow road for 2 km and Aire on right by Cote de Rhone producer.

Sanitation:

Aire Details:

 6

Custom

ℹ️ Cote de Rhone producing cave open 9-12 and 4-6.30 all year. Views across vines. On Cote de Rhone driving tour. Likely to be interesting at harvest time.

COMPS N43°51.257'E004°36.488' 30300 Map ref: 10

Directions: From Beaucaire turn into town sp 'Comps' signed. Follow signs through town (tight) and the service point is in front of you and Aire is 200m on right.

Sanitation:

Aire Details:

50; €5 inc service point

Custom; €3

ℹ️ Like wild camp under trees along edge of river Rhone. Swimming. Canoe hire. Village 2 mins, idyllic. Pay in town (map). 15km from Pont de Gard, impressive Roman aquaduct.

DAUPHIN 43.90057N 5.78401E 04300 Map ref: 11

Directions: Parking area at village hall. Small sign at entrance to old village.

Sanitation:

Aire Details:

5

Custom

ℹ️ No shade; toilets and water taps being rebuilt at time of visit. Visited 2006.

© motorhomeandaway.co.uk

DUILHAC PEYREPERTUSE - 11350 Map ref: 12

If you have a suitable picture for this Aire, please email to: gomotorhoming@hotmail.co.uk

Directions: At village entrance.

Sanitation:

Aire Details:

30

Make unknown

ℹ️ This is the most beautiful place we have found in the Pyrenees. €2 for 5 hours electricity. Visited 2007.

© Phil Peyton

FLORAC	🏛	N44°19.549' E003°35.422'	48400	Map ref: 13

Directions: About 40km south of Mende on N106 - parking Chatemale. Signed. Route de Causse by cemetery.

🚐 20
🛒 Raclet; €2
ℹ Nice spot. Alpine views. Very quiet, good for tarn gorges. Visited 2005.

Sanitation: ♿ 🗑 🚪 ♨ WC ♿ 🚌 F ❄

Aire Details: ● P 🚐 ⚓ 🕯 🎵 🚌 F ❄

GRUISSAN-PLAGE	⚓	N43°05.754'E003°06.591'	11430	Map ref: 14

Directions: Place Alain Colas. Follow sp 'Plage des Chalets'. At end of road by beach.

🚐 40; €6 24hrs; from midday; 01/03 - 05/11
🛒 Custom
ℹ Motorhome campsite; Sandy beach adj; snack bar adj; cycle path to Gruissan. Multiple water sports. Generators may be running.

Sanitation: ♿ 🗑 🚪 ♨ WC ♿ 🚌 F ❄

Aire Details: ● P 🚐 ⚓ 🕯 🎵 🚌 F ❄

GRUISSAN - PORT	⚓	N43°06.256'E003°05.983'	11430	Map ref: 15

Directions: Quai de la Tramontane. At Gruissan follow sp 'Gruissan Port' and 'Aire 4 vents'. Sp through town. At marina.

🚐 100; €6-10; 24hrs from midday; 01/03 - 05/11
🛒 Custom
ℹ Adj to marina with views across water and boats. Town 5 mins. No parking allowed outside official areas from 10pm to 7 am. Showers.

Sanitation: ♿ 🗑 🚪 ♨ WC ♿ 🚌 F ❄

Aire Details: ● P 🚐 ⚓ 🕯 🎵 🚌 F ❄

JAUSIERE	🏛	44.41261N 6.72908E	04850	Map ref: 16

Directions: Quartier Ste Anne.

🚐 4
🛒 Flot Blue; Credit Card
ℹ Small rough parking area. Large parking area across river has sign forbidding overnight camping. Visited 2006.

Sanitation: ♿ 🗑 🚪 ♨ WC ♿ 🚌 F ❄

Aire Details: ● P 🚐 ⚓ 🕯 🎵 🚌 F ❄

Mediterranean

LA LOZERE A75 | N44°52.179'E003°14.947' | - | Map ref: 17

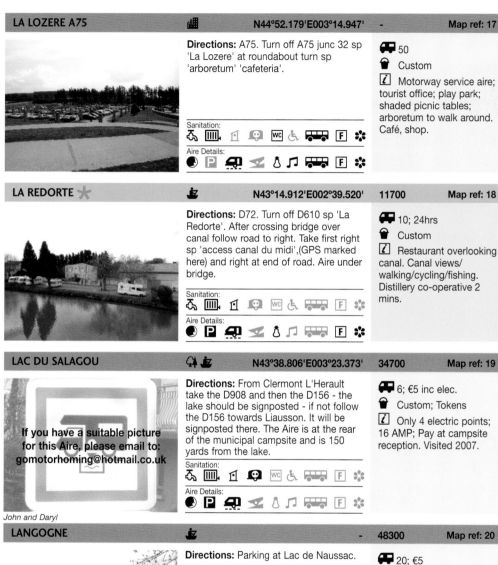

Directions: A75. Turn off A75 junc 32 sp 'La Lozere' at roundabout turn sp 'arboretum' 'cafeteria'.

Sanitation:

Aire Details:

🚐 50
Custom
ℹ️ Motorway service aire; tourist office; play park; shaded picnic tables; arboretum to walk around. Café, shop.

LA REDORTE ✳ | N43°14.912'E002°39.520' | 11700 | Map ref: 18

Directions: D72. Turn off D610 sp 'La Redorte'. After crossing bridge over canal follow road to right. Take first right sp 'access canal du midi',(GPS marked here) and right at end of road. Aire under bridge.

🚐 10; 24hrs
Custom
ℹ️ Restaurant overlooking canal. Canal views/ walking/cycling/fishing. Distillery co-operative 2 mins.

LAC DU SALAGOU | N43°38.806'E003°23.373' | 34700 | Map ref: 19

If you have a suitable picture for this Aire, please email to: gomotorhoming@hotmail.co.uk

John and Daryl

Directions: From Clermont L'Herault take the D908 and then the D156 - the lake should be signposted - if not follow the D156 towards Liausson. It will be signposted there. The Aire is at the rear of the municipal campsite and is 150 yards from the lake.

🚐 6; €5 inc elec.
Custom; Tokens
ℹ️ Only 4 electric points; 16 AMP; Pay at campsite reception. Visited 2007.

LANGOGNE | - | 48300 | Map ref: 20

Directions: Parking at Lac de Naussac.

🚐 20; €5
Flot blue
ℹ️ Lake views; Lake adj. Hotel, restaurants, sailing school. Visited 2007.

© John Barry

108

LAUDUN

  N44°06.470'E004°39.363' 30290 **Map ref: 21**

Directions: At roundabout turn onto D9 sp 'Laudun l'Ardouse' from N86. Then turn off sp 'laudin l'Ardoise' after 4 km to left. Follow rd into town then follow signs and 'parking de Ardens'.

Sanitation:

Aire Details:

3

Flot blue; credit card

i Play area; basket ball courts; seating area adj; quiet; 2 mins downhill to pretty town. Cote de Rhone producing area.

LE CAP D'AGDE

  N43°17.148'E003°31.037' 34300 **Map ref: 22**

Directions: Rue du Gouverneur. As enter Cap d'Agde on D32 turn left at first roundabout and right at second roundabout - signed. The Aire is on right signed.

Sanitation:

Aire Details:

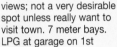€10 per 24 hrs; max 24hrs; pay at machine.

Custom; water from campsite

i Sea 10 mins walk; no views; not a very desirable spot unless really want to visit town. 7 meter bays. LPG at garage on 1st roundabout.

LE MONASTIER

  N44°30.534'E003°15.104' 48100 **Map ref: 23**

Directions: N9. At the train station. From A75 turn off Junc 39. Sp 'Le Monastier' follow road down hill. At roundabout turn left and aire is 150m on right at train station. Signed.

Sanitation:
  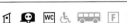

Aire Details:

3

Raclet; Tokens

i At train station.

MENDE

  - 48000 **Map ref: 24**

Directions: Located in town centre.

Sanitation:

Aire Details:

7

Make unknown

i Parking backs onto river with weir under bridge. Visited 2007.

MONFERRAND
N43°21.130'E001°49.442' 11320 Map ref: 25

Directions: N113. D218 Chemin de L'Obelisgue. Driving from Castelnaudary on N113 turn left after obelisk; sp 'P' 'obelisque de Riquet' and 'seuil de Naurouze'. opp Monferrand turning. Parking 200m on left not signed.

Sanitation:

Aire Details:

🚐 15
Custom; Service point broken
ℹ️ Adj Canal du Midi - no views. Walking/cycling canal possible. Shady spot, picnic tables, green open spaces, fishing.

NARBONNE-PLAGE
N43°08.828'E003°09.249' 11100 Map ref: 26

Directions: Turn off D332 towards Gruissan. On right sp 'Aire camping car' sp'Aqua jet'.

Sanitation:

🚐 100; €7
Custom
ℹ️ Motorhome campsite. adj to beach, jet ski hire. Beach popular with wind/kite surfers. No views. Sand kart hire. No shelter from sun, access onto beach, swimming pool adj.

PALAVAS-LES-FLOTS
N43°31.808'E003°55.471' 34250 Map ref: 27

Directions: Rue Frederic Mistral. From D986 as enter town Aire is on right at port. To access go straight across roundabout sp 'halte camping cars' and take next left sp 'halte camping cars', which turns back on itself. Go under 3.5 mt bridge and the Aire is in front of you. GPS taken from top of road to avoid confusion.

Sanitation:

🚐 120; €8-€12 per 24hrs
Custom
ℹ️ Adj to port and river with many boats. Showers; toilet block; boules court. Nice cycle path to Villeneuve les Maguelone. Pleasant seaside town. Motorhome campsite with motorhomes packed in like sardines over Easter, only some with views.

PEZENS
N43°15.329'E002°15.813' 11170 Map ref: 28

Directions: Place de la liberation. Heading towards Carcassoine, car park on left just after crossing river. Difficult access.

🚐 4
Custom
ℹ️ Adj Pezens shops and restaurants. Difficult. Noise from road. No river views - better parking other side of river.

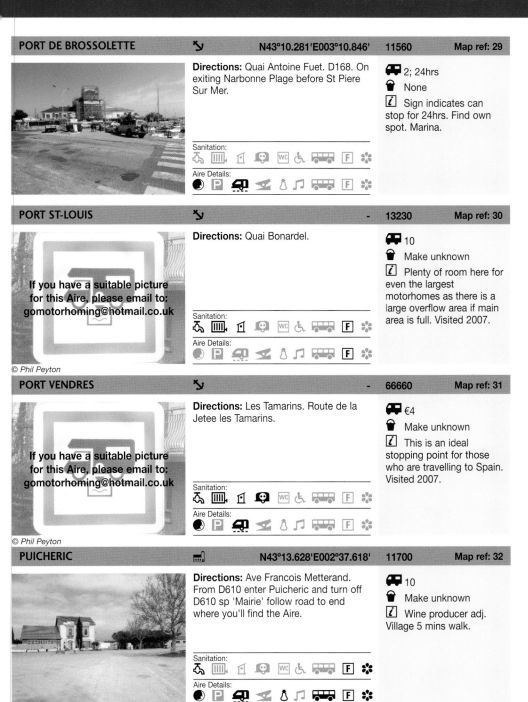

Mediterranean

PORT DE BROSSOLETTE — N43°10.281'E003°10.846' — 11560 — Map ref: 29

Directions: Quai Antoine Fuet. D168. On exiting Narbonne Plage before St Piere Sur Mer.

2; 24hrs

None

Sign indicates can stop for 24hrs. Find own spot. Marina.

Sanitation:

Aire Details:

PORT ST-LOUIS — - — 13230 — Map ref: 30

Directions: Quai Bonardel.

10

Make unknown

Plenty of room here for even the largest motorhomes as there is a large overflow area if main area is full. Visited 2007.

If you have a suitable picture for this Aire, please email to: gomotorhoming@hotmail.co.uk

© Phil Peyton

Sanitation:

Aire Details:

PORT VENDRES — - — 66660 — Map ref: 31

Directions: Les Tamarins. Route de la Jetee les Tamarins.

€4

Make unknown

This is an ideal stopping point for those who are travelling to Spain. Visited 2007.

If you have a suitable picture for this Aire, please email to: gomotorhoming@hotmail.co.uk

© Phil Peyton

Sanitation:

Aire Details:

PUICHERIC — N43°13.628'E002°37.618' — 11700 — Map ref: 32

Directions: Ave Francois Metterand. From D610 enter Puicheric and turn off D610 sp 'Mairie' follow road to end where you'll find the Aire.

10

Make unknown

Wine producer adj. Village 5 mins walk.

Sanitation:

Aire Details:

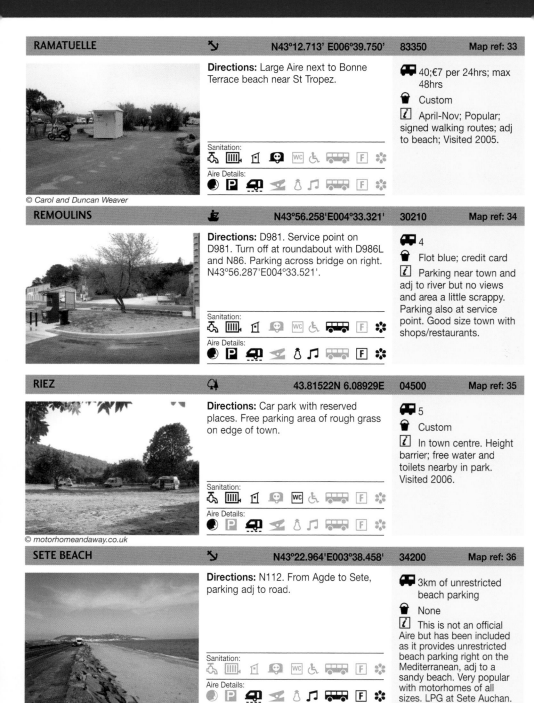

| RAMATUELLE | | N43°12.713' E006°39.750' | 83350 | Map ref: 33 |

Directions: Large Aire next to Bonne Terrace beach near St Tropez.

🚐 40;€7 per 24hrs; max 48hrs

🔧 Custom

ℹ️ April-Nov; Popular; signed walking routes; adj to beach; Visited 2005.

Sanitation:

Aire Details:

© Carol and Duncan Weaver

| REMOULINS | | N43°56.258'E004°33.321' | 30210 | Map ref: 34 |

Directions: D981. Service point on D981. Turn off at roundabout with D986L and N86. Parking across bridge on right. N43°56.287'E004°33.521'.

🚐 4

🔧 Flot blue; credit card

ℹ️ Parking near town and adj to river but no views and area a little scrappy. Parking also at service point. Good size town with shops/restaurants.

Sanitation:

Aire Details:

| RIEZ | | 43.81522N 6.08929E | 04500 | Map ref: 35 |

Directions: Car park with reserved places. Free parking area of rough grass on edge of town.

🚐 5

🔧 Custom

ℹ️ In town centre. Height barrier; free water and toilets nearby in park. Visited 2006.

Sanitation:

Aire Details:

© motorhomeandaway.co.uk

| SETE BEACH | | N43°22.964'E003°38.458' | 34200 | Map ref: 36 |

Directions: N112. From Agde to Sete, parking adj to road.

🚐 3km of unrestricted beach parking

🔧 None

ℹ️ This is not an official Aire but has been included as it provides unrestricted beach parking right on the Mediterranean, adj to a sandy beach. Very popular with motorhomes of all sizes. LPG at Sete Auchan.

Sanitation:

Aire Details:

ST ANDRE LES ALPES

43.96546N 6.50762E 04170 Map ref: 37

Directions: Signed in town.

Sanitation:

Aire Details:

🚐 10

Flot Blue; €3; Tokens

ℹ️ Large tarmac motorhome parking area. No shade. Other motorhomes parked by lake (unofficially) south of town. Visited 2006.

© motorhomeandaway.co.uk

ST CROIX DE VERDON

43.75868N 6.15088E 04500 Map ref: 38

Directions: On road to lakeside beach and campsite.

Sanitation:

Aire Details:

🚐 16; €6

Custom

ℹ️ Good views of lake and near village. Fee collected in evening. Cold shower/washroom; little shade; crowded if full. Visited 2006.

© motorhomeandaway.co.uk

ST MICHEL L'OBSERVATOIRE

43.91308N 5.71592E 04870 Map ref: 39

Directions: On road to observatory north from village; signed.

Sanitation:

Aire Details:

🚐 12

Custom; €2; Token

ℹ️ Some shade (low trees), service point accessed via barrier operated by €2 token from Mairie. Visited 2006.

© motorhomeandaway.co.uk

ST PIERRE DE MER

N43°11.388'E003°11.805' 11560 Map ref: 40

Directions: Enter town from Narbourne, drive through town and at the end of the road just past municipal campsite turn 1st right down road sp 'Ecole de Voile' (sailing school) and 'aire de camping car'.

Sanitation:

Aire Details:

🚐 60; €5 per night; 9am-5pm

Flot Blue; token

ℹ️ Informal 'wild camping' feel. Sailing school adj; sea adj; 5 mins walk to town on footpath along beach; tennis courts.

TREBES

N43°12.539'E002°26.798' 11800 Map ref: 41

Directions: N610. From N113 turn off sp 'Trebes' onto N610 cross over river and follow road. Turn right off N610 into marina adj to canal du midi sp 'Camping Cars'. Aire at far end.

Sanitation:

Aire Details:

🚐 30

Make unknown;difficult

ℹ️ Fantastic Aire. Tree lined dead end road adj to canal du midi. Local products, Boules, marina, restaurants. Always very popular. Tourist office 1 min. Need to be here early. 11am-2pm to guarantee place. Fishing.

VAISON LA ROMAINE

44.24552N 5.07048E 84110 Map ref: 42

Directions: Large parking area in town, signed.

Sanitation:

Aire Details:

🚐 10

None

ℹ️ New; no facilities except bins and bottle bank. Will have some shade when trees grow. Visited 2006.

© motorhomeandaway.co.uk

VALRAS PLAGES

N43°14.600'E003°16.903' 34350 Map ref: 43

Directions: Avenue du Casino. Follow sp 'Casino'. From D19, main route, turn right sp 'Casino' onto D37. Service point on right just before road turns towards sea. Unrestricted parking by Casino.

Sanitation:

Aire Details:

🚐 No designated parking

Aire Services; €2

ℹ️ No designated parking but no restrictions in town either. Many motorhomes parking by Casino. Epitomises many peoples idea of Mediterranean holiday. Beach and town stretching along coast with restaurants etc. Casino parking adj to beach. LPG at Super U Serignan.

VILLEFORT

- 48800 Map ref: 44

Directions: Signed. As enter town from south.

Sanitation:

Aire Details:

🚐 Unknown

Euro Relais Junior

ℹ️ Building works at time of visit. Visited 2005.

© Carol and Duncan Weaver

Mediterranean

D'ANDUZE 30140 Map: 45
Directions: Avenue Rollin; parking de la gare du train touristique; Parking at the tourist train station. • €2 • Suitable large motorhomes

AMELIE LES BAINS 66110 Map: 46
Directions: Aire Municipal.
• €3; tokens • Campsite

ARGELES SUR MER 66700 Map: 47
Directions: Espace loisirs; place for leisure.
• €3

BANYULS DELS ASPRES 66300 Map: 48
Directions: Village Catalan.
• Pay

BANYULS SUR MER 66650 Map: 49
Directions: Aire Municipal.
• €2.30

BARJOLS 83670 Map: 50
Directions: De l'Ancien stade les Tourtouire; Quartier Les Tourtouires; Access via La Place du 19 mars 1962.
• Free • July-Aug; suitable large motorhomes

BEDOIN 84410 Map: 51
Directions: Chemin des Sablieres.

BEDOIN 84410 Map: 52
Directions: Outside campsite Pastory.

BOLQUERE 66210 Map: 53
Directions: Parking du Termanal.

BRIGNOLES 83170 Map: 54
Directions: Supermarket Casino.
• Flot Blue • €2 • All year

CARPENTRAS 84200 Map: 55
Directions: Cours de la pyramide.

CASTEIL 66820 Map: 56
Directions: As enter village on left.

CAVALAIRE-SUR-MER 83240 Map: 57
Directions: Route du Docteur Pardigon; at Station d'épuration;
• €2; Tokens • Open all year except Sunday and public holidays
• Suitable large motorhomes

CUGES LES PINS 13780 Map: 58
Directions: La Ribassee, 200m from the village
• 13

CUGES LES PINS 13780 Map: 59
Directions: RN8 situated at the attraction park OK Corral
• 13

DRAGUIGNAN 83300 Map: 60
Directions: Avenue Pierre Brossolette; Supermarket Intermarché.
• All year • Suitable large motorhomes • A few minutes from town centre

FONT ROMEU 66120 Map: 61
Directions: Parking Terminal.
• €4.50

FONTAINE DE VAUCLUSE 84800 Map: 62
Directions: Aire Municipal.

GREASQUE 13850 Map: 63
Directions: Puits Hely d'Oissel. Parking by the 'musee de la mine'. • Excellent views of Sainte Victoire • 13

GRIMAUD 83310 Map: 64
Directions: St Pons les Mûres; Route Départementale 559. • 10 • 48hrs • pay • Suitable large motorhomes

HYERES-LES-PALMIERS 83400 Map: 65
Directions: Activity/Leisure area on Merou; Bd du Front de Mer; access L'Ayguade. • €3 • Flot Bleu • All year

ISLE SUR LA SORGUE 84800 Map: 66
Directions: Cours Rene Char.

ISTRES 13800 Map: 67
Directions: 163, Chemin du Tour de l'Etang
• CL style • Pay • 13

LA GARDE-FREINET 83680 Map: 68
Directions: Facing the stadium on route D75.
• 5 • All year

LA LONDE LES MAURES 83250 Map: 69
Directions: Round Point Ducournau; Rue Matisse (by the stadium). • €3 • Flot Bleu • All year • Suitable lge motorhomes

LA MOTTE 83920 Map: 70
Directions: Boulevard A. BOUIS.
• 5 • 24 hrs • Free • All year

LE BOULOU   66160   Map: 71

Directions: Near the cemetery.

LE GRAU DU ROI-PORT CAMARGUE   30240   Map: 72

Directions: Parking de la plage (at the beach).

LE GRAU DU ROI-PORT CAMARGUE   30240   Map: 73

Directions: Parking Fanfonne Guillerme.

LES ARCS SUR ARGENS   83460   Map: 74

Directions: Cellier des Archers; Quartier des Laurons; Place de la cave cooperative vinicole; at the community wine producers;
• 55 • Free • All year

LES MAGES   30960   Map: 75

Directions: On D904; as exit village.
• 12 • Free • All year

MALAUCENE   84340   Map: 76

Directions: Near the gendarmerie.
• Payment by credit card

MONT-LOUIS   66210   Map: 77

Directions: Parking des Remparts; RN116.
• Free

PERNES LES FONTAINES   84210   Map: 78

Directions: Outside campsite Coucourelle.

HAVE YOU VISITED AN AIRE?

Don't forget to fill in the form at the back and return to Vicarious Books.

PUYVALADOR   66210   Map: 79

Directions: At the ski station.
• Free.

PUYVERT   84160   Map: 80

Directions: Supermarket Super U.

RIGARDA   66320   Map: 81

Directions: Route de Finestret.

ROQUEBRUNE-SUR-ARGENS : LES ISSAMBRES   83380   Map: 82

Directions: Chez Marcel; Quartier La Gaillarde; Les Issambres.
• 40 • €15 • Custom • Feb-15 Dec • Suitable large motorhomes

SABLET   84110   Map: 83

Directions: Domaine du Parandou RN977.
• 5 • Free • €2 • All year • Suitable large motorhomes

SAILLAGOUSE   66800   Map: 84

Directions: Aire municipal.
• €2

STE-MAXIME   83120   Map: 85

Directions: Rond-Point de Nuenburg - Route du Plan de la Tour n° 68 - Enter by the fire station.
• 80 • €5 / 24 h • All year • Suitable large motorhomes

ST-MANDRIER   83430   Map: 86

Directions: Les Palmiers; Pin Rolland; RD 2018.
• 6 • 48 hrs • Free • €2; Tokens • Tourist Office • All year

ST-TROPEZ   83990   Map: 87

Directions: Private Aire; Chemin Fontaine du Pin - Quartier des Canebiers.

SALIN DE GIRAUD   13129   Map: 88

Directions: By the fire station in town centre.
• 13 • €2

SANARY-SUR-MER   83110   Map: 89

Directions: Campasun Parc Mogador; 167 chemin de Beaucours.
• 800 m from the sea - 800 m town centre • €4,10 • Euros Relais
• 15 March - 4 Nov and 15 - 31 Dec • Suitable lge motorhomes

SANARY-SUR-MER   83110   Map: 90

Directions: Campasun Mas de Pierredon; 652 chemin Raoul Coletta. • 10 • €4 • Euros Relais • April-Sept

SANARY-SUR-MER   83110   Map: 91

Directions: Les Girelles; 1003 chemin de Beaucours.
• By the sea • Flot bleu • April-Sept

ST MARSAL   66110   Map: 92

Directions: Aire Municipal
• €2.30

ST PAUL DE FENOUILLET   66220   Map: 93

Parking du Foyer Rural/Parking Saint-Pierre/ Parking Ecole Primaire. Access from RN117 in town centre. At Place St Pierre.

ST SIFFRET　　30700　Map: 94

Directions: Lieu-dit Les Carrelets, route de Bagnols sur Cèze. (4km d'Uzès) in wine growers.

THUES ENTRE VALLS　　66360　Map: 95

Directions: Gorges de la Caranca .

TRIGANCE　　83840　Map: 96

Directions: Trigance; At the village entrance.
• 12 • €5 • April - Oct • Suitable large motorhomes

VILLECROZE　　83690　Map: 97

Directions: Camping club le Ruou; Route des esparus.
• 10 • €5 • March - Oct • Suitable lge motorhomes

© motorhomeandaway.co.uk

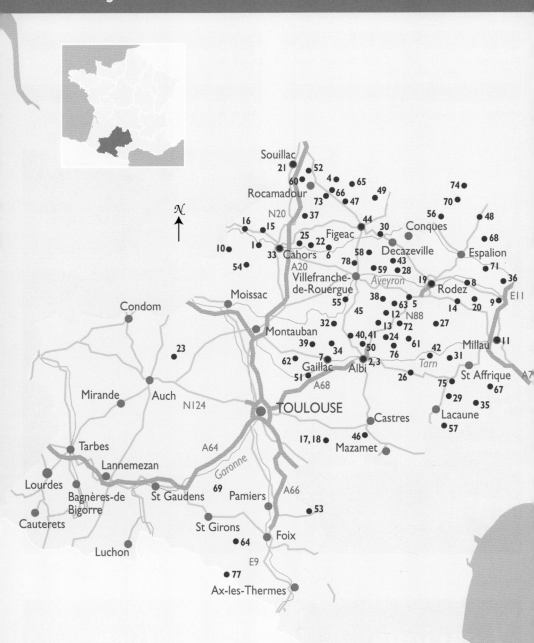

Souillac
21
60
52
4
65
74
Rocamadour
66
70
73
47
49
37
44
56
48
N20
16
15
30
Conques
68
25
22
Figeac
10
1
58
Decazeville
Espalion
33
Cahors
6
78
43
71
A20
59
28
54
Villefranche-
19
8
36
de-Rouergue
Ayeyron
Rodez
E11
Moissac
55
38
9
Condom
45
5
14
20
32
12
N88
27
23
13
72
Montauban
39
40,41
24
61
42
Millau
11
34
50
76
Mirande
62
7
Tarn
31
Auch
Gaillac
Albi
2,3
N124
51
26
St Affrique
A7
A68
75
67
Tarbes
29
35
Lannemezan
Lacaune
Lourdes
Castres
57
A64
Bagnères-de
17,18
46
Bigorre
St Gaudens
Garonne
Mazamet
Cauterets
69
Pamiers
A66
Luchon
53
St Girons
64
Foix
E9
77
Ax-les-Thermes

N

TOULOUSE

© Paul Lammoil

The midi Pyrenees is one of the most beautiful regions of France, offering hot summers and dramatic mountain scenery.

The stunning, brick built city of Albi should be on everyone's agenda, especially as the Aire is within a stones throw of the cathedral.

Breaking all records the Millau toll bridge is the highest of its type in the world. Conveniently situated it is easy to find on the A75 en route to the South of France and Spain.

Head to Pic du Midi, south of Tarbes, then take the disabled friendly cable car from La Mongie to the 2877m summit. Here you can enjoy views across the entire mountain range and the plains of southern France and fully appreciate the glory of the Pyrenees.

Lourdes has been a pilgrimage site for miracle cures for centuries. A fascinating destination for both the converted and the curious.

Skiing in the Pyrenees is excellent, the resorts can be cheaper and quieter than the Alps, but just as challenging.

© C Riviere, CDT Tarn

Midi-Pyrenees

| ALBAS | 🏛 | N44°28.488' E001°13.965' | 46140 | Map ref: 1 |

Directions: On D3, sp 'camping Pech-Del-Gal'.

🚐 Unknown
🚰 Custom
ℹ️ Large area for parking. Visited 2005.

Sanitation:
 🚻 ♿ 🚌 F ❄️

Aire Details:
● P 🚐 ⚓ 🍶 🎵 🚌 F ❄️

© Carol and Duncan Weaver

| ALBI | 🏢 | N43°56.761'E002°09.071' | 81000 | Map ref: 2 |

Directions: Avenue Albert Thomas. Follow N88 into town dir Albi (towards Toulouse). Follow sp 'Centre Ville' on to D988 at roundabout. The service point is on right signed 600 mts.

🚐 At cathedral
🚰 Custom
ℹ️ Toilet service point at waist height. Road parking available but real parking at cathedral.

Sanitation:

Aire Details:
● P 🚐 ⚓ 🍶 🎵 🚌 F ❄️

| ALBI 2 | 🏢 | N43°55.630'E002°08.458' | 81000 | Map ref: 3 |

Directions: Blvd General Sibile. Parking Bondidou. From service point follow sp 'Centre Ville', follow road into and round town. After crossing bridge take turning on right sp 'Coeur Historic' 'Centre hospitalier' when the road opens to a square. Follow road now sp 'Cathedral'. When road ends enter carpark. Follow road in carpark down hill and Aire on left signed.

🚐 9; 48 hrs
🚰 None
ℹ️ Adj to town and cathedral. Over 7 mtrs cannot negotiate car park. Views of cathedral. Historic town worth a visit.

Sanitation:

Aire Details:
 ● P 🚐 ⚓ 🍶 🎵 🚌 F ❄️

| ALVIGNAC | 🏛 | N44°49.502' E001°41.827' | 46500 | Map ref: 4 |

Directions: Route de Padirac. D673 /D20 near west of Rocamadour. Signed.

🚐 5
🚰 Raclet
ℹ️ Village adj. Beware areas of deep gravel. Visited 2004.

Sanitation:
 🚻 ♿ 🚌 F ❄️

Aire Details:

© Carol and Duncan Weaver

BARAQUEVILLE

 N44°16.551'E002°26.055' 12160 **Map ref: 5**

Directions: Rue Caletion. From N88 towards Albi turn left on D507 sp 'Camboulazet'. Turn first right at roundabout and follow road into large car park with toilets. Turn right by toilets and drive down hill - the Aire is on left.

5; 3 days
Euro Relais
Town 2 mins; Free electric.

Sanitation:

Aire Details:

CAJARC

  - 46160 **Map ref: 6**

Directions: 3km west of town on the D24.

10
None
Adj to road so may suffer some noise. Restaurant and bakery nearby. Visited 2006.

Sanitation:

Aire Details:

© John Barry

GAILLAC

N43°53.977'E001°53.696' 81600 **Map ref: 7**

Directions: Aire des Silois - Parking. From D964 from south follow road into town. At square turn left onto D988 then straight over next roundabout signed. Aire is in P des Rives Thomas.

20
Custom
Town car park. 2 mins to town up short slope. Many restaurants and shops. Very pleasant town with nice feel.

Sanitation:

Aire Details:

LAISSAC

N44°23.140'E002°49.282' 12310 **Map ref: 8**

Directions: From N88 turn off sp 'Laissac' at D28 turning. Take first right after bridge, signed. Drive round Intermarche and turn right. Signed. Before bridge. Signed.

6
Custom
Intermarche supermarket 2 mins; adj to N88 - noisy. Town 5 mins. Cattle market adj plenty of parking.

Sanitation:

Aire Details:

L'AVEYRON — N44°19.822'E003°04.948' — 12150 — Map ref: 9

Directions: A75. Exit at junction 42 follow sp 'l'Aveyron'. Signed.

Sanitation:

Aire Details:

🚐 50
Flot blue; tokens
ℹ️ Fuel station; shop; motorway services. Overnight parking not recommended.

MAUROUX — - — 46700 — Map ref: 10

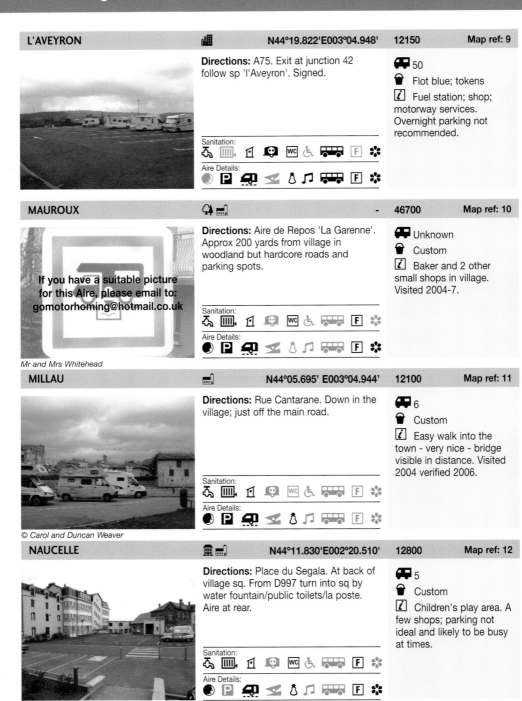

If you have a suitable picture for this Aire, please email to: gomotorhoming@hotmail.co.uk

Mr and Mrs Whitehead

Directions: Aire de Repos 'La Garenne'. Approx 200 yards from village in woodland but hardcore roads and parking spots.

Sanitation:

Aire Details:

🚐 Unknown
Custom
ℹ️ Baker and 2 other small shops in village. Visited 2004-7.

MILLAU — N44°05.695' E003°04.944' — 12100 — Map ref: 11

© Carol and Duncan Weaver

Directions: Rue Cantarane. Down in the village; just off the main road.

Sanitation:

Aire Details:

🚐 6
Custom
ℹ️ Easy walk into the town - very nice - bridge visible in distance. Visited 2004 verified 2006.

NAUCELLE — N44°11.830'E002°20.510' — 12800 — Map ref: 12

Directions: Place du Segala. At back of village sq. From D997 turn into sq by water fountain/public toilets/la poste. Aire at rear.

Sanitation:

Aire Details:

🚐 5
Custom
ℹ️ Children's play area. A few shops; parking not ideal and likely to be busy at times.

PAMPELONNE

 N44°07.334'E002°14.651' 81190 Map ref: 13

Directions: From D78 through village turn onto D53 to 'Tanus'. The Aire is on left at edge of village green. With weigh bridge and public toilets.

 5

🔔 Custom

ℹ️ Play park; village green; pleasant spot; restaurant.

Sanitation:

Aire Details:

PONT-DE-SALARS

 N44°16.688' E002°43.706' 12290 Map ref: 14

Directions: Place de la Riviere, centre of village. In large car park, sp 'Aires'. Near public toilets.

 4; 3 days

🔔 Custom; €2; tokens

ℹ️ River adj; hotel/restaurant opp. Visited 2004.

Sanitation:

Aire Details:

© Carol and Duncan Weaver

PRAYSSAC

 N44°30.222' E001°11.514' 46220 Map ref: 15

If you have a suitable picture
for this Aire, please email to:
gomotorhoming@hotmail.co.uk

 7

🔔 Make unknown

ℹ️ Very pleasant, near road but no noise. Super working type village (no kiss-me-quick hat shops etc) Large grass field that French motorhomes use when spaces filled. Visited 2004-7.

Sanitation:

Aire Details:

Mr and Mrs Whitehead

PUY L'EVEQUE

 N44°30.406' E001°08.140' 46700 Map ref: 16

Directions: The high town. In car park alongside gendarmerie and fire station; signed.

 4

🔔 Custom

ℹ️ Very quiet, real folksy village; very old; close to shops; No parking beginning of August Festivals and Carnival. Visited 2005.

Sanitation:

Aire Details:

© Carol and Duncan Weaver

| REVEL | | N43°27.262'E002°00.934' | 31250 | Map ref: 17 |

Directions: Chemin Des Peupliers. Follow sp 'Piscine', 'Camping' just off D85. Next to campsite. Very well signed.

Sanitation:
Aire Details:

Some parking available on verges.
Raclet; Tokens
Town 1km. Swimming pool opp. Walks along river. Lovely town with many shops and restaurants, interesting covered market houses tourist information. Nice holiday feel.

| REVEL 2 | | N43°27.779'E002°00.318' | 31250 | Map ref: 18 |

Directions: Chemin D'en Besset. At Casino supermarket just off D622 sp in town. Service point in fuel station by gas bottles.

Sanitation:
Aire Details:

20
Aire Services
Supermarket; 5 mins to town.

| RODEZ | | N44°21.467'E002°35.647' | 12000 | Map ref: 19 |

Directions: D162. ZI Cantaranne. Turn off N88 onto D217 sp 'ZI cantaranne' across level crossing. Turn first right and follow road to end. At stop junc turn right And follow road to end. Aire is in front of you across the road.

Sanitation:
Aire Details:

6; 48hrs
Custom
In green fields with walk/cycle to Rodez adj. Substantial amount of gravel footpaths/cycle paths. Map suggests circular walks. Very pleasant.

| SEGUR | | - | 12290 | Map ref: 20 |

Directions: Rue de la Mairie. D29; 25km South Rodez.

Sanitation:
Aire Details:

48hrs
Custom
Shade; seating area; village adj. Visited 2005.

© Carol and Duncan Weaver

124

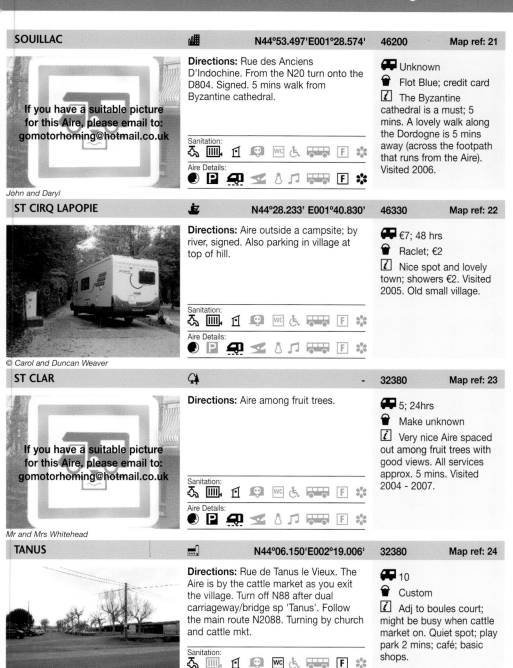

SOUILLAC
N44°53.497'E001°28.574'   46200   **Map ref: 21**

Directions: Rue des Anciens D'Indochine. From the N20 turn onto the D804. Signed. 5 mins walk from Byzantine cathedral.

If you have a suitable picture for this Aire, please email to: gomotorhoming@hotmail.co.uk

Sanitation:

Aire Details:

Unknown

Flot Blue; credit card

The Byzantine cathedral is a must; 5 mins. A lovely walk along the Dordogne is 5 mins away (across the footpath that runs from the Aire). Visited 2006.

John and Daryl

ST CIRQ LAPOPIE
N44°28.233' E001°40.830'   46330   **Map ref: 22**

Directions: Aire outside a campsite; by river, signed. Also parking in village at top of hill.

Sanitation:

Aire Details:

€7; 48 hrs

Raclet; €2

Nice spot and lovely town; showers €2. Visited 2005. Old small village.

© Carol and Duncan Weaver

ST CLAR
-   32380   **Map ref: 23**

Directions: Aire among fruit trees.

If you have a suitable picture for this Aire, please email to: gomotorhoming@hotmail.co.uk

Sanitation:

Aire Details:

5; 24hrs

Make unknown

Very nice Aire spaced out among fruit trees with good views. All services approx. 5 mins. Visited 2004 - 2007.

Mr and Mrs Whitehead

TANUS
N44°06.150'E002°19.006'   32380   **Map ref: 24**

Directions: Rue de Tanus le Vieux. The Aire is by the cattle market as you exit the village. Turn off N88 after dual carriageway/bridge sp 'Tanus'. Follow the main route N2088. Turning by church and cattle mkt.

Sanitation:

Aire Details:

10

Custom

Adj to boules court; might be busy when cattle market on. Quiet spot; play park 2 mins; café; basic shops.

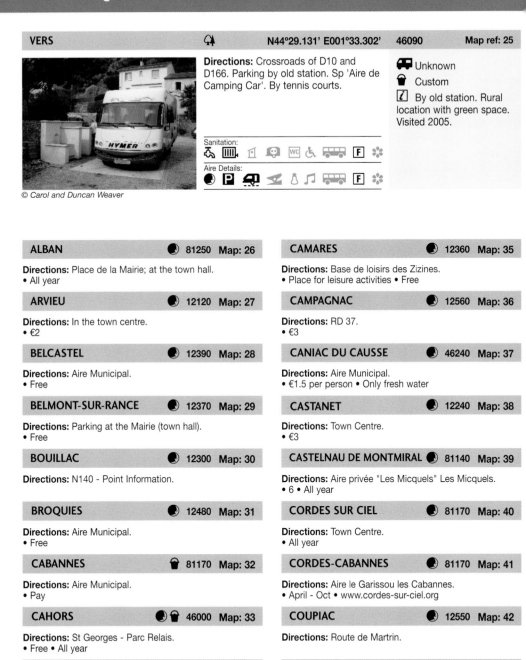

| VERS | 🌳 | N44°29.131' E001°33.302' | 46090 | Map ref: 25 |

Directions: Crossroads of D10 and D166. Parking by old station. Sp 'Aire de Camping Car'. By tennis courts.

🚐 Unknown
👜 Custom
ℹ️ By old station. Rural location with green space. Visited 2005.

Sanitation:
🔧 🛢️ 🚰 🚐 WC ♿ 🚌 F ✿

Aire Details:
⚫ P 🚐 ♨️ 🧴 🎵 🚌 F ✿

© Carol and Duncan Weaver

| ALBAN | ⚫ 81250 Map: 26 |

Directions: Place de la Mairie; at the town hall.
• All year

| ARVIEU | ⚫ 12120 Map: 27 |

Directions: In the town centre.
• €2

| BELCASTEL | ⚫ 12390 Map: 28 |

Directions: Aire Municipal.
• Free

| BELMONT-SUR-RANCE | ⚫ 12370 Map: 29 |

Directions: Parking at the Mairie (town hall).
• Free

| BOUILLAC | ⚫ 12300 Map: 30 |

Directions: N140 - Point Information.

| BROQUIES | ⚫ 12480 Map: 31 |

Directions: Aire Municipal.
• Free

| CABANNES | 👜 81170 Map: 32 |

Directions: Aire Municipal.
• Pay

| CAHORS | ⚫👜 46000 Map: 33 |

Directions: St Georges - Parc Relais.
• Free • All year

| CAHUZAC SUR VERE | ⚫ 81140 Map: 34 |

Directions: Place du Mercadial.
• All year

| CAMARES | ⚫ 12360 Map: 35 |

Directions: Base de loisirs des Zizines.
• Place for leisure activities • Free

| CAMPAGNAC | ⚫ 12560 Map: 36 |

Directions: RD 37.
• €3

| CANIAC DU CAUSSE | ⚫ 46240 Map: 37 |

Directions: Aire Municipal.
• €1.5 per person • Only fresh water

| CASTANET | ⚫ 12240 Map: 38 |

Directions: Town Centre.
• €3

| CASTELNAU DE MONTMIRAL | ⚫ 81140 Map: 39 |

Directions: Aire privée "Les Micquels" Les Micquels.
• 6 • All year

| CORDES SUR CIEL | ⚫ 81170 Map: 40 |

Directions: Town Centre.
• All year

| CORDES-CABANNES | ⚫ 81170 Map: 41 |

Directions: Aire le Garissou les Cabannes.
• April - Oct • www.cordes-sur-ciel.org

| COUPIAC | ⚫ 12550 Map: 42 |

Directions: Route de Martrin.

| CRANSAC | ⚫ 12110 Map: 43 |

Directions: Route de la Gare.
• €6

FIGEAC   46100   Map: 44

Directions: La Foirail; Bd du Colonel Teulie.
• Flot Blue • €2 • All year

LA FOUILLADE   12270   Map: 45

Directions: Aire Municipal.

LABRUGUIERE   81290   Map: 46

Directions: Parc résidentiel de loisirs Domaine d'En Laure.
• 8 • April - Oct • www.ville-labruguiere.com

LACAPELLE MARIVAL   46120   Map: 47

Directions: Place de la Roque.
• Euro Relais Junior • Free • March - Nov

LAGUIOLE   12210   Map: 48

Directions: Outside camping municipal Les Monts D'Aubrac.

LATRONQUIERE   46210   Map: 49

Directions: Place du Foirail; near La Poste (the post office). • Euro Relais Junior • Free • All year

LE GARRIC   81450   Map: 50

Directions: Aire de Cap' Découverte.
• 18 • July - Aug

LISLE SUR TARN   81310   Map: 51

Directions: By lake Bellevue.
• 3 • All year • www.ville-lisle-sur-tarn.fr

MARTEL   46600   Map: 52

Directions: La Fontanelle.
• Free • All year

MIREPOIX   09500   Map: 53

Directions: Paul Dardier; near the old station.
• Pay

MONTCUQ   46800   Map: 54

Directions: Quarter St Jean.
• Euro Relais • €2 • All year

MONTEILS   12200   Map: 55

Directions: RD 47.
• Free

MONTEZIC   12460   Map: 56

Directions: Le Hameau des Prades.
• Free

NAGES   81320   Map: 57

Directions: Aire Rieu Montagné Le Port.
• 10 • All year

NAUSSAC   12700   Map: 58

Directions: Aire de Loisirs de Peyrelevade.
• €3

PEYRUSSE-LE-ROC   12220   Map: 59

Directions: Adj D87.
• Free

PINSAC   46200   Map: 60

Directions: Salle des Fetes - Mairie (town hall).
• Flot Blue • €2 • All year

REQUISTA   12170   Map: 61

Directions: Salle Fetes - place F.-Fabie.
• Free

SALVAGNAC   81630   Map: 62

Directions: Aire naturelle Les Sourigous.
• 8 • June - Sept

SAUVETERRE-DE-ROUERGUE   12800   Map: 63

Directions: D997 as enter town.
• € 2.50

SERRES SUR ARGET   09000   Map: 64

Directions: Salle Polyvalente (village hall); near the Mairie (town hall) • Pay

SOUSCEYRAC   46190   Map: 65

Directions: In village centre.
• Euro Relais • Free • April - Nov

ST CERE   46400   Map: 66

Directions: Parking at the Stadium.
• Flot blue Fountaine • April - Oct

ST JEAN ET ST PAUL   12250   Map: 67

Directions: St jean d'Alcas.
• Free

ST-CHELY-D'AUBRAC   12470   Map: 68

Directions: Aire Municipal.
• Free

ST-CROIX-VOLVESTRE   09230   Map: 69

Directions: Aire Municipal.
• Free

| STE-GENEVIERE-SUR-ARGENCE | 12420 | Map: 70 |

Directions: Rue de l'Argence; near town centre.
• €2

| ST-GENIEZ-D'OLT | 12130 | Map: 71 |

Directions: Avenue de la Gare.
• Free

| ST-JUST-SUR-VIAUR | 12800 | Map: 72 |

Directions: La Fabrie.
• Free

| THEMINES | 46120 | Map: 73 |

Directions: By the church.
• Euro Relais • Free • All year

| THERONDELS | 12600 | Map: 74 |

Directions: Salle des Fetes.
• Free

| VABRES L'ABBAYE | 12400 | Map: 75 |

Directions: CD 999.

| VALDERIES | 81350 | Map: 76 |

Directions: Place de la Mairie; at the town hall.
• All year

| VICDESSOS | 09220 | Map: 77 |

Directions: Salle des Fetes.
• Free

| VILLENEUVE | 12260 | Map: 78 |

Directions: Sol de la Dime.
• Free

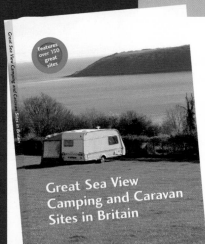

Normandy

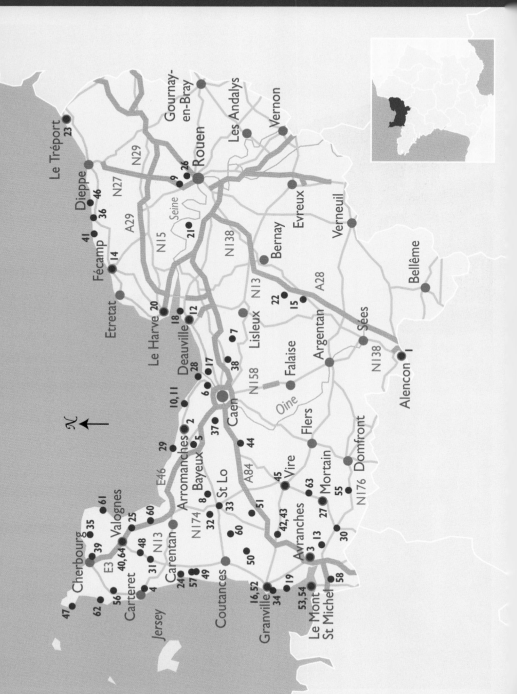

Le Tréport 23
Dieppe 46
36
41
Fécamp 14
N27
A29
N29
Gournay-en-Bray
Rouen
9 26
Les Andalys
Vernon
N15
Seine
21
N138
Evreux
Bernay
Verneuil
Etretat
Le Harve 20
18
12
Deauville
28 17
10,11
6
2
Caen
N158
Lisieux
7
38
Falaise
Oine
Argentan
Sees
N138
Bellême
Alencon 1
A28
N13
22
15
Arromanches
Bayeux 5
St Lo 8
37
Flers
Vire
Mortain
Domfront
Valognes
Cherbourg
E3
40,64
Carteret
Jersey
47
62
56
Jersey
61
35
60
25
N174
32
33
60
50
51
42,43
45
63
27
55
N176
30
Avranches
3 13
Coutances
16,52
34
19
53,54
Le Mont St Michel
58
Granville

130

© CDT Manche

Cliffs and large beaches of either sand or pebbles dominate the coastline. The coastal resorts offer a range of activities.

War history is found all over this region. As early as 1066 the Bayeaux Tapestry depicts the Battle of Hastings. Most recent are the Normandy landing beaches located along the coast north of Caen.

© D Sparrow, CDT Manche

Le Mont St Michel, a medieval city, is one of the most recognisable landmarks in Normandy. Separated from the mainland by a causeway, it is now a major tourist attraction.

Giverny, south of Rouen is home to Monet's garden. Walk the grounds to gain an insight into the artists work.

Honfleur is home to one of the best Aires in France and possibly the most popular. You can spend the day on the beach or watch the boats come and go from the harbour, then while away the evening at the restaurants and bars overlooking the marina.

© A Mauxion, CDT Manche

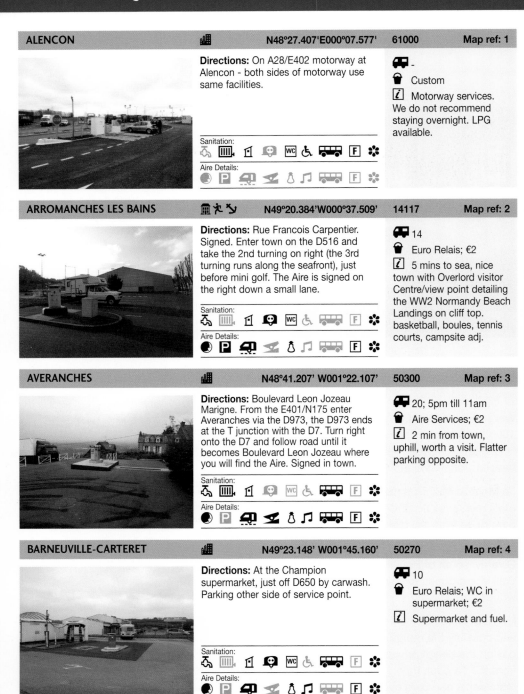

ALENCON
N48°27.407'E000°07.577' 61000 Map ref: 1

Directions: On A28/E402 motorway at Alencon - both sides of motorway use same facilities.

Sanitation:

Aire Details:

🚐 -
🏠 Custom
ℹ️ Motorway services. We do not recommend staying overnight. LPG available.

ARROMANCHES LES BAINS
N49°20.384'W000°37.509' 14117 Map ref: 2

Directions: Rue Francois Carpentier. Signed. Enter town on the D516 and take the 2nd turning on right (the 3rd turning runs along the seafront), just before mini golf. The Aire is signed on the right down a small lane.

Sanitation:

Aire Details:

🚐 14
🏠 Euro Relais; €2
ℹ️ 5 mins to sea, nice town with Overlord visitor Centre/view point detailing the WW2 Normandy Beach Landings on cliff top. basketball, boules, tennis courts, campsite adj.

AVERANCHES
N48°41.207' W001°22.107' 50300 Map ref: 3

Directions: Boulevard Leon Jozeau Marigne. From the E401/N175 enter Averanches via the D973, the D973 ends at the T junction with the D7. Turn right onto the D7 and follow road until it becomes Boulevard Leon Jozeau where you will find the Aire. Signed in town.

Sanitation:

Aire Details:

🚐 20; 5pm till 11am
🏠 Aire Services; €2
ℹ️ 2 min from town, uphill, worth a visit. Flatter parking opposite.

BARNEUVILLE-CARTERET
N49°23.148' W001°45.160' 50270 Map ref: 4

Directions: At the Champion supermarket, just off D650 by carwash. Parking other side of service point.

Sanitation:

Aire Details:

🚐 10
🏠 Euro Relais; WC in supermarket; €2
ℹ️ Supermarket and fuel.

BAYEAUX

🏢 N49°16.812' W000°42.457' | 14400 | **Map ref: 5**

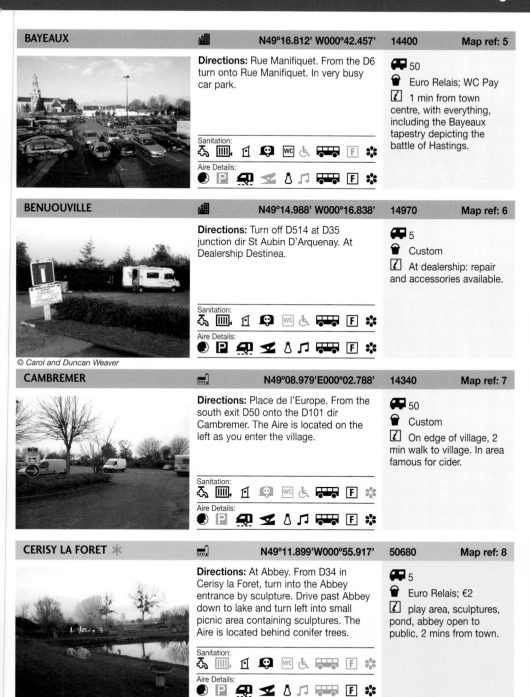

Directions: Rue Manifiquet. From the D6 turn onto Rue Manifiquet. In very busy car park.

Sanitation:

Aire Details:

🚐 50

👝 Euro Relais; WC Pay

ℹ️ 1 min from town centre, with everything, including the Bayeaux tapestry depicting the battle of Hastings.

BENUOUVILLE

🏢 N49°14.988' W000°16.838' | 14970 | **Map ref: 6**

Directions: Turn off D514 at D35 junction dir St Aubin D'Arquenay. At Dealership Destinea.

Sanitation:

Aire Details:

🚐 5

👝 Custom

ℹ️ At dealership: repair and accessories available.

© Carol and Duncan Weaver

CAMBREMER

🏢 N49°08.979'E000°02.788' | 14340 | **Map ref: 7**

Directions: Place de l'Europe. From the south exit D50 onto the D101 dir Cambremer. The Aire is located on the left as you enter the village.

Sanitation:

Aire Details:

🚐 50

👝 Custom

ℹ️ On edge of village, 2 min walk to village. In area famous for cider.

CERISY LA FORET ✳

🏢 N49°11.899'W000°55.917' | 50680 | **Map ref: 8**

Directions: At Abbey. From D34 in Cerisy la Foret, turn into the Abbey entrance by sculpture. Drive past Abbey down to lake and turn left into small picnic area containing sculptures. The Aire is located behind conifer trees.

Sanitation:

Aire Details:

🚐 5

👝 Euro Relais; €2

ℹ️ play area, sculptures, pond, abbey open to public, 2 mins from town.

CLERES  - 76690 Map ref: 9

Directions: Near the sports facilities. Signed.

© Carol and Duncan Weaver

🚐 10; 72 hrs
🚰 Custom
ℹ️ Green space adj; marked bays. Visited 2006.

Sanitation:

Aire Details:

COURSEULLES-SUR-MER N49°20.061'W000°26.733' 14470 Map ref: 10

Directions: Rue de La Liberation. Outside camping Le Champ de Course. Turn off D514, onto Rue de La Liberation on the east edge of town.

🚐 13
🚰 Euro Relais
ℹ️ €5.90 per night; might be cheaper to use campsite, 2 mins to beach.

Sanitation:

Aire Details:

COURSEULLES-SUR-MER N49°20.215'W000°28.166' 14470 Map ref: 11

Directions: Juno Beach, Avenue General de Gaulle. off D514. Motorhomes allowed to use carpark during day. DO NOT use coach bays.

🚐 11, No overnight parking for Motorhomes.
🚰 None
ℹ️ Park to walk and see Juno Beach - one of the beaches used in the Normandy Beach landings WW2 - information and sights on structured walk.

Sanitation:

Aire Details:

DEAUVILLE N49°21.436' E000°05.044' 14800 Map ref: 12

Directions: Boulevard des Sports. Enter via D27A. Large roundabout with A27A/D513 (round-Pont Des Jumelages), from here turn onto D27A drive parallel to sports fields, and take the first turning on right, the Aire is located immediately on your left.

🚐 5
🚰 Euro Relais
ℹ️ By sports facility,10-20 min walk from town. Train station across road.

Sanitation:

Aire Details:

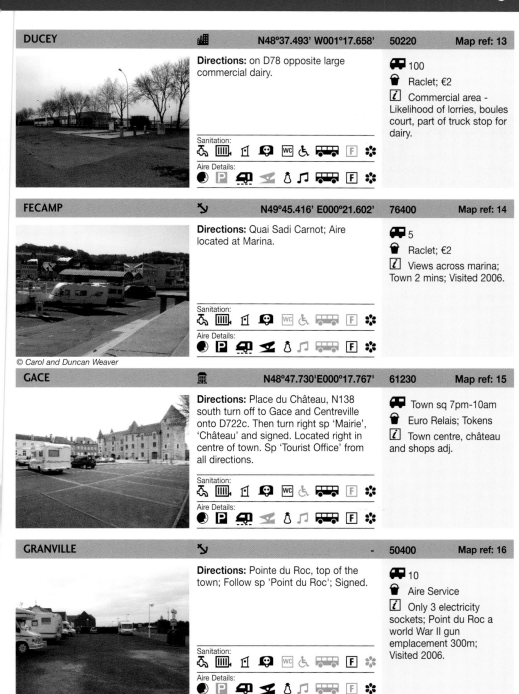

| DUCEY | | N48°37.493' W001°17.658' | 50220 | Map ref: 13 |

Directions: on D78 opposite large commercial dairy.

🚐 100
Raclet; €2
ℹ️ Commercial area - Likelihood of lorries, boules court, part of truck stop for dairy.

Sanitation:

Aire Details:

| FECAMP | | N49°45.416' E000°21.602' | 76400 | Map ref: 14 |

Directions: Quai Sadi Carnot; Aire located at Marina.

🚐 5
Raclet; €2
ℹ️ Views across marina; Town 2 mins; Visited 2006.

Sanitation:

Aire Details:

© Carol and Duncan Weaver

| GACE | | N48°47.730'E000°17.767' | 61230 | Map ref: 15 |

Directions: Place du Château, N138 south turn off to Gace and Centreville onto D722c. Then turn right sp 'Mairie', 'Château' and signed. Located right in centre of town. Sp 'Tourist Office' from all directions.

🚐 Town sq 7pm-10am
Euro Relais; Tokens
ℹ️ Town centre, château and shops adj.

Sanitation:

Aire Details:

| GRANVILLE | | - | 50400 | Map ref: 16 |

Directions: Pointe du Roc, top of the town; Follow sp 'Point du Roc'; Signed.

🚐 10
Aire Service
ℹ️ Only 3 electricity sockets; Point du Roc a world War II gun emplacement 300m; Visited 2006.

Sanitation:

Aire Details:

© Carol and Duncan Weaver

HEROUVILLETTE		N49°13.196' W000°14.678'	14850	Map ref: 17

Directions: D513A, Avenue de Caen. On the main route through Herouvillette, signed.

Sanitation:

🚿 🛁 🏠 🚐 WC ♿ 🚌 F ❄

Aire Details:

⬤ P 🚐 ⛵ 🏕 🎵 🚌 F ❄

🚐 4

🛒 Euro Relais

ℹ️ Village 2 mins, pleasant location. Close to amenities.

HONFLEUR	⚓	N49°25.173' E000°14.513	14600	Map ref: 18

Directions: From A29 exit to Honfleur and follow the D580 into Honfleur. At the roundabout where the road meets the water turn right. The Aire is located directly in front of you.

Sanitation:

🚿 🛁 🏠 🚐 WC ♿ 🚌 F ❄

Aire Details:

⬤ P 🚐 ⛵ 🏕 🎵 🚌 F ❄

© Carol and Duncan Weaver

🚐 100; €7; 24hrs

🛒 Custom

ℹ️ Campsite for motorhomes on edge of waterway. Gypsies in small area at time of visit (January) but motorhomes still using it. Main village 10 mins very pretty.

JOLLOUVILLE-LES-PINS	🏛	N48°50.208'W001°13.456'	50610	Map ref: 19

Directions: Just off main route, surrounded on three sides by height restricted carpark.

Sanitation:

🚿 🛁 🏠 🚐 WC ♿ 🚌 F ❄

Aire Details:

⬤ P 🚐 ⛵ 🏕 🎵 🚌 F ❄

🚐 None

🛒 Aire Services; Credit Card

ℹ️ Not an overnight stop. Tight access.

LE HARVE	🏢⚓	N49°29.536' E000°05.765'	76600	Map ref: 20

Directions: Boulevard Clemenceau. Parking de la piscine du CNH. Located facing the tourist information centre. From the port follow the coast round to the left. The Aire is located on the northern edge of the outer port wall by boat yard.

Sanitation:

🚿 🛁 🏠 🚐 WC ♿ 🚌 F ❄

Aire Details:

⬤ P 🚐 ⛵ 🏕 🎵 🚌 F ❄

🚐 50+

🛒 Flot Blue; Tokens from Tourist Office.

ℹ️ 2 mins from beach, Tourist Office across road, ideal for city shopping, eating, ferrys from Le Harve and nightlife, play area, basketball court, stony beach and short promenade to marina.

LA MAILLERAYE-SUR-SEINE   N49°29.092' E000°46.386'   76940   Map ref: 21

Directions: From D490 turn into town via D131, drive straight through town until you reach river, then turn left parking anywhere, esp grass area. Service point at end of semi-made up road.

Sanitation:

Aire Details:

 20

🪣 Raclet; tokens €2 at maire and shops.

ℹ️ On edge of River Seine, 2 mins from town. Could easily spend a few days here; view, fishing and boat watching.

LE SAP N48°53.722'E000°19.823'   61470   Map ref: 22

Directions: On D12 out of village towards Vimoutiers. By fire station overlooking pond.

Sanitation:

Aire Details:

🚐 3; €6

🪣 Aire Service.

ℹ️ Pond, picnic tables, village 5 mins walk. Brick and Tudor style village with shops. Football pitch opposite.

LE TREPORT N50°03.396' E001°23.215'   76470   Map ref: 23

Directions: By the Tourist Office at the town entrance.

Sanitation:

Aire Details:

🚐 50; pay

🪣 Custom

ℹ️ Large car park style Aire with designated 7 meter bays; Visited 2006.

LESSAY N49°13.134'W001°32.110'   50430   Map ref: 24

Directions: D72, main high street at edge of town, clearly signed through town.

Sanitation:

Aire Details:

🚐 5

🪣 Custom; need to visit Mairie to get access to water.

ℹ️ On edge of pleasant village (2 mins) dominated by large church.

Normandy

MONTEBOURG   🏃   N49°29.137' W001°22.367'   50310   **Map ref: 25**

Directions: At the Louis Lecacheax stadium. The Aire is located in the south of the town before the main shopping area. It is a tight turn on the right by a zebra crossing. Clearly signed. Up steep, pot-holed single track lane.

Sanitation:
🚰 ⬛ 🚻 ☠ WC ♿ 🚐 F ❄

Aire Details:
⬤ P �caravan ⛵ 👄 🎵 🚐 F ❄

🚐 50
👄 Custom
ℹ️ Next to sports facilities, quiet, views of town and fields, 5 mins from town, BBQ.

MONTVILLE   🏢🏃   N49°32.837' E001°04.353'   76710   **Map ref: 26**

Directions: On D155 sp 'camping cars' and 'sports', turn towards church and drive through carpark, in town centre. Problems with bridge heights, ideally approached from south from Malaunay, signed though signs are small.

Sanitation:
🚰 ⬛ 🚻 👄 WC ♿ 🚐 F ❄

Aire Details:
⬤ P 🚐 ⛵ 👄 🎵 🚐 F ❄

🚐 20
👄 Euro Relais; (raised), tokens from l'hexagone, Mairie.
ℹ️ 2 mins from town, with amenities, sports centre, swimming pool and close to lake.

MORTAIN   🏢   N48°38.923'W000°56.697'   50140   **Map ref: 27**

Directions: Place du Château, D133. Signed in town. Turn off D977 onto D133 sp to 'Romagny' & 'Camping'. Located 100m down hill in large carpark with château.

Sanitation:
🚰 ⬛ 🚻 ☠ WC ♿ 🚐 F ❄

Aire Details:
⬤ P 🚐 ⛵ 👄 🎵 🚐 F ❄

🚐 6
👄 Euro Relais
ℹ️ 2 mins to town, marked walking trails to waterfall sp 'Petite Cascade'.

OUISTREHAM   ⚓   N49°17.258' W000°14.998'   14150   **Map ref: 28**

Directions: Follow sp 'car ferry', at ferry follow sp 'plage'. On exiting car ferry turn right, follow road alongside port when road bends sharp left the aire is in front. Signed; 2 entrances.

Sanitation:
🚰 ⬛ 🚻 👄 WC ♿ 🚐 F ❄

Aire Details:

⬤ P 🚐 ⛵ 👄 🎵 🚐 F ❄

🚐 7
👄 Euro Relais; tokens
ℹ️ Boules court, adj sandy beach with attractions. Beach is Sword Beach (British Normandy Landings WW2 - no information), town 5 mins. Fish market located before ferry port; very convenient for car ferry.

PORT EN BESSIN ⚓ N49°20.933' E000°45.300' 14520 Map ref: 29

© Carol and Duncan Weaver

Directions: By Port Huppain, follow sp 'Port Petrollier 1944'. Signed.

🚐 5; €3.30 per night
🚽 Raclet; €2
ℹ️ Fishing community with scallop festival. Visited 2006.

Sanitation:
♿ ▥ 🚻 ☠ WC ♿ 🚌 F ✳️

Aire Details:
● P 🚐 ≺ ⚱ ♫ 🚌 F ✳️

SAINT-HILAIRE-DU-HARCOUET N48°34.554'W001°05.509' 50600 Map ref: 30

Directions: Parking beside large church sp 'plan d'eau'/'Piscine'.

🚐 5
🚽 Raclet; €2
ℹ️ Excellent facility for town. Walks around lake. D177 Fougers-St Hillaire nice road to drive.

Sanitation:
♿ ▥ 🚻 ☠ WC ♿ 🚌 F ✳️

Aire Details:
● P 🚐 ≺ ⚱ ♫ 🚌 F ✳️

SAINT-SAUVEUR-LE-VICOMTE N49°23.192' W001°31.770' 50390 Map ref: 31

Directions: Route de Bricquebec. At town square on the D900, signed on pavement opp town square, right in town centre.

🚐 3
🚽 Custom
ℹ️ Nice Aire, opportunity to enjoy French town, weighbridge on site. Views. Rear of castle.

Sanitation:
♿ ▥ 🚻 ☠ WC ♿ 🚌 F ✳️

Aire Details:
● P 🚐 ≺ ⚱ ♫ 🚌 F ✳️

ST FROMOND N49°13.321'W001°05.377' 50620 Map ref: 32

Directions: In village carpark/square by bridge and roundabout, signed.

🚐 15
🚽 Euro Relais; €2
ℹ️ In village, nice semi rural spot, ideal for tranquil night.

Sanitation:
♿ ▥ 🚻 ☠ WC ♿ 🚌 F ✳️

Aire Details:

● P 🚐 ≺ ⚱ ♫ 🚌 F ✳️

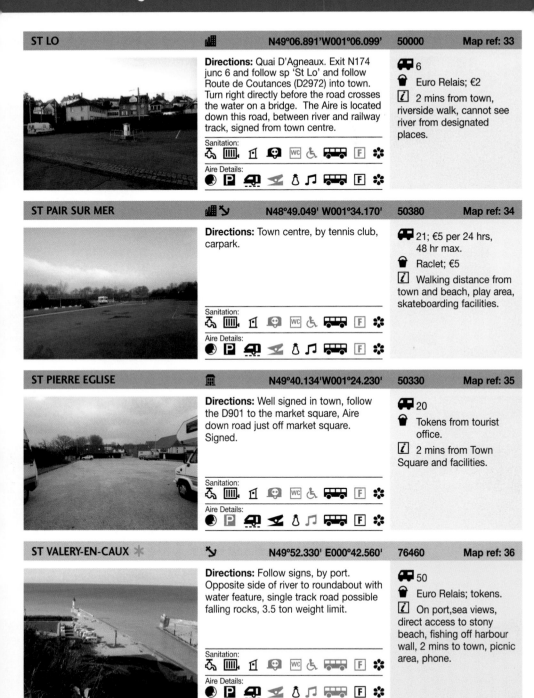

| **ST LO** | | N49°06.891'W001°06.099' | 50000 | **Map ref: 33** |

Directions: Quai D'Agneaux. Exit N174 junc 6 and follow sp 'St Lo' and follow Route de Coutances (D2972) into town. Turn right directly before the road crosses the water on a bridge. The Aire is located down this road, between river and railway track, signed from town centre.

6

Euro Relais; €2

2 mins from town, riverside walk, cannot see river from designated places.

Sanitation:

Aire Details:

| **ST PAIR SUR MER** | | N48°49.049' W001°34.170' | 50380 | **Map ref: 34** |

Directions: Town centre, by tennis club, carpark.

21; €5 per 24 hrs, 48 hr max.

Raclet; €5

Walking distance from town and beach, play area, skateboarding facilities.

Sanitation:

Aire Details:

| **ST PIERRE EGLISE** | | N49°40.134'W001°24.230' | 50330 | **Map ref: 35** |

Directions: Well signed in town, follow the D901 to the market square, Aire down road just off market square. Signed.

20

Tokens from tourist office.

2 mins from Town Square and facilities.

Sanitation:

Aire Details:

| **ST VALERY-EN-CAUX** ✳ | | N49°52.330' E000°42.560' | 76460 | **Map ref: 36** |

Directions: Follow signs, by port. Opposite side of river to roundabout with water feature, single track road possible falling rocks, 3.5 ton weight limit.

50

Euro Relais; tokens.

On port, sea views, direct access to stony beach, fishing off harbour wall, 2 mins to town, picnic area, phone.

Sanitation:

Aire Details:

© Carol and Duncan Weaver

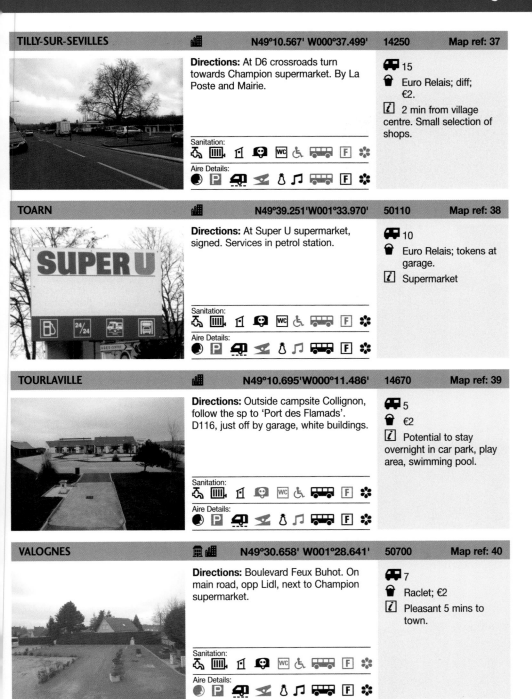

| TILLY-SUR-SEVILLES | | N49°10.567' W000°37.499' | 14250 | Map ref: 37 |

Directions: At D6 crossroads turn towards Champion supermarket. By La Poste and Mairie.

Sanitation:

Aire Details:

🚐 15

Euro Relais; diff; €2.

ℹ 2 min from village centre. Small selection of shops.

| TOARN | | N49°39.251'W001°33.970' | 50110 | Map ref: 38 |

Directions: At Super U supermarket, signed. Services in petrol station.

Sanitation:

Aire Details:

🚐 10

Euro Relais; tokens at garage.

ℹ Supermarket

| TOURLAVILLE | | N49°10.695'W000°11.486' | 14670 | Map ref: 39 |

Directions: Outside campsite Collignon, follow the sp to 'Port des Flamads'. D116, just off by garage, white buildings.

Sanitation:

Aire Details:

🚐 5

€2

ℹ Potential to stay overnight in car park, play area, swimming pool.

| VALOGNES | | N49°30.658' W001°28.641' | 50700 | Map ref: 40 |

Directions: Boulevard Feux Buhot. On main road, opp Lidl, next to Champion supermarket.

Sanitation:

Aire Details:

🚐 7

Raclet; €2

ℹ Pleasant 5 mins to town.

VEULETTES-SUR-MER   N49°51.151' E000°36.124' 76450 Map ref: 41

© Vicky and Nick Church

Directions: On seafront behind tourist office.

Sanitation:

Aire Details:

🚐 20

🛏 Unknown

ℹ️ Short walk to small village; large pitches. Visited 2006.

VILLEDIEU LES POELES 1 N48°50.502' W001°13.363' 50800 Map ref: 42

Directions: Place des Quais. Signed from D9. Exit the E401/A84 onto the D924 into Villedieu Les Poeles centre. Turn left onto the D9/Bourg Abbesse then right onto Jean Gaste. Signed in Town Centre.

Sanitation:

Aire Details:

🚐 See next entry

🛏 Euro Relais; €2

ℹ️ Cobbled carpark with 5 large bays. By river, close to town 5-10 min urban but pleasant, backs onto park. Restaurants and Hospital.

VILLEDIEU LES POELES 2 N48°50.243 W001°13.415' 50800 Map ref: 43

Directions: Place de la Commanderie. Signed in town centre on D924 up small side street to carpark.

Sanitation:

Aire Details:

🚐 30

🛏 See last entry

ℹ️ 1 min walk from town, surrounded by water with weir situated in a wooded dell, poss swimming in weir but unknown. children's play park and grassy area.

VILLERS-BOCAGE N49°04.802'W000°39.640' 14310 Map ref: 44

Directions: D67. Follow D675 through town at end of high street by chemist, turn right and right Aire on left by tennis courts. Sp 'tennis'.

Sanitation:

Aire Details:

🚐 4

🛏 Aire Services; €2

ℹ️ Park surround, shops in town and restaurants to amuse for a few hours, tennis and basketball courts. Picnic tables and boules court. Pretty town 1 min walk, nice location.

VIRE		N48°50.458'W000°53.350'	14500	Map ref: 45

Directions: Champ de Foire. North edge of town. Easy approach from D577/N174/ D407 junction turn into town on the N174. Turning signed on left at bottom of hill (carpark rd then goes up hill) before the town centre.

🚐 50
Custom
Large town 2 mins.

Sanitation:
Aire Details:

VOULES-LES-ROSES		N49°52.549'E000°48.132'	76980	Map ref: 46

Directions: Avenue Jean Moulin D68. Located on the D68 on the edge of the village, on a corner directly in front of campsite, turn into campsite entrance and drive past reception. The Aire is in front of you running parallel to D68.

🚐 18
Raclet; €3, tokens campsite reception.
Use of campsite facilities available at extra charge. Walking distance from village.

Sanitation:
Aire Details:

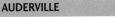

AUDERVILLE	50440	Map 47

Directions: Exit the village on the D901 towards Goury.

BRICQUEBEC	50260	Map 48

Directions: Route de Cherbourg.

CREANCES	50710	Map 49

Directions: At the Supermarket Champion, Rue Haut Chemin.

GAYRAY	50450	Map 50

Directions: Impasse de l'ancienne gare.

GOUVETS	50420	Map 51

Directions: Aire de Service de La Vallee de la Vire (A84).

GRANVILLE	50400	Map 52

Directions: In the carpark of the Aquarium (l'Aquarium).
• €5 from 19h-10h

LE MONT SAINT MICHEL	50170	Map 53

Directions: Parking outside Campsite Le Mont St Michel.

LE MONT SAINT MICHEL 2	50170	Map 54

Directions: Parking at Mont St Michel.
• Service point €2.70 • 150 spaces • €8 24h.

LE TEILLEUL	50640	Map 55

Directions: Route de Domfront.

LES PIEUX	50340	Map 56

Directions: Sciotot.

PIROU	50770	Map 57

Directions: Chemin des Matelots.
• €2

PONTORSON	50170	Map 58

Directions: Supermarket Champion - Route du Mont Saint-Michel.

Normandy

REMILLY-SUR-LOZON	50340	Map 59

Directions: At the entrance to the village.
• €2

SAINT-MERE-EGLISE	50480	Map 60

Directions: Beside the church.
• €4 per night

SAINT-VAAST-LA-HOUGUE	50550	Map 61

Directions: Aire de la Gallouette. Outside the campsite.
• Services €2 • €7 per night

SIOUVILLE-HAGUE	50340	Map 62

Directions: Avenue des Peupliers.
• €2

SOURDEVAL	50150	Map 63

Directions: Parc Saint-Lys, Rue Jean-Baptiste Janin.
• €2

VALOGNES	50700	Map 64

Directions: Elephant blue, Route de Sottevast. (car wash)
• €2 • €5 arrive after 19h, services & elec.

© Carol and Duncan Weaver

© Ken Croft

© Carol and Duncan Weaver

© G Targat, CDT Marche

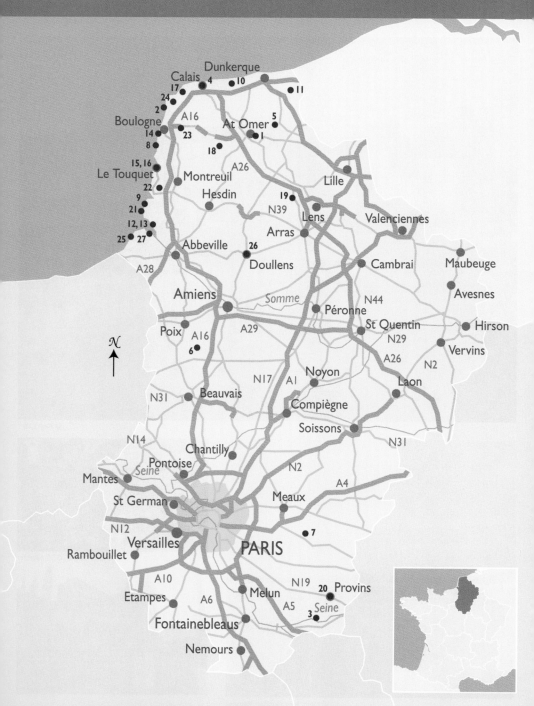

Dunkerque
Calais
17
24
2
Boulogne
14
8
15, 16
Le Touquet
22
9
21
12, 13
25 27
Abbeville
A28
Amiens
Poix
6
4
10
11
A16
At Omer
5
1
23
18
A26
Montreuil
Hesdin
19
N39
Lille
Lens
Valenciennes
Arras
26
Doullens
Cambrai
Maubeuge
Avesnes
Somme
Péronne
N44
N29
St Quentin
Hirson
Vervins
A16
A29
A26
N2
N17
A1
Noyon
Laon
N31
Beauvais
Compiègne
N14
Chantilly
Soissons
N31
Pontoise
Seine
N2
Mantes
St German
Meaux
A4
N12
7
Versailles
PARIS
Rambouillet
A10
N19
20 Provins
Etampes
A6
Melun
A5
Seine
Fontainebleaus
3
Nemours

N

Sandy beaches can be found from the borders of Belgium all the way to Normandy, offering some of the best Aires in the region. Being so close to Calais and Dunkerque these can be enjoyed for a weekend break or at the beginning and end of longer trips.

War history scars this region. Vimy Ridge near Arras has well preserved World War One trenches. There are interesting and humbling museums, cemeteries and battlefields between Arras and Amiens.

Why not visit the world famous châteaux of Versailles to the west of Paris and Chantilly to the north. Both are impressive buildings with excellent gardens and grounds. Chantilly is home to a horse museum with 2,500 thoroughbred horses and the Conde Museum of art.

Oise-idays de France is a regional park surrounding Chantilly, ideal for walking, cycling, horse riding and fishing. The Park also houses the theme park 'Parc Asterix'. Disneyland Paris is to the west of Paris.

© John Barry

ARQUES

N50°44.731'E002°18.276'   62510   **Map ref: 1**

Directions: Rue Michelet. Located behind camping Beausejour. Sp 'Beausejour' off D210 as exit town towards Clairmarais. Turn onto Rue Michelet and follow road through residential streets to campsite. Sp in town. Drive round behind reception to parking.

Sanitation:

Aire Details:

30; €2 24hrs

Euro Relais; Tokens

Pay at campsite reception. Partial views of lake, pleasant. English speaking vet in town. Fishing - pay.

AUDRESSELLES

N50°49.184'E001°35.820'   62164   **Map ref: 2**

Directions: D940. On southern edge of Audresselles outside campsite 'Les Ajoncs' adj to main road; signed.

Sanitation:

Aire Details:

5

Inside campsite; €1.90

Aire on gravelled area. Plenty of WW2 remnants. Beach 10 mins. Showers in campsite €1.10.

BRAY-S-SEINE

N48°25.033'E003°14.349'   77480   **Map ref: 3**

Directions: Turn off D412 at south side of river just by bridge sp 'Aire Camping Car' and 'P 200 spaces'. Turn towards large industrial building then turn right under bridge into car park. Large car park adj to river Seine.

Sanitation:

Aire Details:

20

Custom

River views; town with shops adj; park adj; river walks/cycles. Pleasant spot unlikely to be busy.

CALAIS

N50°57.962'E001°50.622'   62100   **Map ref: 4**

Directions: Avenue Raymond Poincare. From ferry port follow sp 'Calais centre ville'. Then follow sp 'camping'. This will mean veering to right when approaching Calais centre. Follow the sp 'P camping car'. Always keep ferry terminals on right. You are literally driving round the port. On right just past campsite and adj beach.

Sanitation:

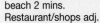

Aire Details:

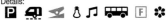

50; €7 per night

Raclet

Views of harbour/ferries. Fishing off harbour wall 2 mins. Sandy beach 2 mins. Restaurant/shops adj. Toilets open 01/06-30/09

© John Barry

CASSEL

   N50°47.596'E002°29.314'   **59670**   **Map ref: 5**

Directions: C301. South of town. From D933 turn off just after Bauinchore on to c301 to Oxelaere. Drive past Oxelaere heading to Cassel. The Aire is on your left at the sports ground before entering Cassel.

5

🔓 Custom

ℹ Shaded; views over fields but roadside location. Nice town 15 mins walk. Cycle route adj.

Sanitation:

Aire Details:

CONTY

  N49°44.595'E002°09.347'   **80160**   **Map ref: 6**

Directions: Rue du Marais. In village centre signed off D920.

🚐20

🔓 Custom

ℹ Play park adj. Motorhome parking opp service point. Village 2 mins.

Sanitation:

Aire Details:

COULOMMIERS

  N48°47.848'E003°05.765'   **77120**   **Map ref: 7**

If you have a suitable picture for this Aire, please email to: gomotorhoming@hotmail.co.uk

Directions: N34 Rue du Grand Morin. Leave coulonimiers on N34 dir le Ferte Gaucher as exit Coloumbier the Aire is on left.

🚐20

🔓 Custom

ℹ Under construction at time of visit.

Sanitation:

Aire Details:

EQUIHEN-PLAGE

  N50°40.787'E001°34.117'   **62224**   **Map ref: 8**

Directions: Rue du Beurre Fondu. From D119 at Equihen-Plage enter roundabout and turn onto D236E into the high street. Take first right, turning down road by café Le Ocean, signed. In 200m turn right and Aire on left.

🚐10

🔓 Make unknown

ℹ On cliff overlooking sea. Possibility of walk to beach down grassy area. Next to small sewerage works. Town 5 mins.

Sanitation:

Aire Details:

FORT MAHON PLAGE N50°20.320'E001°33.345' 80120 Map ref: 9

Directions: At Fort-Mohan-Plage drive down the main road, D32 heading towards the sea. Turning left off D32 just before sea. The Aire is located behind car park and in front of Dune. Well signed.

Sanitation:

Aire Details:

🚐 50; €6

🛒 Custom

ℹ️ In town centre, backs onto sand dunes, town 1 min, beach 2 mins. Very pleasant. Sheltered, total suntrap. Very nice town. Cycle routes through dunes/woods.

GRAVELINES N50°58.966'E002°08.487' 59820 Map ref: 10

Directions: Rue du Pont de Pierre D11. Caravanning Municipal - station sanitaire signed in town. A16 exit junc 23 dir Gravelines at roundabout go straight across and Aire on right sp 'Caravanning Municipal - Station Sanitaire'.

Sanitation:

Aire Details:

🚐 50

🛒 Station Sanitaire; €1.50

ℹ️ Service point takes 3x 50 cents. Might be campsite some of year.

HONDSCHOOTE N50°58.588'E002°34.836' 59122 Map ref: 11

Directions: Impasse Spynnewyn. On D110 from Bergues as enter town turn right sp 'Moulin de la Victorie'. Service point on right just past turning to windmill. Parking at windmill.

Sanitation:

Aire Details:

🚐 10; at windmill

🛒 Raclet; Tokens; €2

ℹ️ Sports park adj; by windmill. Town 2 mins. Pleasant; no shade.

LE CROTOY N50°13.713'E001°36.738' 80550 Map ref: 12

Directions: Des Dunes. From D940 at roundabout turn onto D4 then right at roundabout with D4/D104 onto D104 sp 'Le Crotoy Centre' then turn immediately right, and right again the Aire is on the left signed.

Sanitation:

Aire Details:

🚐 30; €5; Pay at meter

🛒 Aire Service; €2

ℹ️ On beach; sand dunes adj. Town 10 minutes. Cycle routes adj. Town 5 mins cycle. Pleasant but a little isolated.

LE CROTOY 2

N50°13.094'E001°37.992'   80550   Map ref: 13

Directions: Le Port. Ave des Escoles. From D940 at roundabout turn onto D104 into Le Crotoy sp 'le port'. At town turn first left sp 'P Port', at end of road turn left. The Aire is in the parking straight in front of you.

Sanitation:

Aire Details:

🚐 70; €5; pay at machine
🚰 Aire Service; €2
ℹ️ Views over port. Town 2 mins; restaurants; walks around seafront/harbour. Plenty of cycle routes. Pleasant spot - busier than Des Dunes Aire.

LE PORTEL

N59°42.647'E001°34.566'   62480   Map ref: 14

Directions: Rue des Champs. Just off D236. At roundabout opposite E'leclerc supermarket turn right, then follow sp 'Le Portel'. Turning on right after total garage on steep left hand bend sp 'Le Portel'. Aire by sports facilities on right past Bricomarche.

Sanitation:

Aire Details:

🚐 25
🚰 Custom
ℹ️ Service point at far end on blue and white building 'Stade Portelois'. Water available 8.30-9.30 5.30-6.30. Just off main route. Some roads 3.5ton weight limited.

LE TOUQUET PARIS PLAGE

N50°32.142'E001°35.593'   62520   Map ref: 15

Directions: Avenue Jean Ruet. At the Centre Nautique Touquet. Follow N39 'centre ville' until reach sea - turn right and follow the road along until you can go no further - turning off onto Route en Corniche. Aire at end Route en Corniche well sp through town.

Sanitation:

Aire Details:

🚐 50; €6.50 per 24hrs
🚰 Aire Service; €2
ℹ️ Adj to boat yard/marina. Adj beach. Very well maintained beach resort with an expensive feel.

LE TOUQUET PARIS PLAGE 2

N50°31.585'E001°35.907'   62520   Map ref: 16

Directions: Boulevard de la Canche. Park International de la Canche. Follow sp 'Hippotel' and 'Parking International de la canches'. At Hippotel follow sp 'Office du Tourisme' Aire 200m on right. Marked by horse on Michelin map.

Sanitation:

Aire Details:
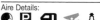

🚐 100
🚰 Aire Service; €2
ℹ️ Walks to sea, partial sea views. Walks to town 5 mins.

LES ERABLES

 N50°54.738'E001°43.231' 62179 **Map ref: 17**

Directions: Rue du Chateau Eau. From Calais drive on D940 towards Boulogne. At Escalles turn first left and second right. Signed.

Sanitation:

Aire Details:

25; €8
Custom
At Aire Natural; caravans accepted; Cap Blanc Nez ideal for walking - bunkers.

LUMBRES

N50°42.854'E002°06.614' 62380 **Map ref: 18**

Directions: Centre Commercial. Exit A26 junction 3, take N42 turn off sp 'Lumbres' turn left under road bridge sp 'Lumbres' then at roundabout turn left sp 'centre commercial' the Aire is at the kiosk in petrol station.

Sanitation:

Aire Details:

10
Raclet
Large E'Leclerc supermarket.

NOEUX-LES-MINES

N50°29.182'E002°40.208' 62290 **Map ref: 19**

Directions: Rue de L'egalite. Outside dechetterie (recycling). Turn at roundabout with ESSO garage sp 'Dechetterie'. Left at traffic lights sp 'Dechetterie'. Aire on right at recycling centre. Barriered when recycling not open.

Sanitation:

Aire Details:

None
Aire Service; Tokens; €4; open office hrs
Really difficult. So suggest only use if desperate and in office hours. Parking opportunities at Salle Polyvente (on route).

PROVINS

N48°33.629'E003°16.778' 77160 **Map ref: 20**

Directions: Chemin de Villecran. From D231/N19 roundabout turn into Provins sp 'Centre' 'City Medeival'. Turn next left sp 'tourist info'. The Aire is in the parking on right.

Sanitation:

Aire Details:

20; €20 24hrs
Custom
Adj to very imposing hill top medieval city. Walking distance. City closed to traffic March-Nov. Tourist office adj. Even lower non-tourist town has shopping.

QUEND-PLAGE-LES-PINS
 N50°19.533'E001°32.919' 80120 **Map ref: 21**

Directions: From D32 follow road to end (main high street towards sea). Turn right then follow round aire on right in car park by sand dune.

Sanitation:

Aire Details:

🚐 50

Aire Service; €2

i Sea Views. Sea/sandy beach 2 mins; town centre 2 mins; cycle path adj. Area has plenty of excellent cycle paths through woods/dunes to Fort Mahon Plage. Golf course 5 mins. Pleasant seaside town, 3 slipways adj.

RANG-DU-FLIERS-BERCK
N50°24.879'E001°36.472' 62180 **Map ref: 22**

Directions: Le Boure Etoile. On D917 at centre commercial adj the Bricomarche (behind the Ecomarche).

Sanitation:

Aire Details:

🚐 5

Custom

i In commercial area. €3 for 4 hours electric. Sea 10 mins drive. LPG at Ecomarche.

ST MARTIN BOULOGNE
N50°43.982'E001°40.119' 62200 **Map ref: 23**

Directions: At St Martin Boulogne. Exit A16 junc 3 and follow sp 'centre commercial' away from town. The service point is at Auchan petrol station.

Sanitation:

Aire Details:

🚐 1

Raclet; Tokens

i In large commercial out of town shopping area. LPG at Auchan.

TARDINGHEN
N50°51.771'E001°38.955' 62179 **Map ref: 24**

Directions: D249. From D940 at Tardighen as enter village towards Boulogne turn left sp 'Ferme de l'horge' follow road. Farm on left 1.5km sp.

Sanitation:

Aire Details:

🚐 5

Custom; €3

i If no one available post money through letterbox. No evidence of parking but could take 5 motorhomes.

Northern France

CAYEUX-SUR-MER 📞 80410 Map: 25	**SAINT-VALERY-SUR-SOMME** 📞 80230 Map: 27
Directions: Outside the campsite.	**Directions:** Rue de la Croix-l'Abbe.

DOULLENS 📞 80600 Map: 26

Directions: As enter the village Rue du Pont a l'Avoine.

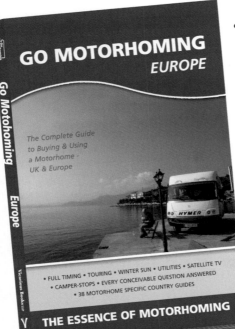

Pays

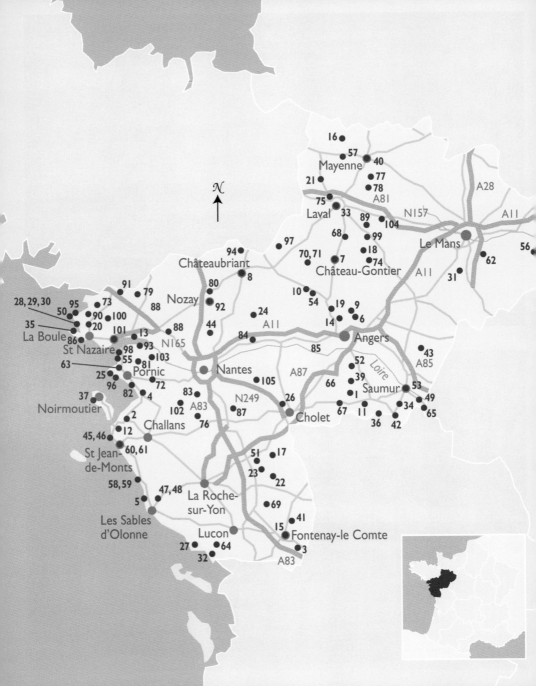

156

The Loire River is a key feature of this region, an untamed section between Angers to Samur has world heritage status. Cliffs and hillsides are dotted with troglodyte (cave) dwellings. There is an abundance of Aires down this river making it ideal for a motorhome meander during the regions famed long summers.

Known the world over the Le Mans 24-hour race is held in June. Visit www.lemans.org for information on the 24hr and other races. Part of the track is a national road so visit on non-race days and get racing driver experience without the speed.

Most of the coastline is within the Vendee region. Working salt marsh dominates the southern part of the region; many birds take advantage of the natural and man-made environment. Coast ports tend to be on tidal rivers so people looking for sandy holiday resorts should drive the D38 from St Jean-de-Monts.

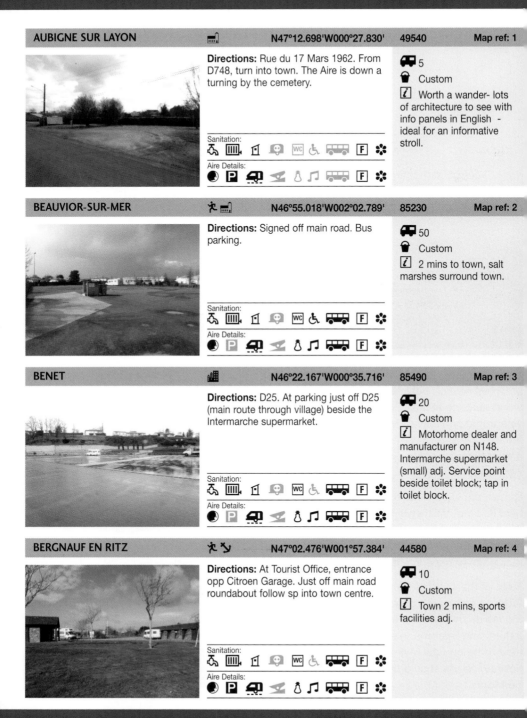

| AUBIGNE SUR LAYON | | N47°12.698'W000°27.830' | 49540 | Map ref: 1 |

Directions: Rue du 17 Mars 1962. From D748, turn into town. The Aire is down a turning by the cemetery.

Sanitation:

Aire Details:

🚐 5
Custom
ℹ️ Worth a wander- lots of architecture to see with info panels in English - ideal for an informative stroll.

| BEAUVIOR-SUR-MER | | N46°55.018'W002°02.789' | 85230 | Map ref: 2 |

Directions: Signed off main road. Bus parking.

Sanitation:

Aire Details:

🚐 50
Custom
ℹ️ 2 mins to town, salt marshes surround town.

| BENET | | N46°22.167'W000°35.716' | 85490 | Map ref: 3 |

Directions: D25. At parking just off D25 (main route through village) beside the Intermarche supermarket.

Sanitation:

Aire Details:

🚐 20
Custom
ℹ️ Motorhome dealer and manufacturer on N148. Intermarche supermarket (small) adj. Service point beside toilet block; tap in toilet block.

| BERGNAUF EN RITZ | | N47°02.476'W001°57.384' | 44580 | Map ref: 4 |

Directions: At Tourist Office, entrance opp Citroen Garage. Just off main road roundabout follow sp into town centre.

Sanitation:

Aire Details:

🚐 10
Custom
ℹ️ Town 2 mins, sports facilities adj.

BRETIGNOLLES SUR MER

 N46°37.592'W001°51.341' 85470 **Map ref: 5**

Directions: On D38. At Super U petrol Station.

 10

Euro Relais; €2

i Supermarket, 2 mins from town, LPG.

Sanitation:

Aire Details:

BRIOLLAY

N47°34.051'W000°30.434' 49125 **Map ref: 6**

Directions: Just off Grande Rue. From D52 follow sp to 'campsite'. First turning on right as enter village from North. Turn right again then left. Signed.

5

Euro Relais

i View across river. Prone to flooding, can be very dramatic. Village 2 mins walk. Plenty of sp walking opportunities. Fishing.

Sanitation:

Aire Details:

CHATEAU GONTIER

N47°49.486'W000°42.201' 53200 **Map ref: 7**

Directions: Quai D'Alsace. Centre town, on river edge. N162 river bridge adj. Turn off roundabout with Champion supermarket.

12

Custom

i Walks with map in English, fishing, walk along river into town 5 mins. Slip way. LPG at E'leclerc supermarket.

Sanitation:

Aire Details:

CHATEAUBRIANT

N47°42.165'W000°22.690' 44110 **Map ref: 8**

Directions: Rue de Tugny. On D178 just before outer ring road with N171 sp outside Camping Municipal.

5

Custom

i Outside campsite, urban area a good distance from town.

Sanitation:

Aire Details:

Pays

CHATEAUNEUF-SUR-SARTHE

 N47°40.657'W000°29.227' 49330 **Map ref: 9**

Directions: D89. By bridge as enter town on D89 from south. Outside campsite.

Sanitation:

Aire Details:

 15; €5.15 per night 30/04-29/09

Custom

Fishing available with permit. Washing sink; showers available, village 2 mins.

CHENILLE-CHANGE

 N47°41.960'W000°40.023' 49220 **Map ref: 10**

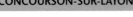

Directions: Signed off main road, by cemetery.

Sanitation:

Aire Details:

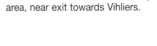 10

Custom; tokens €2

On terrace overlooking campsite to river. Small village on rivers edge. Adj to small campsite. Bus stop.

CONCOURSON-SUR-LAYON

 N47°10.439'W000°20.589' 49700 **Map ref: 11**

Directions: Located on D960 at picnic area, near exit towards Vihliers.

Sanitation:

Aire Details:

5

Custom - toilet waste down toilet

Park and river adj - Picnic tables, open air table tennis, riverside stroll possible. Village 2 mins.

DE BARRE DE MONTS

 N46°53.114'W002°07.135' 85550 **Map ref: 12**

Directions: Route de Saint Jean de Monts D22. Follow main road around edge of town. Aire is behind the Mairie which is beside the church. Signed from road.

Sanitation:

Aire Details:

8

Euro Relais; tokens

Sandy beach, sailing school at Fromentine - 10 mins. Marked cycle route leaving from Aire. July and August additional parking in school car park. Bells! Play park adj.

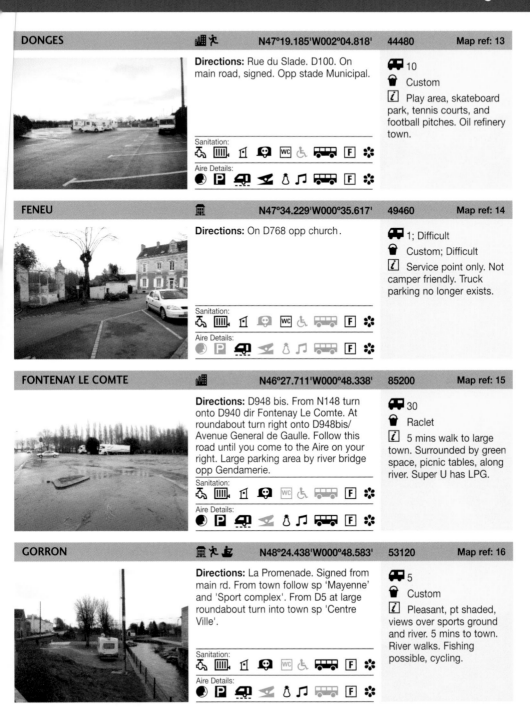

DONGES   N47°19.185'W002°04.818'   44480   **Map ref: 13**

Directions: Rue du Slade. D100. On main road, signed. Opp stade Municipal.

10
Custom
Play area, skateboard park, tennis courts, and football pitches. Oil refinery town.

Sanitation:

Aire Details:

FENEU   N47°34.229'W000°35.617'   49460   **Map ref: 14**

Directions: On D768 opp church.

1; Difficult
Custom; Difficult
Service point only. Not camper friendly. Truck parking no longer exists.

Sanitation:

Aire Details:

FONTENAY LE COMTE   N46°27.711'W000°48.338'   85200   **Map ref: 15**

Directions: D948 bis. From N148 turn onto D940 dir Fontenay Le Comte. At roundabout turn right onto D948bis/ Avenue General de Gaulle. Follow this road until you come to the Aire on your right. Large parking area by river bridge opp Gendamerie.

30
Raclet
5 mins walk to large town. Surrounded by green space, picnic tables, along river. Super U has LPG.

Sanitation:

Aire Details:

GORRON   N48°24.438'W000°48.583'   53120   **Map ref: 16**

Directions: La Promenade. Signed from main rd. From town follow sp 'Mayenne' and 'Sport complex'. From D5 at large roundabout turn into town sp 'Centre Ville'.

5
Custom
Pleasant, pt shaded, views over sports ground and river. 5 mins to town. River walks. Fishing possible, cycling.

Sanitation:

Aire Details:

GRAND PARC DU PUY DE FOU
N46°53.515'W000°56.153' | 85590 | Map ref: 17

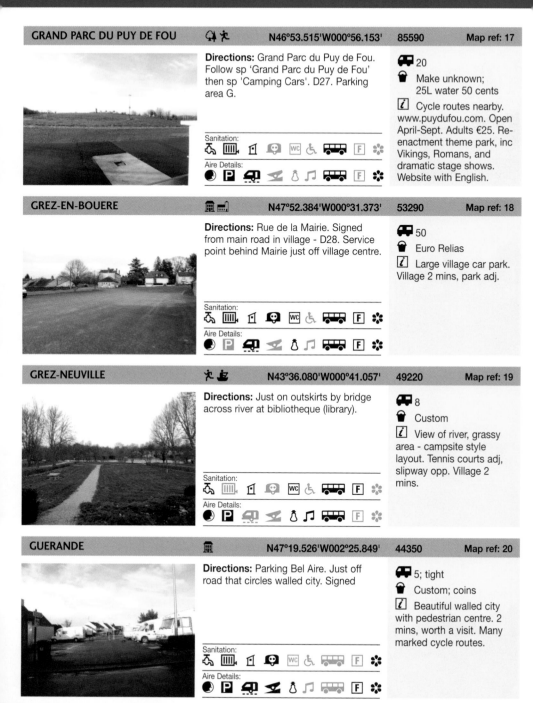

Directions: Grand Parc du Puy de Fou. Follow sp 'Grand Parc du Puy de Fou' then sp 'Camping Cars'. D27. Parking area G.

Sanitation:

Aire Details:

20
Make unknown; 25L water 50 cents
Cycle routes nearby. www.puydufou.com. Open April-Sept. Adults €25. Re-enactment theme park, inc Vikings, Romans, and dramatic stage shows. Website with English.

GREZ-EN-BOUERE
N47°52.384'W000°31.373' | 53290 | Map ref: 18

Directions: Rue de la Mairie. Signed from main road in village - D28. Service point behind Mairie just off village centre.

Sanitation:

Aire Details:

50
Euro Relias
Large village car park. Village 2 mins, park adj.

GREZ-NEUVILLE
N43°36.080'W000°41.057' | 49220 | Map ref: 19

Directions: Just on outskirts by bridge across river at bibliotheque (library).

Sanitation:

Aire Details:

8
Custom
View of river, grassy area - campsite style layout. Tennis courts adj, slipway opp. Village 2 mins.

GUERANDE
N47°19.526'W002°25.849' | 44350 | Map ref: 20

Directions: Parking Bel Aire. Just off road that circles walled city. Signed

Sanitation:

Aire Details:

5; tight
Custom; coins
Beautiful walled city with pedestrian centre. 2 mins, worth a visit. Many marked cycle routes.

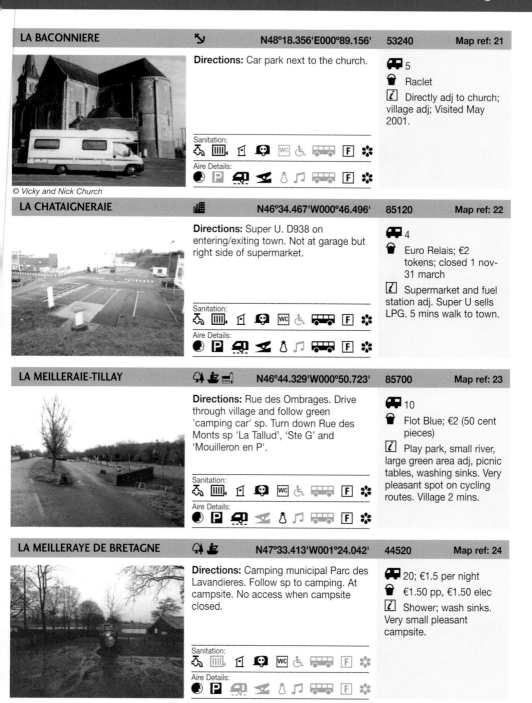

LA BACONNIERE

N48°18.356'E000°89.156'　　53240　　Map ref: 21

Directions: Car park next to the church.

🚐 5

🪣 Raclet

ℹ️ Directly adj to church; village adj; Visited May 2001.

© Vicky and Nick Church

Sanitation:

Aire Details:

LA CHATAIGNERAIE

N46°34.467'W000°46.496'　　85120　　Map ref: 22

Directions: Super U. D938 on entering/exiting town. Not at garage but right side of supermarket.

🚐 4

🪣 Euro Relais; €2 tokens; closed 1 nov-31 march

ℹ️ Supermarket and fuel station adj. Super U sells LPG. 5 mins walk to town.

Sanitation:

Aire Details:

LA MEILLERAIE-TILLAY

N46°44.329'W000°50.723'　　85700　　Map ref: 23

Directions: Rue des Ombrages. Drive through village and follow green 'camping car' sp. Turn down Rue des Monts sp 'La Tallud', 'Ste G' and 'Mouilleron en P'.

🚐 10

🪣 Flot Blue; €2 (50 cent pieces)

ℹ️ Play park, small river, large green area adj, picnic tables, washing sinks. Very pleasant spot on cycling routes. Village 2 mins.

Sanitation:

Aire Details:

LA MEILLERAYE DE BRETAGNE

N47°33.413'W001°24.042'　　44520　　Map ref: 24

Directions: Camping municipal Parc des Lavandieres. Follow sp to camping. At campsite. No access when campsite closed.

🚐 20; €1.5 per night

🪣 €1.50 pp, €1.50 elec

ℹ️ Shower; wash sinks. Very small pleasant campsite.

Sanitation:

Aire Details:

Pays

| LA PLAINE SUR MER | 🏃 | N47°08.413'W002°11.414' | 44770 | Map ref: 25 |

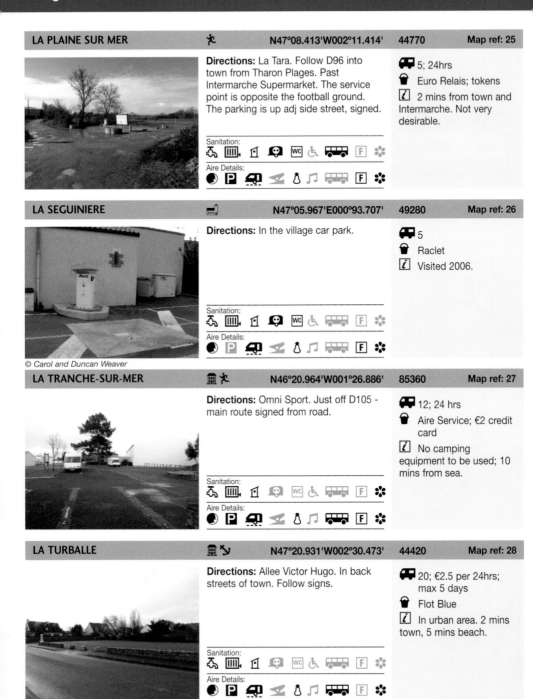

Directions: La Tara. Follow D96 into town from Tharon Plages. Past Intermarche Supermarket. The service point is opposite the football ground. The parking is up adj side street, signed.

Sanitation:

Aire Details:

🚐 5; 24hrs
🪣 Euro Relais; tokens
ℹ️ 2 mins from town and Intermarche. Not very desirable.

| LA SEGUINIERE | 🏭 | N47°05.967'E000°93.707' | 49280 | Map ref: 26 |

Directions: In the village car park.

Sanitation:

Aire Details:

🚐 5
🪣 Raclet
ℹ️ Visited 2006.

© Carol and Duncan Weaver

| LA TRANCHE-SUR-MER | 🏛🏃 | N46°20.964'W001°26.886' | 85360 | Map ref: 27 |

Directions: Omni Sport. Just off D105 - main route signed from road.

Sanitation:

Aire Details:

🚐 12; 24 hrs
🪣 Aire Service; €2 credit card
ℹ️ No camping equipment to be used; 10 mins from sea.

| LA TURBALLE | 🏛⚓ | N47°20.931'W002°30.473' | 44420 | Map ref: 28 |

Directions: Allee Victor Hugo. In back streets of town. Follow signs.

Sanitation:

Aire Details:

🚐 20; €2.5 per 24hrs; max 5 days
🪣 Flot Blue
ℹ️ In urban area. 2 mins town, 5 mins beach.

LA TURBALLE 2

🏛 ⚓   N47°21.842'W002°31.563'   44420   **Map ref: 29**

Directions: D99. From La Turballe head towards Piriac-Sur-Mer. The Aire is along this rd, signed.

Sanitation:
🛁 🚽 🚪 💩 WC ♿ 🚐 F ✻

Aire Details:
● P 🚐 ⬦ 🛢 🎵 🚐 F ✻

🚐 20; €2.5 per 24hrs; max 5 days

♙ Flot Blue

ℹ️ Adj to D99. Sandy beach 2 mins accessible from car park across rd. No amenities but walking/cycling to La Turballe/Piriac-sur-Mer possible.

LA TURBALLE 3

🏛 🏃 ⚓   N47°19.867'W002°29.947'   44420   **Map ref: 30**

Directions: Follow D92, sp 'campsite', sp on right. Rd 3.5 ton weight limit.

Sanitation:
🛁 🚽 🚪 💩 WC ♿ 🚐 F ✻

Aire Details:
● P 🚐 ⬦ 🛢 🎵 🚐 F ✻

🚐 10; €2.5 per 24hrs; max 5 days

♙ Flot Blue

ℹ️ Beach 5 mins, boules, Crazy Golf adj, Town 10 mins. Cycle routes, walking routes through salt marsh (still producing salt).

© Carol and Duncan Weaver

LAIGNE-EN-BELIN

🏚   N47°52.698'E000°13.633'   72220   **Map ref: 31**

Directions: Just off junc D144 and D139. By church behind Casino mini market.

If you have a suitable picture for this Aire, please email to: gomotorhoming@hotmail.co.uk

Sanitation:
🛁 🚽 🚪 💩 WC ♿ 🚐 F ✻

Aire Details:
● P 🚐 ⬦ 🛢 🎵 🚐 F ✻

🚐 5

♙ Custom

ℹ️ In heart of village. 10 km from Le Mans race circuit. LPG E Leclerc and Auchan in Le Mans.

L'AIGUILLON SUR MER

⚓   N46°19.901'W001°18.503'   85460   **Map ref: 32**

Directions: D46. Follow sp 'L'Aiguillion sur Mer' then 'Centre Ville'. Aire is signed by Marina, water slide, and tourist info along seafront. Sp 'Ecole de Voile' (sailing school).

Sanitation:
🛁 🚽 🚪 💩 WC ♿ 🚐 F ✻

Aire Details:
● P 🚐 ⬦ 🛢 🎵 🚐 F ✻

🚐 20; €5 per night

♙ Custom

ℹ️ Skate board park, sailing school, seafront location, 2 mins town and tourist info.

LAVAL

 N48°04.561'W000°46.270'   53000   **Map ref: 33**

Directions: Bottom of railway viaduct. In town centre. Signed. Follow sp 'Centre Ville' and 'Tourist Info', then sp 'Mayenne', 'Toutes Directions'.

Sanitation:

Aire Details:

140 spaces

Euro Relais

Nice large town. 2 mins to centre, river walks. LPG E Leclerc supermarket. A tight car park not suitable for 6m+ motorhomes.

LE COURDRAY MACOUARD

N47°11.288'W000°07.053'   49260   **Map ref: 34**

Directions: D163 (road to Brun). From N147 turn into village. From village follow route to Brun, Aire as exit village.

Sanitation:

Aire Details:

10

Custom

Pleasant shaded parking between trees in wooded area. Play park, table tennis, football pitch, and village 5 mins - quite attractive. Very interesting weathervane shop.

LE CROISIC

N47°17.398'W002°30.328'   44490   **Map ref: 35**

Directions: Rue des Courlis - gare SNCF. Turn right by train station, right at roundabout then next left. Free.

Sanitation:

Aire Details:

10

Flot Blue

By train station, working area, coach parking on site. 2 mins to salt farm, town.

LE PUY NOTRE DAME

N47°07.434'W000°13.935'   49260   **Map ref: 36**

Directions: Rue du Parc. Approach only from D178 from Montreuel-Bellay. Going into town not an option, too narrow. Aire is signed off D178 before entering town down lane and is opposite the cemetery.

Sanitation:

Aire Details:

3

Custom

Nice town. Church and centre 2 mins. Plenty of wine tasting opportunities, narrow streets, possibility to discover troglodyte caves.

L'EPINE

 N46°59.174'W002°17.626' 85740 **Map ref: 37**

Directions: Follow signs to 'L'Epine', then to 'Port Morin'. Road will end, go straight on towards boats. Parking area on right.

Sanitation:

Aire Details:

20

Custom €1

[i] Aire directly on beach overlooking sand dunes and sea. Ideal beach holiday stop. Town 10 mins walk. Busy in Summer. Ground dump may need excavating! LPG at Intermarche on Island.

HAVE YOU VISITED AN AIRE?

FILL IN THE FORM AT THE BACK AND SEND TO VICARIOUS BOOKS.

Sanitation:

Aire Details:

[i] We need your help to make this guide bigger and better. Don't forget to send us your Aires.

MARTIGNE BRIAND

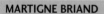 N47°14.129'W000°25.740' 49540 **Map ref: 39**

Directions: Jardin des Vieux Pressoirs. D748. On exiting village dir Angers located at the D748/D70 junction. Signed through town.

Sanitation:

Aire Details:

5

Custom

[i] 2 mins town, picnic tables some green space but adj to main road. Abbey in town. Market in town centre on Saturday. In wine producing region, wine caves and vines 2 mins.

MAYENNE

 N48°17.976'W000°37.232' 53100 **Map ref: 40**

Directions: Quai Carnot. Sp 'Euro Relais' in town centre. Situated beside river directly underneath road viaduct.

Sanitation:

Aire Details:

5

Euro relais

[i] River view from parking - 2 nights. Other parking opportunities in town. N48°18.082'W000°37.124' opp large riverside parking. E Leclerc supermarket has LPG. Large town, large river.

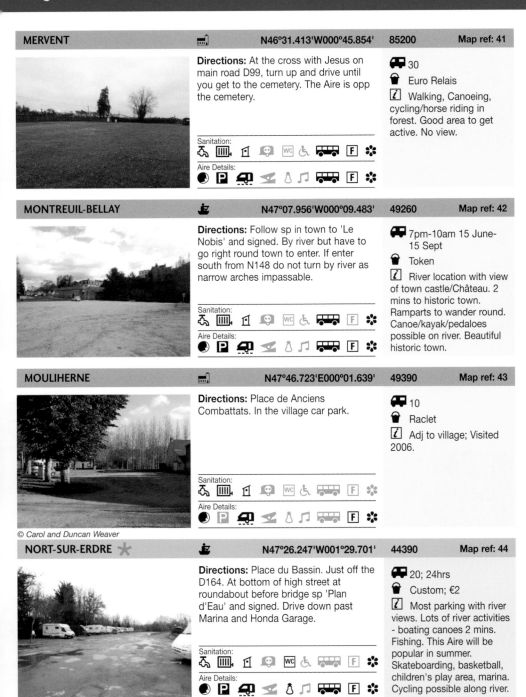

MERVENT | N46°31.413'W000°45.854' | 85200 | Map ref: 41

Directions: At the cross with Jesus on main road D99, turn up and drive until you get to the cemetery. The Aire is opp the cemetery.

Sanitation:

Aire Details:

🚐 30
Euro Relais
ℹ️ Walking, Canoeing, cycling/horse riding in forest. Good area to get active. No view.

MONTREUIL-BELLAY | N47°07.956'W000°09.483' | 49260 | Map ref: 42

Directions: Follow sp in town to 'Le Nobis' and signed. By river but have to go right round town to enter. If enter south from N148 do not turn by river as narrow arches impassable.

Sanitation:

Aire Details:

🚐 7pm-10am 15 June-15 Sept
Token
ℹ️ River location with view of town castle/Château. 2 mins to historic town. Ramparts to wander round. Canoe/kayak/pedaloes possible on river. Beautiful historic town.

MOULIHERNE | N47°46.723'E000°01.639' | 49390 | Map ref: 43

Directions: Place de Anciens Combattats. In the village car park.

Sanitation:

Aire Details:

🚐 10
Raclet
ℹ️ Adj to village; Visited 2006.

© Carol and Duncan Weaver

NORT-SUR-ERDRE ⭐ | N47°26.247'W001°29.701' | 44390 | Map ref: 44

Directions: Place du Bassin. Just off the D164. At bottom of high street at roundabout before bridge sp 'Plan d'Eau' and signed. Drive down past Marina and Honda Garage.

Sanitation:

Aire Details:

🚐 20; 24hrs
Custom; €2
ℹ️ Most parking with river views. Lots of river activities - boating canoes 2 mins. Fishing. This Aire will be popular in summer. Skateboarding, basketball, children's play area, marina. Cycling possible along river.

| NOTRE DAME DE MONTS | ⇘ | N46°50.078'W002°08.528' | 85690 | Map ref: 45 |

Directions: Rue de la Clairiere. Signed from main road through, also sp 'Jardin de Vent' and 'Camping Car Clairiere' or 'Camping Car'. Small but frequent signs.

🚐 20; €5 per 24h pay at ticket machine
🚰 Custom
ℹ️ 2 mins from beach, nice wooded area adj.

Sanitation:

Aire Details:

| NOTRE DAME DE MONTS 2 | 🏛 ⇘ | N46°49.871'W002°07.793' | 85690 | Map ref: 46 |

Directions: On main road through town.

🚐 10; €5 per 24h pay at ticket machine
🚰 Custom; Difficult
ℹ️ 2 mins from town.

Sanitation:

Aire Details:

| OLONNE-SUR-MER | 🏛 | N46°33.199'W001°48.610' | 85340 | Map ref: 47 |

Directions: Restaurant. Located north of Olonne sur Mer just off the D80, the forest road. Clearly signed.

🚐 10; €3
🚰 Custom; €4
ℹ️ Restaurant adj, swings, Washing up sinks pleasant CL feel.

Sanitation:

Aire Details:

| OLONNE-SUR-MER 2 | 🏢 | N46°32.551'W001°46.336' | 85340 | Map ref: 48 |

Directions: At Super U. Service point by Lavarge (carwash).

🚐 10
🚰 Euro Relais Mini
ℹ️ Supermarket, Bus stop

Sanitation:

Aire Details:

PARNAY

N47°13.870'E000°00.665'   49730   Map ref: 49

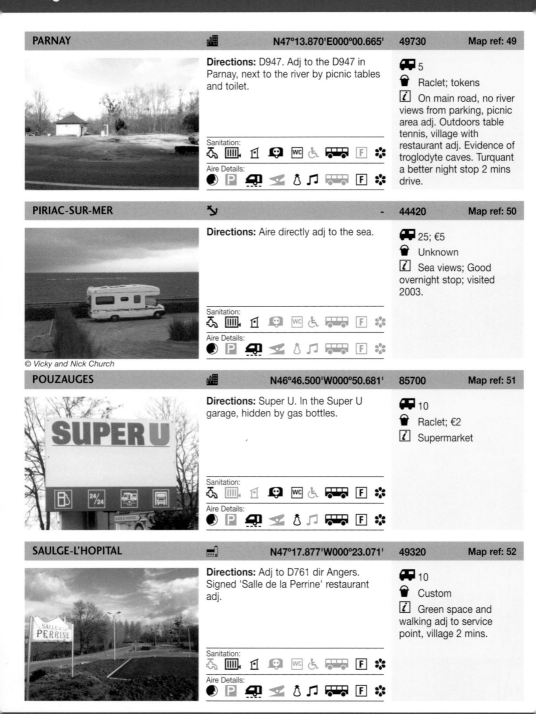

Directions: D947. Adj to the D947 in Parnay, next to the river by picnic tables and toilet.

Sanitation:

Aire Details:

🚐 5

🪣 Raclet; tokens

ℹ️ On main road, no river views from parking, picnic area adj. Outdoors table tennis, village with restaurant adj. Evidence of troglodyte caves. Turquant a better night stop 2 mins drive.

PIRIAC-SUR-MER

-    44420   Map ref: 50

Directions: Aire directly adj to the sea.

Sanitation:

Aire Details:

🚐 25; €5

🪣 Unknown

ℹ️ Sea views; Good overnight stop; visited 2003.

© Vicky and Nick Church

POUZAUGES

N46°46.500'W000°50.681'   85700   Map ref: 51

Directions: Super U. In the Super U garage, hidden by gas bottles.

Sanitation:

Aire Details:

🚐 10

🪣 Raclet; €2

ℹ️ Supermarket

SAULGE-L'HOPITAL

N47°17.877'W000°23.071'   49320   Map ref: 52

Directions: Adj to D761 dir Angers. Signed 'Salle de la Perrine' restaurant adj.

Sanitation:

Aire Details:

🚐 10

🪣 Custom

ℹ️ Green space and walking adj to service point, village 2 mins.

SAUMER — 49400 — Map ref: 53

Directions: Daytime parking located in the car park by the château. At the top of the town.

🚐 10
👤 None
ℹ️ Adj to château. Restaurant adj to carpark.

Sanitation:

Aire Details:

© Carol and Duncan Weaver

SEGRE ⭐ — N47°41.062'W000°52.406' — 49500 — Map ref: 54

Directions: From D775 turn onto D71 into Segre, follow this road and turn left onto Rue E Zola, the Aire can be found on your left in the car park at the bottom of the hill.

🚐 20
👤 Custom
ℹ️ Town 2 mins along river. Cobbled streets and hidden restaurants. Idyllic. Skate park, slip way, weir.

Sanitation:

Aire Details:

ST BREVIN L'OCEAN — N47°17.399'W002°30.328' — 44250 — Map ref: 55

Directions: Follow sp 'Base Nautique' at St Beven l'Ocean. Aire adj in car park.

🚐 10; 24hrs
👤 Euro Relais - tokens
ℹ️ Adj to beach - ideal sailing/windsurfing - walk into town along beach 10 mins. Large duned sandy beach adj. Kite surfing.

Sanitation:

Aire Details:

ST CALAIS — N47°55.425'E000°44.657' — 72120 — Map ref: 56

Directions: D249 Boulevard Gigon. At the swimming pool sp 'Piscine' through town. From N157 from Le Mans turn left onto D249, the Aire is on right.

🚐 10
👤 Euro Relais
ℹ️ By sports facilities, (boules court, basketball, play park, green space, tennis, swimming pool adj). Town 2 mins through park.

Sanitation:

Aire Details:

Pays

| ST GEORGES BUTTAVENT | | N48°18.594'W000°41.680' | 53100 | Map ref: 57 |

Directions: N12. In car park of Vinenco mini market at the D5/N12 traffic lighted junctions.

Sanitation:

Aire Details:

5

Euro Relais; tokens €2

ℹ Small mini market adj, on busy road junction.

| ST GILLES CROX DE VIE | | N46°42.187'W001°56.823' | 85800 | Map ref: 58 |

Directions: Rue de la Rabalette. From D38 turn into town, signed. Follow signs.

Sanitation:

Aire Details:

50; 48hrs

Custom; tokens €2.5; office du Tourism

ℹ Sports facilities adj, lake to walk around. On cycle route.

| ST GILLES CROX DE VIE 2 | | N46°42.041'W001°56.315' | 85800 | Map ref: 59 |

Directions: From main roundabout turn right follow road. Aire on left sp 'P Quai Goron'.

Sanitation:

Aire Details:

50

-

ℹ Views over river, town 2 mins. Area so full of motorhomes when visited, difficult to assertain any details.

| ST JEAN-DE-MONTS | | N46°47.587'W002°04.757' | 85160 | Map ref: 60 |

Directions: Rue de la Paree Jesus. From D38 from north take third roundabout onto Bvd des Maraichins Sp 'La Paree Jesus'. At next roundabout turn right and next right and the Aire is on the right.

Sanitation:

Aire Details:

28; €5 1/04-30/09; Max 48hrs

Flot Blue; tokens; €2

ℹ 5 mins to beach. High rope adj, walking, wooded area, petite train stop. Cycle routes. LPG at Super U. Pay at Tennis courts, need reg and pitch number.

ST JEAN-DE-MONTS 2

N46°47.697'W002°02.805'   85160   **Map ref: 61**

Directions: D753. Super U direction Challans.

🚐 10
🔧 Raclet; tokens
ℹ️ Supermarket, LPG available.

Sanitation:

Aire Details:

ST MARS-D'OUTILLE

N47°52.219'E000°19.991'   72220   **Map ref: 62**

Directions: D32. Located on D32 as you exit village towards Le Grand-Luce.

🚐 5; 48hrs
🔧 Custom
ℹ️ Village 2 mins. Toilet disposal down toilet.

Sanitation:

Aire Details:

ST-MICHEL-CHEF-CHEF

N47°10.949'W002°08.844'   44730   **Map ref: 63**

Directions: Rue du Chevecier. As you drive into centre from the D213 on the left opp Mairie.

🚐 26; €5 24hrs; pay at machine.
🔧 €2.5; tokens
ℹ️ Town Hall, tourism. Parking restricted outside Aire. 2 mins from village shops.

Sanitation:

Aire Details:

ST-MICHEL-EN-L'HERM

N46°21.104'W001°14.898'   85580   **Map ref: 64**

Directions: D746 Rue Basse, On main route through village on D746.

🚐 7
🔧 Custom; €2 tokens
ℹ️ By small square, pleasant. 2 min to main square, shops and restaurants.

Sanitation:

Aire Details:

TURQUANT N47°13.430'E000°01.754' 49730 Map ref: 65

Directions: Rue des Ducs D'Anjou. Turn off D947 into village, take the first turning on right before entering village opp stonewall with featured turret.

Sanitation:

Aire Details:

 5

Custom; tokens €2

Basketball, table tennis, picnic and BBQ, troglodyte village, play park, pretty village in wine region.

VALANJOU N47°12.996'W000°36.199' 49670 Map ref: 66

Directions: D84. Signed off D84 on west side of village sp 'Camping Cars' and 'Picnic', tight entrance.

Sanitation:

Aire Details:

5

Custom; 1 two-pin socket

River views, river walk back to village, village has ruined abbey. Green space adj. Lovely spot; village 2 mins.

VIHIERS N47°08.605'W000°32.145' 49310 Map ref: 67

Directions: Rue du Champ des Fares. Drive into town following sp 'Centre Ville'. The Aire is located just off the main town square behind the large church signed on way in.

Sanitation:

Aire Details:

 5

Custom

Adj to town, green park adj. Large pleasant town with nice town square.

VILLERS-CHARLEMAGNE N47°55.234'W000°40.919' 53170 Map ref: 68

Directions: Rue des Sports. Follow sp 'Village Vacances et Peche'. At lake outside holiday village.

Sanitation:

Aire Details:

 10

Euro Relais

On edge of fishing lake. Play area. Walks around lake, carp and course fishing lake - tickets available on site. Card operated weighbridge opp Mairie in village.

VOUVANT

N46°34.462'W000°46.498'   85120   Map ref: 69

Directions: From the main road D938ter follow sp to 'Vouvant'. On entering village follow road and the Aire is the first parking area on left.

20
Custom
Views, edge of forest.

Sanitation:

Aire Details:

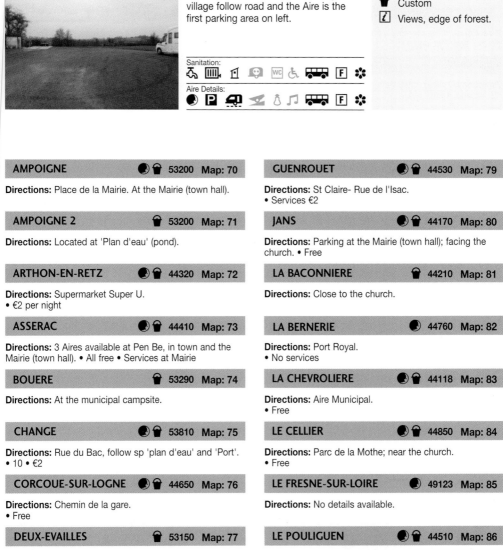

AMPOIGNE — 53200 Map: 70
Directions: Place de la Mairie. At the Mairie (town hall).

AMPOIGNE 2 — 53200 Map: 71
Directions: Located at 'Plan d'eau' (pond).

ARTHON-EN-RETZ — 44320 Map: 72
Directions: Supermarket Super U.
• €2 per night

ASSERAC — 44410 Map: 73
Directions: 3 Aires available at Pen Be, in town and the Mairie (town hall). • All free • Services at Mairie

BOUERE — 53290 Map: 74
Directions: At the municipal campsite.

CHANGE — 53810 Map: 75
Directions: Rue du Bac, follow sp 'plan d'eau' and 'Port'.
• 10 • €2

CORCOUE-SUR-LOGNE — 44650 Map: 76
Directions: Chemin de la gare.
• Free

DEUX-EVAILLES — 53150 Map: 77
Directions: Leisure/activity place Fenderie.

EVRON — 53600 Map: 78
Directions: Outside the campsite.

GUENROUET — 44530 Map: 79
Directions: St Claire- Rue de l'Isac.
• Services €2

JANS — 44170 Map: 80
Directions: Parking at the Mairie (town hall); facing the church. • Free

LA BACONNIERE — 44210 Map: 81
Directions: Close to the church.

LA BERNERIE — 44760 Map: 82
Directions: Port Royal.
• No services

LA CHEVROLIERE — 44118 Map: 83
Directions: Aire Municipal.
• Free

LE CELLIER — 44850 Map: 84
Directions: Parc de la Mothe; near the church.
• Free

LE FRESNE-SUR-LOIRE — 49123 Map: 85
Directions: No details available.

LE POULIGUEN — 44510 Map: 86
Directions: Bd de l'Atlantique.
• Free

MAISDON SUR SEVRE — 44690 Map: 87
Directions: Domaine des Croix; take the D74 towards St Fiacre; the Aire is 1km from the church on your left. • €4 elec

Pays

MALVILLE 🌐 44260 Map: 88

Directions: Aires l'Espace Herlareg.

MESLAY DU MAINE 🌐 🪣 53170 Map: 89

Directions: At the swimming pool. Follow sp 'Salle des Sports' and 'Piscine.'

MESQUER 🌐 🪣 44420 Map: 90

Directions: 2 Aires; route de Kerlagadec and port de l'Echouage. • Free

MISSILLAC 🌐 🪣 44780 Map: 91

Directions: Aire de la chinoise.
• Pay for services

NOZAY 🌐 🪣 44170 Map: 92

Directions: Entrance of leisure/activity place; adj RD121.
• Free

PAIMBOEUF 🌐 🪣 44560 Map: 93

Directions: Parking on the quai Sadi Carnot.
• Free

PIERRIC 🌐 🪣 44290 Map: 94

Directions: 3 Aires.
• Parking free • Services pay

PIRIAC-SUR-MER 🌐 🪣 44420 Map: 95

Directions: 2 Aires at Brambell and Lerat.
• Pay

PREFAILLES 🌐 44770 Map: 96

Directions: Pte St Gildas.

ST AIGNAN SUR ROE 🪣 53390 Map: 97

Directions: At the campsite.
• Open all year

ST BREVIN-LES-PINS 🌐 🪣 44250 Map: 98

Directions: Base Nautique; Le Pointeau.
• Parking free • Services pay

ST DENIS DU MAINE 🌐 🪣 53170 Map: 99

Directions: Base de Loisirs (leisure) de la Chesnaie a Saint Denis du Maine.

ST LYPHARD 🪣 44410 Map: 100

Directions: Outside the campsite.
• Services • Free

ST NAZAIRE 🪣 44600 Map: 101

Directions: Route de l'Ocean; St Marc sur Mer.
• Pay

ST PHILBERT-DE-GRANDLIEU 🌐 🪣 44310 Map: 102

Directions: Base de loisirs (leisure); La Businiere.
• Parking free • Services pay

ST VIAUD 🌐 🪣 44320 Map: 103

Directions: Base de Loisirs (leisure); plan d'eau (pond).
• Services pay; tokens

VAIGES 🪣 53480 Map: 104

Directions: At the 'Plan d'eau' - pond.

VALLET 🌐 44330 Map: 105

Directions: Place A Barre, Bd Dejoie.
• Free

© Carol and Duncan Weaver

© Carol and Duncan Weaver

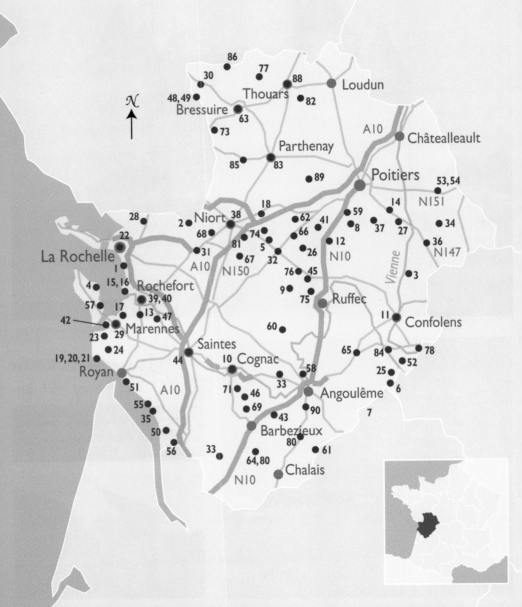

N

86
30   77
48,49   88   Loudun
Bressuire   Thouars   82
63
73   A10
Parthenay   Châtealleault
85   83
89   Poitiers   53,54
N151
18   14
28   38   62   37   27   34
2   Niort   68   59   8   36
22   74   41   N147
La Rochelle   31   81   5   66   12
1   A10   67   32   26   N10   3
4   15,16   N150   76   45   Vienne
57   17   9   75   Ruffec
42   39,40   60   11   Confolens
13   47   65   84   78
23   29   Marennes   52
24   Saintes   10   Cognac   58   25   6
19,20,21   44   33   Angoulême   7
Royan   51   A10   71   46   90
55   69   43
35   50   Barbezieux   80
56   33   64,80   61   Chalais
N10

© Carol and Duncan Weaver

Poitou is said to be the sunniest area on the Atlantic coast and claims to have a microclimate with Mediterranean temperatures.

Think of Cognac and you probably think brandy but this is the town that accommodates brand names which have wonderful buildings there. Famous producers of cognac brandy such as Hennessay, Martell and Remy Martin open their doors to the public.

© Carol and Duncan Weaver

For something a little different head to 'Green Venice' just west of Niort. Enjoy a little boating, and retire to one of the quiet town Aires.

The church of St Jean at Aubeterre is one of the largest carved cave churches in Europe, started in the tenth century it can be found on the southern border of the region.

© Carol and Duncan Weaver

Poitou

ANGOULINS

N46°06.778'W001°07.381'   17690   Map ref: 1

Directions: Drive out of Angoulins towards Aytre. Turn left onto Route de la Plage and cross the railway track. Take next left at Camping de la Plage. Drive through parking area to end.

Sanitation:

Aire Details:

🚐 10

Custom

ℹ️ Coastal walk, large grass area, enclosed bay of sand and stone. Cycle paths signed from Aire. Idyllic. Huge out of town shopping area at Anguilins.

ARCAIS

N46°17.739'W000°41.442'   79210   Map ref: 2

If you have a suitable picture for this Aire, please email to: gomotorhoming@hotmail.co.uk

Directions: D101. At town sq just off D101.

Sanitation:

Aire Details:

🚐 -

-

ℹ️ Aire under renovation at time of visit. Pleasant town with restaurants. Many of the towns in this area offer the opportunity to punt up river inc St Hilaire le Palud, Coulon and la Garette.

AVAILLES LIMOUZINE

N46°07.385'E000°39.626'   86460   Map ref: 3

Directions: D34, just off D34 by bridge over river.

Sanitation:

Aire Details:

🚐 20

Custom

ℹ️ 2 mins river, 5 mins town, may have to pay at campsite.

BOYARDVILLE

N45°58.140'W001°14.268'   17190   Map ref: 4

Directions: From D126 at bridge that crosses river turn into town sp 'Centre Ville' and 'Camping Cars'. Follow signs through town past large car park to the Aire - well sp. Sp 'Plages'.

Sanitation:

Aire Details:

🚐 30; €5-7

Euro Relais

ℹ️ Sandy beach adj, views of exit/entrance of harbour. Views of Fort Boyard from beach. Forest adj. Island dominated by salt marsh and shellfish farming of mussels and oysters.

CELLES-SUR-BELLE
N46°15.735'W000°12.507' 79370 Map ref: 5

Directions: Rue des Halles. Follow the main road through, then turn off signed and drive down cobbled streets past church and tourist office and turn left at the bottom of hill opp impressive gates.

Sanitation:

Aire Details:

🚐 20
Custom
ℹ️ Tourist office and town 2 mins. Abbey adj, gardens and buildings. Part shaded. Easy place to spend a day. Goats cheese made locally.

CHASSENON
N45°51.025'E000°46.352' 16150 Map ref: 6

Directions: D29. Off D29 as exit the village signed 'Auto Cars'.

Sanitation:

Aire Details:

🚐 3
Custom
ℹ️ Village 5 Mins, picnic area, tables. Unusually quiet and rural spot. Water point in toilet.

CHATAIN BESSON / ECURAS
N45°40.983'E000°33.579' 16220 Map ref: 7

Directions: D699. Clearly signed off D699 in Chatain Besson, opp Le Poste and Salle Municipal.

🚐 10
Raclet
ℹ️ In village, picnic area at edge of village, east side; with children's play area and ample parking.

Sanitation:

Aire Details:

CHATEAU-LARCHER
N46°24.869'E000°18.938' 86160 Map ref: 8

Directions: D88. Signed from D88 'Camping Stad'. Located at the sports ground. Gate has digital lock but was chained open at time of visit.

Sanitation:

Aire Details:

🚐 10
Custom
ℹ️ Sports ground, river adj, nice walk through sports ground to castle and village. Pleasant spot.

CHEF BOUTONNE
 N46°06.607'W000°04.626'   79110   Map ref: 9

Directions: Chemin du Park. Drive through the town sp 'Melle'. Turn off opp cemetery of Jauarzay sp 'Aire Naturelle' and signed.

Sanitation:

Aire Details:

🚐 10

Custom

ℹ️ The best parking is at the top and the water is turned off 1 Nov-30 March. Town 5 mins. Large grassy area with river adj. Tent camping allowed and washing sinks provided.

COGNAC
 N45°41.910'W000°19.962'   16100   Map ref: 10

Directions: D731, Place de La Levade. Enter town on D48, sp 'Centre Ville', follow sp 'Centre Ville' at roundabout then in 50m turn sp 'Parking Gratuit' and 'Aire de Camping Car'. Follow sp 'Parking Gratuit' then drive towards river. Aire by river just past tanker depot. Adj to bridge that crosses river.

Sanitation:

Aire Details:

🚐 4

Raclet

ℹ️ View across river. Town 2 mins.

© Carol and Duncan Weaver

CONFOLENS
 N46°00.768'E000°40.047'   16500   Map ref: 11

Directions: Adj to D952. From river bridge in centre head south on D952 towards St Claud.

Sanitation:

Aire Details:

🚐 20

Flot Blue

ℹ️ River views, pretty town 2 mins, play park and large green space opp. Slipways available, picnic tables and river walks/cycles.

COUHE
 N46°17.907'E000°10.705'   86700   Map ref: 12

Directions: At covered market in town centre turn off D2. Drive through the parking area and take 2nd turning on left, into huge parking area. Service point on left by toilet.

Sanitation:

Aire Details:

🚐 20

Custom

ℹ️ Views. Open space adj. Town centre 2 mins. Some road noise from N10. Restaurants etc in town.

| ECHILLAIS | 🏛️🏘️ | N45°53.847'W000°57.335' | 17620 | Map ref: 13 |

Directions: Route de l'Eglise. Signed from D733. Church visible from parking.

🚐 10
💧 Custom
ℹ️ Newly constructed with care, has motorhome weather vane. Village and tourist office 2 mins walk. Picnic area.

Sanitation:
🚰 🔲, 🚽 😀 WC ♿ 🚌 F ✳️

Aire Details:
⚫ P 🚐 🛶 🜂 🎵 🚌 F ✳️

| FLEURE | 🏘️ | N46°28.718'E000°31.420' | 86340 | Map ref: 14 |

Directions: D2. Located just off D2 the parking is at the church. Signed from N147.

🚐 5
💧 None
ℹ️ Church adj, village 2 mins, picnic tables.

Sanitation:
🚰 🔲, 🚽 😀 WC ♿ 🚌 F ✳️

Aire Details:
⚫ P 🚐 🛶 🜂 🎵 🚌 F ✳️

| FOURAS | 🏛️⚓ | N45°58.894'W001°05.210' | 17450 | Map ref: 15 |

Directions: Place Jean Moulin. Signed from main road.

🚐 10
💧 Custom; Token €1
ℹ️ Beach opp, sea views and views of regional fishing huts. Town 5 mins walk, main road adj.

Sanitation:
🚰 🔲, 🚽 😀 WC ♿ 🚌 F ✳️

Aire Details:
⚫ P 🚐 🛶 🜂 🎵 🚌 F ✳️

| FOURAS 2 | 🏭⚓ | N45°59.528'W001°05.202' | 17450 | Map ref: 16 |

Directions: Avenue du Cadoret. Outside Camping de Caderet, just off roundabout. Signed from main road

🚐 20
💧 Custom; Token €1
ℹ️ Next to campsite and mini golf. 5 mins to town. Motorhomes banned from all other parking areas.

Sanitation:
🚰 🔲, 🚽 😀 WC ♿ 🚌 F ✳️

Aire Details:
⚫ P 🚐 🛶 🜂 🎵 🚌 F ✳️

| HIERS-BROUGE | 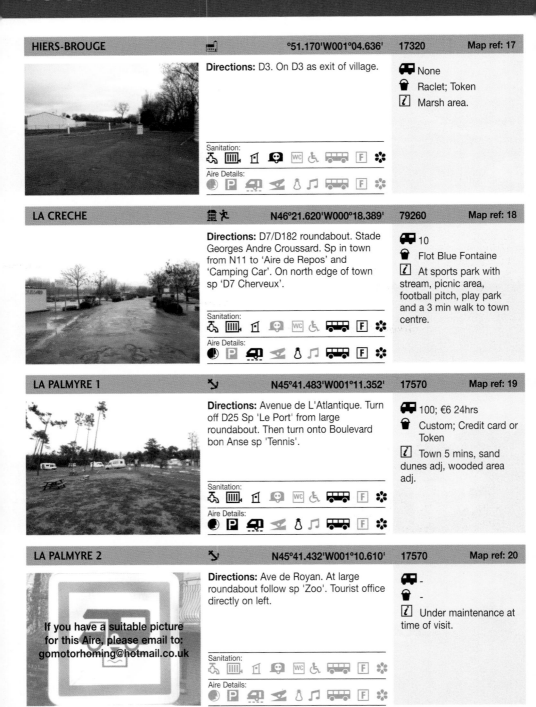 | °51.170'W001°04.636' | 17320 | Map ref: 17 |

Directions: D3. On D3 as exit of village.

None
Raclet; Token
Marsh area.

Sanitation:

Aire Details:

| LA CRECHE | | N46°21.620'W000°18.389' | 79260 | Map ref: 18 |

Directions: D7/D182 roundabout. Stade Georges Andre Croussard. Sp in town from N11 to 'Aire de Repos' and 'Camping Car'. On north edge of town sp 'D7 Cherveux'.

10
Flot Blue Fontaine
At sports park with stream, picnic area, football pitch, play park and a 3 min walk to town centre.

Sanitation:

Aire Details:

| LA PALMYRE 1 | | N45°41.483'W001°11.352' | 17570 | Map ref: 19 |

Directions: Avenue de L'Atlantique. Turn off D25 Sp 'Le Port' from large roundabout. Then turn onto Boulevard bon Anse sp 'Tennis'.

100; €6 24hrs
Custom; Credit card or Token
Town 5 mins, sand dunes adj, wooded area adj.

Sanitation:

Aire Details:

| LA PALMYRE 2 | | N45°41.432'W001°10.610' | 17570 | Map ref: 20 |

Directions: Ave de Royan. At large roundabout follow sp 'Zoo'. Tourist office directly on left.

-
-
Under maintenance at time of visit.

If you have a suitable picture for this Aire, please email to:
gomotorhoming@hotmail.co.uk

Sanitation:

Aire Details:

LA PALMYRE 3

N45°40.936'W001°10.692' 17570 Map ref: 21

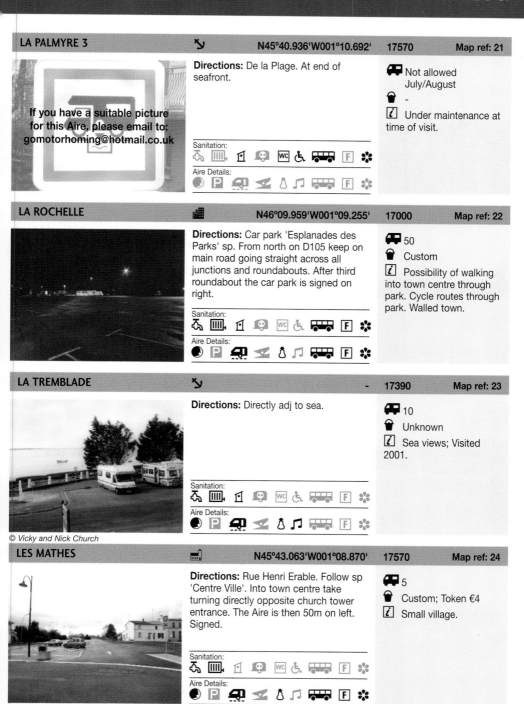

Directions: De la Plage. At end of seafront.

Not allowed July/August

-

ℹ Under maintenance at time of visit.

Sanitation:

Aire Details:

LA ROCHELLE

N46°09.959'W001°09.255' 17000 Map ref: 22

Directions: Car park 'Esplanades des Parks' sp. From north on D105 keep on main road going straight across all junctions and roundabouts. After third roundabout the car park is signed on right.

50

Custom

ℹ Possibility of walking into town centre through park. Cycle routes through park. Walled town.

Sanitation:

Aire Details:

LA TREMBLADE

- 17390 Map ref: 23

Directions: Directly adj to sea.

10

Unknown

ℹ Sea views; Visited 2001.

Sanitation:

Aire Details:

© Vicky and Nick Church

LES MATHES

N45°43.063'W001°08.870' 17570 Map ref: 24

Directions: Rue Henri Erable. Follow sp 'Centre Ville'. Into town centre take turning directly opposite church tower entrance. The Aire is then 50m on left. Signed.

5

Custom; Token €4

ℹ Small village.

Sanitation:

Aire Details:

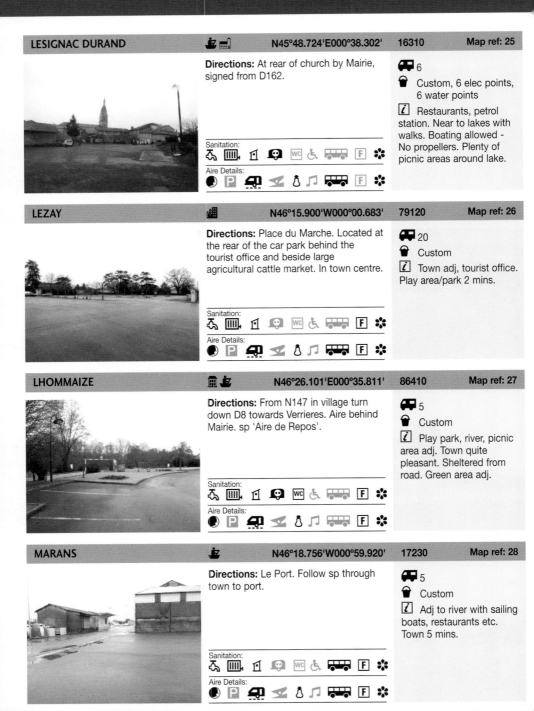

| LESIGNAC DURAND | | N45°48.724'E000°38.302' | 16310 | Map ref: 25 |

Directions: At rear of church by Mairie, signed from D162.

Sanitation:

Aire Details:

🚐 6

Custom, 6 elec points, 6 water points

ℹ️ Restaurants, petrol station. Near to lakes with walks. Boating allowed - No propellers. Plenty of picnic areas around lake.

| LEZAY | | N46°15.900'W000°00.683' | 79120 | Map ref: 26 |

Directions: Place du Marche. Located at the rear of the car park behind the tourist office and beside large agricultural cattle market. In town centre.

Sanitation:

Aire Details:

🚐 20

Custom

ℹ️ Town adj, tourist office. Play area/park 2 mins.

| LHOMMAIZE | | N46°26.101'E000°35.811' | 86410 | Map ref: 27 |

Directions: From N147 in village turn down D8 towards Verrieres. Aire behind Mairie. sp 'Aire de Repos'.

Sanitation:

Aire Details:

🚐 5

Custom

ℹ️ Play park, river, picnic area adj. Town quite pleasant. Sheltered from road. Green area adj.

| MARANS | | N46°18.756'W000°59.920' | 17230 | Map ref: 28 |

Directions: Le Port. Follow sp through town to port.

Sanitation:

Aire Details:

🚐 5

Custom

ℹ️ Adj to river with sailing boats, restaurants etc. Town 5 mins.

MARENNES

N45°49.399'W001°06.127' 17320 Map ref: 29

Directions: E'leclerc Supermarket. Follow sp in town. Service point by Fuel station.

🚐 10
🚰 Raclet
ℹ️ In town, supermarket.

Sanitation:

Aire Details:

MAULEON

N46°55.070'W000°45.133' 79700 Map ref: 30

Directions: Rue de la Bachelette. Follow sp 'Noirt', exit town on D744 towards Noirt. Turn to right up lane after exiting town, sp 'Complex Sportif'. Signed. Follow lane into housing estate until reach sports fields. Aire signed on left.

🚐 5, 48hrs
🚰 Custom
ℹ️ At sports centre. Green areas (sports field) adj. Town 20 mins.

Sanitation:

Aire Details:

MAUZE-SUR-LE-MIGNON

N46°11.990'W000°40.857' 79210 Map ref: 31

Directions: Route de Saint Hilliare/Rue de Port. Off route de Saint Hilliare, edge of town outside campsite but diff area. Sp 'Camping'.

🚐 10
🚰 Flot blue; Token
ℹ️ Nice pond/water feature adj, possibility to launch canoes down river. Town 10 mins.

Sanitation:

Aire Details:

MELLE

N46°13.907'W000°08.643' 79500 Map ref: 32

Directions: Outside Municipal Campsite. Turn off D737 and follow sp 'Camping'.

🚐 2
🚰 Custom
ℹ️ There is a possibility of parking at this Aire but really it is just a service point. Picnic area, river, walking by multiple marked trails, large grassy area. Church 5 mins.

Sanitation:

Aire Details:

Poitou

MERIGNAC		-	16200	Map ref: 33

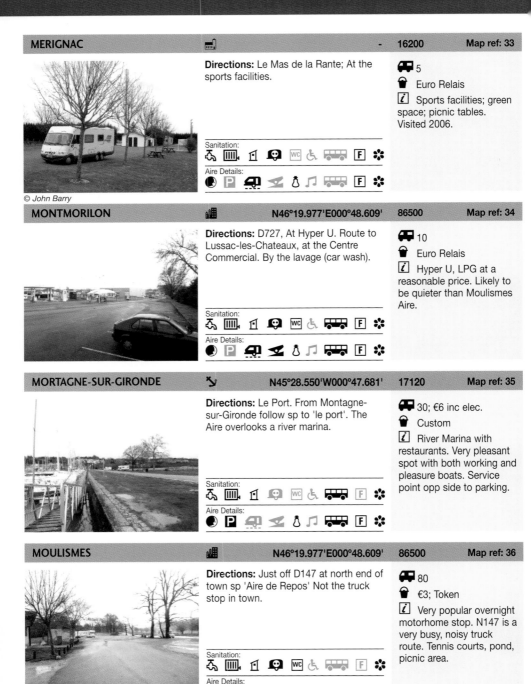

Directions: Le Mas de la Rante; At the sports facilities.

Sanitation:

Aire Details:

🚐 5
Euro Relais
ℹ️ Sports facilities; green space; picnic tables. Visited 2006.

© John Barry

MONTMORILON		N46°19.977'E000°48.609'	86500	Map ref: 34

Directions: D727, At Hyper U. Route to Lussac-les-Chateaux, at the Centre Commercial. By the lavage (car wash).

Sanitation:

Aire Details:

🚐 10
Euro Relais
ℹ️ Hyper U, LPG at a reasonable price. Likely to be quieter than Moulismes Aire.

MORTAGNE-SUR-GIRONDE		N45°28.550'W000°47.681'	17120	Map ref: 35

Directions: Le Port. From Montagne-sur-Gironde follow sp to 'le port'. The Aire overlooks a river marina.

Sanitation:

Aire Details:

🚐 30; €6 inc elec.
Custom
ℹ️ River Marina with restaurants. Very pleasant spot with both working and pleasure boats. Service point opp side to parking.

MOULISMES		N46°19.977'E000°48.609'	86500	Map ref: 36

Directions: Just off D147 at north end of town sp 'Aire de Repos' Not the truck stop in town.

Sanitation:

Aire Details:

🚐 80
€3; Token
ℹ️ Very popular overnight motorhome stop. N147 is a very busy, noisy truck route. Tennis courts, pond, picnic area.

NIEUL-L'ESPOIR

N46°29.113'E000°27.268' | 86340 | Map ref: 37

Directions: D1. On D1 as enter village sp 'Camping Car' (from N147).

Sanitation:

Aire Details:

🚐 10

🚰 Euro Relais, token

ℹ Very pleasant spot, river flooded at time of visit (but not dangerously). Park, river walk, green space adj, town 2 mins.

NIORT

N46°19.763'W000°27.870' | 79000 | Map ref: 38

Directions: Rue de Bessac. North/west side of town. From N148 enter town, Follow sp 'Centre Ville', drive south on Rue Leon Gambett. Signed down turning on left Rue Gustave Effel. If get to E'leclerc supermarket have gone too far. Must exit way entered.

Sanitation:

Aire Details:

🚐 10; €6 24hrs; max 7 days.

🚰 Euro Relais

ℹ Nice stop, park and river adj and can walk directly into town over bridges from Aire. Motorhome campsite.

ROCHEFORT

N45°56.597'W000°57.518' | 17300 | Map ref: 39

Directions: Port de Plaisance, Esplanade Pierre Sournet. Sp in town to Aire and to 'Capitainerie Corderie Royal'. Parking in old fort.

Sanitation:

Aire Details:

🚐 10

🚰 -

ℹ Motorhomes parking here - no restriction visable. Not sure if official, adj to marina and town.

ROCHEFORT 2

N45°56.648'W000°57.443' | 17300 | Map ref: 40

Directions: Quai Lemoigne de Serigny. Just by road swing bridge for marina. Just off Avenue William Ponty signed.

Sanitation:

Aire Details:

🚐 No overnight parking

🚰 Custom

ℹ See Rochefort for parking suggestion.

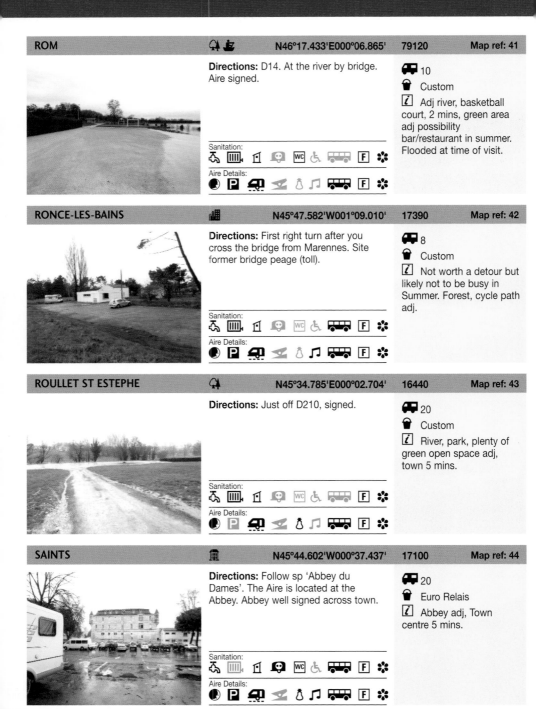

| ROM | 🏕️⚓ | N46°17.433'E000°06.865' | 79120 | Map ref: 41 |

Directions: D14. At the river by bridge. Aire signed.

🚐 10

🔧 Custom

ℹ️ Adj river, basketball court, 2 mins, green area adj possibility bar/restaurant in summer. Flooded at time of visit.

Sanitation:

Aire Details:

| RONCE-LES-BAINS | 🏢 | N45°47.582'W001°09.010' | 17390 | Map ref: 42 |

Directions: First right turn after you cross the bridge from Marennes. Site former bridge peage (toll).

🚐 8

🔧 Custom

ℹ️ Not worth a detour but likely not to be busy in Summer. Forest, cycle path adj.

Sanitation:

Aire Details:

| ROULLET ST ESTEPHE | 🏕️ | N45°34.785'E000°02.704' | 16440 | Map ref: 43 |

Directions: Just off D210, signed.

🚐 20

🔧 Custom

ℹ️ River, park, plenty of green open space adj, town 5 mins.

Sanitation:

Aire Details:

| SAINTS | 🏛️ | N45°44.602'W000°37.437' | 17100 | Map ref: 44 |

Directions: Follow sp 'Abbey du Dames'. The Aire is located at the Abbey. Abbey well signed across town.

🚐 20

🔧 Euro Relais

ℹ️ Abbey adj, Town centre 5 mins.

Sanitation:

Aire Details:

Poitou

SAUZE-VAUSSAIR · N46°08.123'E000°06.399' · 79190 · Map ref: 45

Directions: Place des Halles. In main town sq. Follow sp 'Tourist Information'. Aire in back corner by Sapeurs Pompiers (Fire Station).

🚐 10
Flot Blou; token
ℹ In town sq, town, tourist office.

Sanitation:
Aire Details:

SEGONZAC · N45°36.869'W000°13.255' · 16130 · Map ref: 46

Directions: Place du Jardin Public. Signed from all directions but is located down side street off D736.

🚐 4 (each with electric point)
Custom
ℹ Play park adj, seating area, village 5 mins, Sign showing local Cognac producers.

Sanitation:
Aire Details:

ST AGNANT · N45°51.987'W000°57.908' · 17620 · Map ref: 47

Directions: Place de Verdun. Signed from traffic lighted crossroads; turn down Avenue Charles de Gaulle. In car park with memorial sp 'Place de Verdon' and 'Medi@theque'.

🚐 10
Custom; €2
ℹ Marked walk, boules court, basketball hoop, 2 mins to village.

Sanitation:
Aire Details:

ST-AMAND-SUR-SEVRE · N46°52.154'W000°47.998' · 79700 · Map ref: 48

Directions: Rue des Fontaines. Located directly on C56.

🚐 3
Custom
ℹ Grass area, walks adj, village 2 mins. Riverside 2 mins.

Sanitation:
Aire Details:

ST-AMAND-SUR-SEVRE 2   N46°53.079'W000°49.449'   79700   Map ref: 49

Directions: Sp 'Bar Moulin de Chaligny' from road. Located on C2. Between St Amand s Sevre and Treize-Vents.

Sanitation:

Aire Details:

Unknown

Unknown

i Under water at time of visit. Bar/restaurant surrounded by fields adj to river. Idyllic rural spot.

ST DIZANT DU GUA   N45°25.840'W000°42.343'   17240   Map ref: 50

Directions: D145. Directly as you exit the village towards Cognac.

Sanitation:

Aire Details:

5

Euro Relais Junior; €2

i Mini market adj, small river adj with picnic spots. Village 5 mins. Large green area adj. Cycle down lanes around vines.

ST GEORGES-DE-DIDONNE   N45°36.261'W000°59.974'   17110   Map ref: 51

Directions: Rue du Docteur Maudet/Rue du Stade. Opposite stadium. From beachfront travel to large roundabout, go straight across. At next roundabout turn right. Follow road until opposite stadium.

Sanitation:

Aire Details:

8

Custom

i 5 mins to beach, 5 mins to town centre. Opp sports facilities. Pleasant seaside town with large sandy beach.

ST QUENTIN S CHARENTE   N45°49.633'E000°41.287'   16150   Map ref: 52

Directions: Sp off D161, sp 'Les Versennes'. Well signed from St Quentin.

Sanitation:

Aire Details:

10; April - Oct

Custom

i Resevoir/Lake adj, Boat Launch- canoe/sailing no propellers. Play area, picnic area views of lake. Cycling routes marked and walk around water.

ST SAVIN   N45°08.401'W000°26.541'   86310   Map ref: 53

Directions: At roundabout with D18, D115, D250 by the Intermarche Supermarket, follow signs - by Office Tourisme.

🚐 -
Custom
ℹ️ For parking see St Savin 2.

Sanitation:

Aire Details:

ST SAVIN 2   N45°08.292'W000°26.808'   86310   Map ref: 54

Directions: D18. Just off main high street, sp from Intermarche supermarket. Clearly signed on D18.

🚐 20
🪣 -
ℹ️ Part Shaded, High Street Adj.

Sanitation:

Aire Details:

ST SEURIN-D'UZET   N45°30.061'W000°50.097'   17120   Map ref: 55

Directions: Signed from main road through (D145). Next to river.

🚐 4; €6 inc elec.
Custom
ℹ️ Overlooking boats in village centre. Idyllic.

Sanitation:

Aire Details:

ST THOMAS DE CONAC   N45°25.824'W000°42.365'   17150   Map ref: 56

Directions: On D145. Signed off D145, adj to village Boules Court. 100m from church.

🚐 5
Custom
ℹ️ Small Aire with view and boules court adj.

Sanitation:

Aire Details:

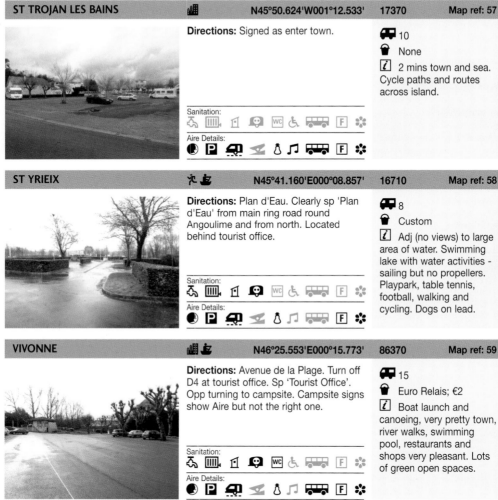

ST TROJAN LES BAINS — N45°50.624'W001°12.533' — 17370 — Map ref: 57

Directions: Signed as enter town.

🚐 10
🛢 None
ℹ️ 2 mins town and sea. Cycle paths and routes across island.

Sanitation:

Aire Details:

ST YRIEIX — N45°41.160'E000°08.857' — 16710 — Map ref: 58

Directions: Plan d'Eau. Clearly sp 'Plan d'Eau' from main ring road round Angoulime and from north. Located behind tourist office.

🚐 8
🛢 Custom
ℹ️ Adj (no views) to large area of water. Swimming lake with water activities - sailing but no propellers. Playpark, table tennis, football, walking and cycling. Dogs on lead.

Sanitation:

Aire Details:

VIVONNE — N46°25.553'E000°15.773' — 86370 — Map ref: 59

Directions: Avenue de la Plage. Turn off D4 at tourist office. Sp 'Tourist Office'. Opp turning to campsite. Campsite signs show Aire but not the right one.

🚐 15
🛢 Euro Relais; €2
ℹ️ Boat launch and canoeing, very pretty town, river walks, swimming pool, restaurants and shops very pleasant. Lots of green open spaces.

Sanitation:

Aire Details:

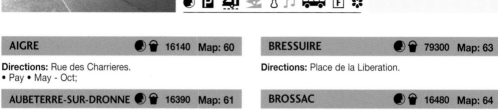

AIGRE — 16140 — Map: 60

Directions: Rue des Charrieres.
• Pay • May - Oct;

AUBETERRE-SUR-DRONNE — 16390 — Map: 61

Directions: Base de loisirs (leisure place).
• Pay • All year

BOUGON — 79800 — Map: 62

Directions: Situated in the car park of the 'Musee des Tumulus'. • Open all year

BRESSUIRE — 79300 — Map: 63

Directions: Place de la Liberation.

BROSSAC — 16480 — Map: 64

Directions: Rue du Château d'Eau.
• Pay • All year;

CHASSENEUIL — 16260 — Map: 65

Directions: Place du Champ de Mars.
• Pay • All year

CHEY — 79120 Map: 66
Directions: Place du Bourg.

CHIZE — 79170 Map: 67
Directions: Parking du Zoorama.

COULON — 79510 Map: 68
Directions: By the school.

CRITEUIL-LA-MAGDELEINE — 16300 Map: 69
Directions: In the town.
• All year;

HAVE YOU VISITED AN AIRE?
Don't forget to fill in the form at the back and return to Vicarious Books.

GENTE — 16130 Map: 71
Directions: In the town.
• June - Oct

JARNAC — 16200 Map: 72
Directions: Gondeville.
• All year

LA FORET SUR SEVRE — 79380 Map: 73
Directions: Rue de Beauchene.

LA MOTHE ST HERAY — 79800 Map: 74
Directions: La Mothe Pont labbe.

LONDIGNY — 16700 Map: 75
Directions: Place de l'eglise (church).

MAIRE-L'EVESCAULT — 79190 Map: 76
Directions: In the town, service point at the Municipal Campsite.

MASSAIS — 79150 Map: 77
Directions: Aire Natural at camping 'Le Moulin Bernard'.
• €5

MASSIGNAC — 16310 Map: 78
Directions: In the town.
• All year

MERIGNAC — 16200 Map: 79
Directions: Near Echangeur; RN 141.
• All year

MONTMOREAU — 16190 Map: 80
Directions: Place de Tude.
• Pay • All year

NOIRT/VOUILLE — 79180 Map: 81
Directions: Aire d'autoroute A10.

OIRON — 79100 Map: 82
Directions: At the Church.
• Tokens

PARTHENAY — 79200 Map: 83
Directions: Base de Loisirs (Leisure place) Pierre Beaufort. • Open all year

ROUMAZIERES-LOUBERT — 16270 Map: 84
Directions: In the town, adj RN141.
• All year

SECONDIGNY — 79130 Map: 85
Directions: D748; at base de loisir (leisure place) and Camping.

ST MAURICE LA FOUGEREUSE — 79150 Map: 86
Directions: Place of the river Juliot.
• Tokens

ST VARENT — 79330 Map: 87
Directions: Avenue des Platenes.
• Service point at the campsite

THOUARS — 79100 Map: 88
Directions: Place Ferdinand Buisson.
• Tokens • Open all year

VASLES — 79340 Map: 89
Directions: Tourist place Mouton Village.

VOEUIL-ET-GIGET — 16400 Map: 90
Directions: Place de la Mairie (town hall).
• Pay • All year

Rhone-Alps

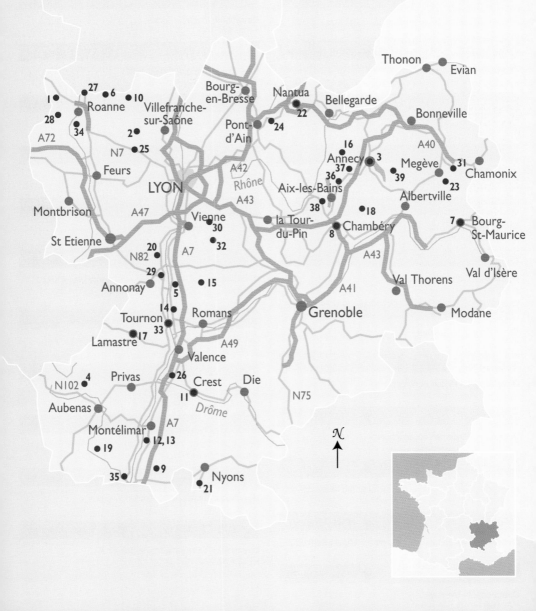

Thonon
Evian
Bourg-en-Bresse
Nantua
Bellegarde
Bonneville
27 6
1   10
28   Roanne   Villefranche-sur-Saône
34   2   Pont-d'Ain   24   22
A72   25
N7   Rhône   16
Feurs   A42   Annecy 37 3   Megève   31
             A43 36   39   Chamonix
Montbrison   LYON   Aix-les-Bains   23
             A47   Vienne   38   la Tour-   Albertville
St Etienne   30   du-Pin   18 7 Bourg-St-Maurice
             20 A7   32   8 Chambéry
             N82   29   Val d'Isère
Annonay   5   A43
             15   A41   Val Thorens
             14   Modane
Tournon 33 Romans   Grenoble
17
Lamastre
             A49
             Valence
Privas 26
4 N102   Crest   Die
Aubenas 11   Drôme   N75
Montélimar A7
19   12,13
35   9   Nyons
     21

N

196

© Carol and Duncan Weaver

A region of two halves. To the west the beautiful river Rhone winds through grape lined valleys. Still an important navigation, barges transport goods to riverside factories. The vineyards here produce Rhone and Beaujolais wines.

The Alps dominate the east of the region providing lovely mountain resorts along lakeshores. Skiers enjoy the stunning views in the winter and the summer sees people boating, walking and cycling. At the foot of Mont Blanc, Europe's tallest mountain, nestles the town of Chamonix, the famous destination for skiing in winter and world capital for climbing in summer.

AMBIERLE

 N46°06.395'E003°53.623' 42820 Map ref: 1

Directions: Rue du 19 Mars 1962. Follow sp from D52 in Ambierle centre by château. When road ends go straight across and follow road. Imperative to follow correct route - 7 metres only!

Sanitation:

Aire Details:

🚐 5

🎫 Custom

ℹ️ Parking at new sports complex; near cemetery. Views. Interesting church/château complex in centre. Area scrappy as still developing site but village pleasant.

AMPLEPUIS

N45°58.198'E004°19.854' 69550 Map ref: 2

Directions: Rue Paul de la Goulte. Entering on D8 from south at D8/D10 roundabout exit sp 'Thurzy D8'. 150m first right turn sp 'Aire Camping Car' then first right the Aire is down slope, signed. 7.5 ton weight limit.

Sanitation:

Aire Details:

🚐 10; 48hrs

🎫 Custom

ℹ️ At sports facility in town. Difficult to find. Hard football court marked on car park; large town.

ANNECY LE VIEUX

N45°54.382'E006°09.365' 74940 Map ref: 3

Directions: D909 Rue du Pre Vernet. Adj to lake.

Sanitation:

Aire Details:

🚐 10

🎫 Flot Blue; €2

ℹ️ Lovely resort town; cycle/walking path around lake. Swimming; sunbathing; skiing; LPG at Auchan.

AUBIGNAS

N44°35.236'E004°37.899' 07400 Map ref: 4

Directions: D363. From N102 follow signs 'Aubignas' then 'le village' as enter village Aire in car park on left.

Sanitation:

Aire Details:

🚐 10

🎫 Raclet

ℹ️ Hillside village. Aire has panoramic views. Very quiet and peaceful. Village 2 mins.

BEAUSEMBLANT N45°13.085'E004°49.980' 26240 Map ref: 5

Directions: D122; Rue du 11 Nov 1918. Turn off D122 in town sp 'Aire de Camping Car', turning opposite boulangerie.

🚐 6

Custom

ℹ️ Fruit and veg shop across car park and boulangery 2 mins. Play park and green space.

Sanitation:

Aire Details:

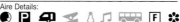

BELMONT DE LA LOIRE N46°09.928'E004°20.772' 42670 Map ref: 6

Directions: At the church. Sp from village roundabout by church follow D4 then left at roundabout then immediately left. Service point against church.

🚐 5

Custom

ℹ️ Small village with aged service point and limited parking. Looks better than it is!

Sanitation:

Aire Details:

BOURG ST MAURICE - 73700 Map ref: 7

Directions: Huge car park.

🚐 10

Custom

ℹ️ Mountain views. Visited 2004.

Sanitation:

Aire Details:

© Carol and Duncan Weaver

CHAMBERY   N45°33.772'E005°55.982' 73000 Map ref: 8

Directions: Espace Sportif Delphine et Jonathen. Exit junction 18 and head into town on N6. Stay on N6 following sp 'Lyches', at second roundabout turn left. Aire at end of road.

🚐 10

Custom

ℹ️ Town 10 mins walk. Indian restaurant in town. Cycle path to green park.

Sanitation:

Aire Details:

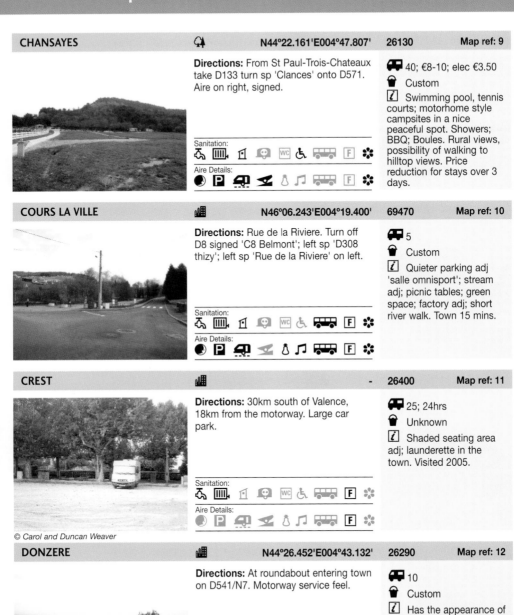

CHANSAYES

N44°22.161'E004°47.807'   26130   Map ref: 9

Directions: From St Paul-Trois-Chateaux take D133 turn sp 'Clances' onto D571. Aire on right, signed.

Sanitation:

Aire Details:

🚐 40; €8-10; elec €3.50

Custom

ℹ️ Swimming pool, tennis courts; motorhome style campsites in a nice peaceful spot. Showers; BBQ; Boules. Rural views, possibility of walking to hilltop views. Price reduction for stays over 3 days.

COURS LA VILLE

N46°06.243'E004°19.400'   69470   Map ref: 10

Directions: Rue de la Riviere. Turn off D8 signed 'C8 Belmont'; left sp 'D308 thizy'; left sp 'Rue de la Riviere' on left.

Sanitation:

Aire Details:

🚐 5

Custom

ℹ️ Quieter parking adj 'salle omnisport'; stream adj; picnic tables; green space; factory adj; short river walk. Town 15 mins.

CREST

    -    26400   Map ref: 11

Directions: 30km south of Valence, 18km from the motorway. Large car park.

Sanitation:

Aire Details:

🚐 25; 24hrs

Unknown

ℹ️ Shaded seating area adj; launderette in the town. Visited 2005.

© Carol and Duncan Weaver

DONZERE

N44°26.452'E004°43.132'   26290   Map ref: 12

Directions: At roundabout entering town on D541/N7. Motorway service feel.

Sanitation:

Aire Details:

🚐 10

Custom

ℹ️ Has the appearance of a motorway service stop. Very noisy from N7. Village 2 mins walk.

DONZERE (MARKET)

 N44°26.600'E004°42.598' 26290 **Map ref: 13**

Directions: Place Henri Dunant. From D213 turn into town, sp 'Centre Ville'. Just off main market square, signed.

Sanitation:

Aire Details:

🏍 10

☂ Raclet

ℹ️ Adj to market square in heart of village. Saturday 8-2pm no motorhomes allowed due to market. Chocolate park; play park and seated park 2 mins.

GERVANS

N45°06.546'E004°49.831' 26600 **Map ref: 14**

Directions: Rue de l'Ecole. From N7 turn off sp 'Gervans village' and signed. Follow signs through village; tight access.

Sanitation:

Aire Details:

🏍 5

☂ Custom; donation

ℹ️ Very pleasant village. Views across Rhone grape vines on hills. Skateboard park; basketball courts. Ideal if Tournon Aire full.

HAUTERIVES

45.25494N 50.02896E 26390 **Map ref: 15**

Directions: Near 'Palais Ideal' signed in town.

Sanitation:

Aire Details:

🏍 10

☂ Custom

ℹ️ New services and large gravel parking area. No shade. Visited 2006.

© Motorhomeandaway.co.uk

LA BALME DE SILLINGY

N45°58.290'E006°01.888' 74330 **Map ref: 16**

Directions: N508. Just off N508 at exit to village by lake.

Sanitation:

Aire Details:

🏍 14; 48hrs; 01/04 - 30/11

☂ Custom

ℹ️ By lake; children's play area; walk around lake; green space; fishing; swimming; café

LAMASTRE

If you have a suitable picture for this Aire, please email to: gomotorhoming@hotmail.co.uk

motorhomeandaway.co.uk

44.98701N 4.57933E   07270   **Map ref: 17**

Directions: Place Pradon; Town centre. Parking and two service points in town.

Sanitation:

Aire Details:

Unknown

€1.70; Tokens; tourist office

Not available Monday night/Tuesday due to large market. Possible to park in large car park behind market next to river but would be noisy and busy on market day. Visited 2006.

LE FECLAZ

N45°38.515'E005°59.016'   73230   **Map ref: 18**

Directions: 206A. From D912 turn onto D913 sp 'le Feclaz' at entrance to village turn left sp 'P camping cars' follow road and parking on right signed.

Sanitation:

Aire Details:

40; pay at tourist office

Raclet; Tokens

Button ski lift 100m; small down hill resort; cross country skiing; ski passes €200. Good for walking in summer. Play area 2 mins.

LES CROTTES/ST-THOME

N44°30.045'E004°38.052'   07220   **Map ref: 19**

Directions: D107. Adj D107 just before entrance to Le Crottes from Viviers. Signed.

Sanitation:

Aire Details:

None

Raclet

Service point only at this small village.

LES ROCHES DE CONDRIEU

N45°27.239'E004°46.094'   38370   **Map ref: 20**

Directions: D4. Cross bridge from Condrieu and drive straight on. The Aire is in the first car park on right signed adj to D4.

Sanitation:
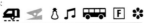

Aire Details:

20

Custom

2 mins from Rhone river with port, shops etc. Disappointing as not on river but on market square.

MIRABEL AUX BARONNIERS 44.31454N 5.10007E 26110 Map ref: 21

Directions: Signed just north of town. Narrow approach lane.

🚐 6

🚰 Unknown

ℹ️ Small Aire. Visited 2006.

Sanitation:

Aire Details:

© Motorhomeandaway.co.uk

NANTUA N46°09.260'E005°35.827' 01130 Map ref: 22

Directions: D74. At lake turn off sp 'Aire de picnic' and 'Monument aux Deportes' signed. Follow rd around lake signed.

🚐 10

🚰 Custom

ℹ️ Amazing lake/mountain views. Lake suitable fishing/swimming/boating. Town 5 mins walk, lots of shops. Pleasant spot. Lidl 2 mins, occasional road noise. Play area/pedaloes 300m.

Sanitation:

Aire Details:

PLAINE-JOUX - 74120 Map ref: 23

Directions: At plateau D'Assy; Car park at skiing and paragliding area. Large parking area before restaurants and paragliding centre on road to le Lac Vert.

🚐 15

🚰 Flot Blue; €2; tokens

ℹ️ Skiing and paragliding area adj. Camping fee payable if parking on grass fields past campsite sign. Fantastic views of Mont Blanc. Lac Vert 1.5km worth a visit and church in Plateau d'Assy has works of art by famous artists. Visited 2005.

Sanitation:

Aire Details:

© Motorhomeandaway.co.uk

PONCIN N46°05.274'E005°24.280' 01450 Map ref: 24

Directions: Off N1084 onto D91 sp 'Tourist Office' and 'Foyer Rural'. Enter town signed then over bridge turn left and follow road then turn left.

🚐 20

🚰 Custom

ℹ️ At sports facilities; basketball; boules; tennis; football; village 5 mins. N1084 to Nantua a scenic, twisty drive past French Resistance monument.

Sanitation:

Aire Details:

PONTCHARRA SUR TURDINE N45°52.464'E004°29.496' 69490 Map ref: 25

Directions: D33. From N7 turn into village at square with mini Casino supermarket. Turn left when Casino supermarket is behind you, then left sp 'Poste' then Aire on left before la Poste.

4

Custom

Play park; seating area; dog toilet adj; town 2 mins.

Sanitation:
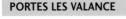

Aire Details:

PORTES LES VALANCE N44°50.993'E004°52.153' 26800 Map ref: 26

Directions: D7, Intermarche. Just off D7 as enter town from south towards Valance.

50

Custom

Service point in 24hr petrol station. Parking at supermarket 50 meters.

Sanitation:

Aire Details:

POUILLY SOUS CHARLIEU N46°08.589'E004°06.515' 42720 Map ref: 27

Directions: At D4/D482 junction turn onto D482 sp 'Roanne' Aire 200m on left opp mini market Casino sp. Just before D35 junc on left.

10

Aire Service

Play park; boules; small green space adj; town 2 mins with large shops.

Sanitation:

Aire Details:

ST ANDRE D'APCHON N46°02.040'E003°55.625' 42370 Map ref: 28

Directions: Rue du 11 Novembre 1918. Between church and cemetery, turn off D8 at roundabout into St Andre d'Apchon and follow signs through town.

2

Custom

Really just a service point; tight access through village; village 2 mins; additional parking adj.

Sanitation:

ST DESERAT
  N45°15.515'E004°47.546'   07340   **Map ref: 29**

Directions: D291. From N82 turn sp 'St Desirant' at roundabout turn right sp 'Museum'. Aire 500m on right. Aire in visitor parking.

🚐 10
Custom
ℹ️ At wine producer and museum. Restaurant. Pleasant rural spot, two pin plugs.

Sanitation:

Aire Details:

ST GEORGES D'ESPERANCHE
  N45°33.348'E005°04.504'   38790   **Map ref: 30**

Directions: Rue des Bougettes. From D75, main road, exit roundabout onto D53 sp 'St Georges d'Esperanche'. At village turn left then right sp 'centre ville' then follow sp through village.

🚐 10
Custom
ℹ️ Tight access through town. Town with shops and restaurants 5 mins. Pleasant stop. Green space with dog toilet. Boules court adj.

Sanitation:

Aire Details:

ST GERVAIS LES BAINS
    -   74170   **Map ref: 31**

If you have a suitable picture for this Aire, please email to: gomotorhoming@hotmail.co.uk

Directions: By Ice rink. Follow signs to 'Patinoire' on road towards Megeve.

🚐 Unknown
Service point being installed at time of visit.
ℹ️ Possible noise from ice rink cooling plant. Visited 2005.

Sanitation:
Aire Details:

motorhomeandaway.co.uk

ST JEAN DE BOURNAY
  N45°30.060'E005°08.300'   38440   **Map ref: 32**

Directions: Place du Marche. From roundabout on D518 follow truck route into town. Turn right then left.

🚐 50
Custom
ℹ️ Not on a Monday - market day. LPG at Intermarche 2 mins, town 2 mins. Town with restaurants; some shops; pleasant squares.

Sanitation:

Aire Details:

Rhone-Alps

TOURNON-SUR-RHONE N45°04.230'E004°49.716' 07300 Map ref: 33

Directions: N86 Quai Farconnet. Directly off N86, main route through town. Service point directly adj to large town parking area on Rhone opp post office down side street.

Sanitation:

Aire Details:

No designated parking
Euro relais junior
Lively town on Rhone good for entertainment; restaurants; shops; boat watching.

VILLEREST N45°59.189'E004°02.578' 42300 Map ref: 34

Directions: D18; South Roanne sp off D53 'Lac de Villerest'. In Villerest follow sp 'plan d'eau'. By road bridge that crosses reservoir.

Sanitation:

Aire Details:

20; pay at adj mini golf
Flot blue; Tokens
Walking; sailing; fishing; fantastic views; crazy golf; play area; bar adj; waterslides/beach 5 mins walk. Narrow concrete slipway. Deep shelving water by Aire.

VIVIERS N44°29.161'E004°41.534' 07220 Map ref: 35

Directions: D861. Turn down road adj to river bridge on D861 on right as exit Viviers sp 'Port Plesance' signed.

Sanitation:

Aire Details:

4
Custom
Views over town, some interesting architecture. Bar in season. Town nice walk 5 mins. Boules adj; river adj but no views; water sports likely. Very interesting, worth a visit.

LA BIOLLE 73410 Map: 36

Directions: Aire Naturelle sous la Colline, Villette.
• 01/04 - 30/10

MONTAGNY LES LANCHES 74600 Map: 37

Directions: Aire Naturelle La Vidome; Avulliens; adj N201. • €4.8
• €3.40 per per • elec €2.10 • Open all year • Caravans accepted

SAINT PAUL 73170 Map: 38

Directions: Aire Natural Le Bol d'Air; Le Lutrin RN504.
• elec and showers

SERRAVAL 74230 Map: 39

Directions: Aire Naturelle La Bottiere; La Bottiere
• elec and showers

© Motorhomeandaway.co.uk

Index

Index

Index

Index

Index

Index

Index

Index

If Aire is already listed, complete only sections where changes apply. Please fill in answers in capital letters and circle appropriate symbols.

Town/Village:

Region:

Road name/number:

Page Number:

Ambience (type of area):

↘	Coastal	♧	Rural	🚜	Farm
🏛	Residential	🏘	Village	🏃	Park
🏢	Urban	⛴	Riverside or lakeside		

Please circle 1 or more symbols as appropriate

GPS reference: Postcode – if known:

Number of Spaces: Time limit:

Cost:

Aire details symbols:

●	Overnight parking possible	🚐	Hard surface	🚌	Large motorhomes
P	Designated motorhome parking	⬎	Sloping	**F**	Free of charge
		⌂	Illuminated	❖	Open all year
		♪	Noisy		

Please circle 1 or more symbols as appropriate

Service Point type: Cost:

Payment type:

Sanitation symbols:

⚸	Water	⚡	Electric hook up	**F**	Free of charge
▦	Grey water disposal	WC	Toilets	❖	Open all year
⌂	Toilet disposal	♿	Disabled toilet		

Please circle 1 or more symbols as appropriate

Please turn over

All the Aires - Report Form

Directions - Brief, specific directions to Aire:

Information - Brief description of location and amenities:

Location of nearest LPG:

Photo(s) included/emailed:

email pictures to: gomotorhoming@hotmail.com

Name and email or address - so information can be credited:

Please use a separate form (photocopy) for each Aire. Send completed forms to:

Vicarious books, PO Box 72, Minehead, TA24 9AL.

Thank you very much for your time.

By supplying details and photography you are giving un-restricted publication and reproduction rights to Vicarious Books LLP.